21世纪国际经济与贸易学专业精品教材

Cross-Border E-Commerce

跨境电子商务双语教程

易露霞 尤彧聪◎主编

U0361904

清华大学出版社

北京

内 容 简 介

本书系统地阐述了跨境电子商务的基本原理和实际应用，基础理论以应用为目的，以必需、够用为度，尽量体现新知识、新技术和新方法；同时，理论联系实际，以跨境电子商务知识体系为导向基础，以跨境电子商务专员工作过程为线索，强调各环节对跨境电子商务操作能力的训练。

本书共 13 个单元，每个单元包括 4 部分：第 1 部分为课文，按照跨境电子商务业务交易发展的规律，同时用中英文系统地阐述了跨境电子商务中的各个重要环节。第 2 部分为专业术语解释，对跨境电子商务中经常出现的重要术语进行了简要、精确的解释，使读者能够正确、清晰地理解这些术语的含义。第 3 部分为实用表达，紧扣课文内容，提供与课文内容相关的实用表达。第 4 部分为练习，充分体现双语特点，既有中文练习，又有英文练习，便于读者自学。

本书理论与实际相结合，内容深入浅出，通俗易懂，重点、难点突出，适合高等院校经济类、管理类、商贸类的学生作为教材使用，同时也可以作为公务员、企业管理者、信息技术人员学习跨境电子商务知识的参考用书或培训教材。

图书在版编目（CIP）数据

跨境电子商务双语教程 / 易露霞，尤彧聪主编. —北京：清华大学出版社，2019（2024.2重印）
（21 世纪国际经济与贸易学专业精品教材）
ISBN 978-7-302-51337-7

Ⅰ. ①跨… Ⅱ. ①易… ②尤… Ⅲ. ①电子商务－双语教学－高等学校－教材 Ⅳ. ①F713.36

中国版本图书馆 CIP 数据核字（2018）第 229846 号

责任编辑：杜春杰
封面设计：刘 超
版式设计：周春梅
责任校对：毛姗姗
责任印制：丛怀宇

出版发行：清华大学出版社
网　　址：https://www.tup.com.cn，https://www.wqxuetang.com
地　　址：北京清华大学学研大厦 A 座　　　　邮　编：100084
社 总 机：010-83470000　　　　　　　　　　邮　购：010-62786544
投稿与读者服务：010-62776969，c-service@tup.tsinghua.edu.cn
质 量 反 馈：010-62772015，zhiliang@tup.tsinghua.edu.cn
印 装 者：北京嘉实印刷有限公司
经　　销：全国新华书店
开　　本：185mm×260mm　　　　印　张：13.25　　　字　数：329 千字
版　　次：2019 年 3 月第 1 版　　　　　　　印　次：2024 年 2 月第 7 次印刷
定　　价：49.80 元

产品编号：080357-01

前　言

随着全球经济一体化时代的来临，以及对外开放的不断扩大和深入，中国对外经济发展也越来越快。随着对外经济贸易的进一步高速发展，中国贸易国际化程度将进一步加深，各行各业对外贸易业务往来将更加频繁，更多的企业和部门将直接参与到对外经济贸易活动中去，这毫无疑问地需要大量既懂外语又懂外贸业务的专业人才。而进入互联网时代，国际贸易与"互联网+"紧密联系，出现了新的业态，即"跨境电子商务"；互联网和英语共同成为当前开展对外经济贸易业务和相关国际商务活动的最主要工具。

如何适应国内外经济贸易发展的需要，促进中国跨境电子商务与国际的进一步接轨，推广外贸业务跨境电子商务英语的实际应用，正确掌握跨境电子商务的基本知识并熟练地加以运用，准确地了解和表达跨境电子商务，是外贸工作者必须具备的专业技能和素质。现在国内高等院校非常重视对外经济贸易人才的培养，社会对这方面人才也有旺盛的需求，越来越多的人关注跨境电子商务英语方面的知识，希望不断提升自身的跨境电子商务英语水平和技能。正是因为如此，现在市场上的跨境电子商务英语书籍非常受欢迎。

为使本书更能符合教学要求，满足学习者适应对外经济贸易业务活动中跨境电子商务学习与运用的需要，帮助学习者系统、完整地学习和掌握对外经济贸易业务跨境电子商务的各个流程、专业用语、英语表达等知识，提高学习者正确使用英语的能力，增加其对外进行跨境电子商务各项业务联系活动的竞争力，笔者结合多年的教学经验，通过与跨境电子商务公司和平台的相关人员的直接合作，并参考在英国做访问学者期间所获得的相关资料，经多年努力编写了此书。

本书以中英文双语对照为特色，系统地阐述了跨境电子商务的基本原理和实际应用，基础理论以应用为目的，以必需、够用为度，尽量体现新知识、新技术和新方法。同时，理论联系实际，以跨境电子商务知识体系为导向基础，以跨境电子商务专员工作过程为线索，强调各环节对跨境电子商务操作能力的训练，依据课程标准，分为13个学习情境章节，其中包括核心环节，如跨境电子商务营运方式，第三方跨境电子商务平台，跨境电子商务询盘，商品展示和产品质量，跨境电子商务国际支付与国际物流，跨境电子商务订单流程，跨境电子商务市场选品和跨境电子商务监管，等等。每单元后附有专业术语部分，介绍跨境电子商务相关专业术语和跨境电子商务活动中经常用到的专业表达；实用表达部分提供了数十个短语，以帮助学习者掌握更多的跨境电子商务英文表达方式，有利于写出更多、更好、更标准的跨境电子商务外贸信函；练习部分提供了大量灵活多样的跨境电子商务训练题，有利于学习效果的强化和进一步检验。

除了参考相关资料外，本书许多跨境电子商务信函、数据和图表等来自外贸进出口公司的第一手资料，在此一并表示感谢。由于编者水平和学识有限，书中难免出现差错，敬请读者指正。

本书作为研究基金项目，受到广东省哲学社会科学"十三五"规划 2016 年度学科共建项目（广东外贸"供给侧改革"驱动发展路径分析，项目编号 GD16XYJ30），广州市哲学社会科学发展"十三五"规划 2017 年度共建课题（供给侧结构性改革视阈下的广州外贸企业资源配置和创新驱动路径研究，项目编号 2017GZGJ20），广州工商学院 2016 年本科"质量工程"重点建设项目（在线 MOOC 示范课程，项目编号 ZL20161226），广东省国际贸易特色重点学科项目和广东省职业教育信息化研究会 2016—2017 科研规划项目（"互联网+职业教育"商务英语课程建设信息化推广实践，项目编号 YZJY161739）的资助。

特此感谢！

编　者

2018 年 10 月

Contents

目　　录

Chapter One　Overview of Cross-Border E-Commerce

第一章　跨境电子商务概述

Part A　Text

A Brief Introduction to Cross-Border E-Commerce

Cross-border e-commerce is developed based on the network. The network space is a new space, relatively speaking, to the physical space, and is a virtual reality of net address and password. Cyberspace's unique values and behavior patterns profoundly affect cross-border e-commerce, making it different from the traditional way of trade and showing its own characteristics.

跨境电子商务是基于网络发展起来的，网络空间相对于物理空间来说是一个新空间，是一个由网址和密码组成的虚拟但客观存在的世界。网络空间独特的价值标准和行为模式深刻地影响着跨境电子商务，使其不同于传统的交易方式，并呈现出自己的特点。

Cross-border e-commerce is a new-type mode of trade. It is to digitalize and electronize the exhibition, negotiation and conclusion of a business of the traditional trade by Chinese production and trade enterprises through e-commerce, means to finally realizing the import and export of products. At the same time, it is also an effective way to broaden overseas marketing channel, promote China's brand competitiveness and realize the transformation and upgrading of China's foreign trade.

跨境电子商务是我国生产和贸易企业通过电子商务手段将传统贸易中的展示、洽谈和成交环节数字化、电子化，最终实现产品进出口的新型贸易方式；同时，也是扩大海外营销渠道，提升我国品牌竞争力，实现我国外贸转型升级的有效途径。

Section One　Features of Cross-Border E-Commerce（跨境电子商务的特征）

1. Global Forum

Network is a medium body with no boundary, sharing the characteristics of globalization and decentralization. Cross-border e-commerce, attached to the network, also has the characteristics of the globalization and decentralization. E-commerce, compared with the traditional way of trade, boasts its important feature: a borderless trade, losing the geographical factors brought by the traditional exchanges. Internet users do convey products, especially high value-added products, and services to the market without crossing borders. The positive effect brought by features of network is the greatest sharing degree of information, whilst its negative impact is that the users confront risks due to different cultural, political and legal factors. Anyone, who has a certain technical means, can

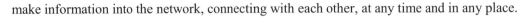
make information into the network, connecting with each other, at any time and in any place.

1. 全球性

网络是一个没有边界的媒介体，具有全球性和非中心化的特征。依附于网络发生的跨境电子商务也因此具有了全球性和非中心化的特性。电子商务与传统的交易方式相比，其一个重要特点在于电子商务是一种无边界交易，没有传统交易所具有的地理因素。互联网用户不需要跨越国界就可以把产品，尤其是高附加值产品和服务提交到市场。网络的全球性特征带来的积极影响是信息的最大限度的共享，消极影响是用户必须面临因文化、政治和法律的不同而产生的风险。任何人只要具备了一定的技术手段，在任何时候、任何地方都可以让信息进入网络，与其他人建立相互联系并进行交易。

2. Intangibility

The development of the network promotes the transmission of digital products and services. And digital transmission is done through different types of media, such as data, voices and images in the global focus of the network environment. Since the media in the network are in the form of computer data code, they are invisible. Digital products and services on the basis of the characteristics of digital transmission activities also have feature of intangibility, although traditional trade in kind is given priority to the physical objects, in the electronic commerce, intangible products can replace physical objects.

2. 无形性

网络的发展使数字化产品和服务的传输盛行。而数字化传输是通过不同类型的媒介（如数据、声音和图像）在全球化网络环境中集中而进行的，这些媒介在网络中是以计算机数据代码的形式出现的，因而是无形的。数字化产品和服务基于数字传输活动的特性也必然具有无形性，传统交易以实物交易为主，而在电子商务中，无形产品却可以替代实物成为交易的对象。

3. Anonymity

Due to the decentralization of cross-border e-commerce and global features, it is difficult to identify the e-commerce user's identity and its geographical location. Online transactions of consumers often do not show their real identities and their geographical location, but the important thing is that this doesn't affect trade. Network anonymity also allows consumers to do so. In the virtual society, the convenience of concealing the identity quickly leads to asymmetric freedom and responsibility. People here can enjoy the greatest freedom, but only bear the smallest responsibility, or even simply evade responsibility.

3. 匿名性

由于跨境电子商务的非中心化和全球性的特性，很难识别电子商务用户的身份和其所处的地理位置。在线交易的消费者往往不显示自己的真实身份和所处的地理位置，重要的是这丝毫不影响交易的进行，网络的匿名性也允许消费者这样做。在虚拟社会里，隐匿身份的便利迅捷导致自由与责任的不对称。人们在这里可以享受最大的自由，却只承担最小的责任，甚至干脆逃避责任。

4. Real-time

For network, the transmission speed is irrelevant to geographical distance. Information communication means of traditional trade, such as letter, telegraph, fax, etc., are with a length in different time between the sending and receiving of information. With regard to the information exchange in the e-commerce, regardless of the actual distance of time and space, one party sends a message to the other party who receives that information almost at the same time, just like talking face to face in life. Some digital products (such as audio and video products, software, etc.), can also get instant settlement, ordering, payment, delivery done in a flash.

4. 即时性

对于网络而言，传输的速度和地理距离无关。传统交易模式中的信息交流方式，如信函、电报、传真等，在信息的发送与接收间，存在着长短不同的时间差。而电子商务中的信息交流，无论实际时空距离远近，一方发送信息与另一方接收信息几乎是同时的，就如同生活中的面对面交谈。某些数字化产品（如音像制品、软件等）的交易，还可以即时结算、订货、付款、交货。

5. Paperlessness

Electronic commerce mainly takes the way of the paperless operation, which serves as the main characteristic of trade in the form of electronic commerce. In e-commerce, electronic computer communication records files instead of a series of paper trading. Users send or receive electronic information. Now that the electronic information exists in the form of bits and transmission, the whole process is realized by the paperless information. Paperlessness brings positive effects in terms of making information transferred without the limitation of paper. However, many specifications of the traditional law are with the standard "paper trades" as the starting point, therefore, paperlessness brings chaos in the law, to a certain extent.

5. 无纸化

电子商务主要采取无纸化操作的方式，这是以电子商务形式进行交易的主要特征。在电子商务中，计算机通信记录取代了一系列的纸面交易文件。用户发送或接收电子信息时，由于电子信息以比特的形式存在和传送，整个信息发送和接收过程实现了无纸化。无纸化带来的积极影响是使信息传递摆脱了纸张的限制，但由于传统法律的许多规范是以标准的"有纸交易"为出发点的，因此，无纸化在法律层面带来了一定程度上的混乱。

Section Two　Features of China's Cross-Border E-Commerce Development（我国跨境电子商务发展特征）

Currently, China's cross-border e-commerce is developing rapidly with outstanding features. Firstly, new business subjects spring up. According to incomplete statistics, the number of platform enterprises has been over 5 000, and the number of foreign trade enterprises that conduct cross-border e-commerce through kinds of platforms has been over 0.2 million. Secondly, the trade scale is expanding rapidly. It is estimated that in 2012, the turnover of the nationwide cross-border e-commerce was beyond USD 200 billion including over USD 15 billion of export of retails in cross-border e-commerce, which goes up by over 30% year-on-year, far beyond the growth rate of general trade in the same period. The momentum is expected to remain in 2013 with huge development potentials. Thirdly, the threshold for small and medium-sized enterprises conducting cross-border trade lowers. Small and medium-sized enterprises have established the international marketing channel through which they could directly connect with foreign buyers, reduce trade cost and shorten operation period. It is estimated that among the newly registered business entities on cross-border e-commerce platforms every year, the number of small and medium-sized enterprises and self-employed businessmen has taken up more than 90%. Fourthly, emerging markets have become the highlights. Turnover with emerging markets such as Brazil, Russia and India has soared, making important contributions to the rapid development of domestic cross-border e-commerce retail and export platforms. Fifthly, import size is small, but export one develops to the contrary. Import goods are mainly food such as milk powder, and luxuries like cosmetics with a small scale; export goods are mainly such goods for everyday consumption as cloths, accessories, small household appliances, and digital products with a large scale and a yearly fast growth rate.

当前，我国跨境电子商务发展迅速，特征突出。一是新的经营主体大量涌现。据不完全统计，平台企业已超过 5 000 家，境内通过各类平台开展跨境电子商务业务的外贸企业已超过 20 万家。二是贸易规模迅速扩张。据测算，2012 年全国跨境电子商务交易额已超过 2 000 亿美元，其中跨境电子商务零售出口突破 150 亿美元，较上年增长超过 30%，远高于同期我国一般贸易增长水平。2013 年有望继续保持这一态势，发展潜力巨大。三是中小企业从事跨境贸易的门槛降低。中小企业建立直接面向国外买家的国际营销渠道，以降低交易成本，缩短运营周期。据估算，目前每年在跨境电子商务平台上注册的新经营主体中，中小企业和个体商户已经占到 90% 以上。四是新兴市场成为亮点。巴西、俄罗斯和印度等新兴市场交易额大幅提升，为境内众多跨境电子商务零售出口平台快速发展做出重要贡献。五是进口规模小，出口规模大。进口商品主要包括奶粉等食品，化妆品等奢侈品的进口规模较小；出口商品主要包括服装、饰品、小家电和数码产品等日用消费品，规模较大，每年增速很快。

Section Three　Regulations on China's Cross-Border E-Commerce(我国跨境电子商务的法规）

The rapid development of cross-border e-commerce has attracted great attention from the government and business circle. On July 26, 2013, the General Office of the State Council issued Several Opinions of the General Office of the State Council on Promoting Steady Growth and Adjusting Structures in Foreign Trade (Guo Ban Fa [2013] No. 83), putting forward explicit requirements to develop cross-border e-commerce. On August 21, 2013, in order to encourage enterprises to broaden foreign trade through cross-border e-commerce, the General Office of the State Council forwarded the Opinions Concerning the Implementation of the Policies to Support Retail and Export in Cross-Border E-Commerce (Guo Ban Fa [2013] No.89)formulated by Ministry of Commerce and other Departments (hereinafter referred to as the "Opinions"), which aiming at the prominent problems that limit the development of cross-border e-commerce, have pointed out six measures on customs, quality inspection, taxes, foreign exchange, payment and credit to support the development of cross-border e-commerce. The Opinions were put into effect on October 1, 2013, in favorable regions of the country. The policies and measures concerning encouraging enterprises to conduct cross-border e-commerce retail and export, and taking retail and export into the trade statistics are favorably received by local governments and enterprises.

跨境电子商务的迅猛发展，引起政府和企业界高度重视。2013 年 7 月 26 日，国务院办公厅下发的《国务院办公厅关于促进进出口稳增长、调结构的若干意见》（国办发〔2013〕83 号）对发展跨境电子商务提出明确要求。同年 8 月 21 日，为鼓励企业利用跨境电子商务扩大对外贸易，国务院办公厅转发了商务部等部门制定的《关于实施支持跨境电子商务零售出口有关政策的意见》（国办发〔2013〕89 号），针对制约跨境电子商务零售出口发展的突出问题，提出通过海关、质检、税收、外汇、支付和信用 6 项措施支持跨境电子商务发展。该意见自 2013 年 10 月 1 日起在全国范围内有条件的地区实施，其中有关鼓励企业开展跨境电子商务零售出口，并将零售出口纳入贸易统计等政策措施，受到了各地和企业的普遍欢迎。

Section Four　Pattern of Trade（贸易模式）

Basic pattern of trade of Cross-border e-commerce in China is mainly divided into business to business (B2B) and business to consumer (B2C). With B2B mode, enterprises applies e-commerce with priority to use of advertisement and information release, with its deals and customs clearance process fulfilled in an offline manner. Therefore, it is still in the essence of the traditional trade, incorporated into the customs statistics of general trade. With B2C mode, our country's enterprises , directly facing the foreign customers, are mainly involved with sales of personal consumer goods; logistics is mainly carried out by aviation packets, mail, express way, and its declaration entity is Postal or Courier, which is not included in the customs registration at present.

我国跨境电子商务主要分为企业对企业（B2B）和企业对消费者（B2C）的贸易模式。B2B模式下，企业运用电子商务以广告和信息发布为主，成交和通关流程基本在线下完成，本质上仍属传统贸易，已纳入海关一般贸易统计。B2C模式下，我国企业直接面对国外消费者，以销售个人消费品为主，物流方面主要采用航空小包、邮寄、快递等方式，其报关主体是邮政或快递公司，目前大多未纳入海关登记。

As shown in Figure 1-1, the cross-border e-commerce process consists of four main entities, namely, authority, intermediary agencies, buyers/customers and suppliers. Among them, customers and suppliers are the main body of the entire cross-border e-commerce process, authority plays the role of supervision and policy formulation, and the intermediary agencies mainly play the role of service or third-party platform. The customer purchases cross-border e-commerce goods and pays the supplier, who effects delivery accordingly. The three processes involve cross-border e-commerce platform and "Internet +" payment means, as well as the realization of cross-border e-commerce process, which is also an embodiment of O2O online (purchase and payment) to offline (logistics delivery).

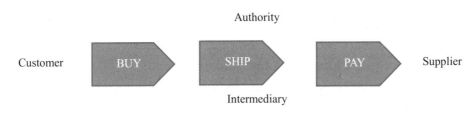

Figure 1-1　Procedure of Cross-Border E-Commerce

如图 1-1 所示，跨境电子商务流程包括四个主体，分别是政府部门、中间机构、顾客和供应商。其中，顾客和供应商是整个跨境电子商务流程的主体，政府部门起着监督与政策制定的作用，中间机构主要是起服务或第三方平台的作用。顾客购买跨境电子商务商品，并支付货款给供应商，供应商发货，这中间的三个流程涉及跨境电子商务平台与"互联网+"支付手段，跨境电子商务流程的实现，也是 O2O 线上（购买与支付）对线下（物流发货）的一种体现。

图 1-1　跨境电子商务流程图

Section Five　Policy Defects of Cross-Border E-Commerce（跨境电子商务面临的政策缺陷）

1．The Ownership Management Problems of E-Commerce Transactions

Based on the analysis of e-commerce transactions mode, pure electronic trading, to a great extent, belongs to the category of service trade, which is under the rule of GATS rules according to the trade in services. Those orders by electronic commerce, contract, etc., are transported by the traditional mode of transportation, and classified as trade in goods category, which belong to the category of the management of the GATT. In addition, for special types of e-commerce, trade in services is neither service trade nor goods trade, such as electronic products provided by means of electronic commerce (such as cultural products, software, entertainment, etc.), whether this kind of e-commerce trade belongs to services trade or trade in goods is still under discussion.

1．电子商务交易归属管理问题

从电子商务交易形式上分析，纯粹的电子交易在很大程度上属于服务贸易范畴，国际普遍认可归入 GATS（《服务贸易总协定》）的规则中，按服务贸易进行管理。对于只是通过电子商务方式完成定购、签约等，但要通过传统的运输方式将货物运送至购买人所在地的交易，则归入货物贸易范畴，属于 GATT（《关税及贸易总协定》）的管理范畴。此外，对于特殊的电子商务种类，既非明显的服务贸易也非明显的货物贸易，如通过电子商务手段提供电子类产品（如文化、软件、娱乐产品等），国际上对此类电子商务交易归属服务贸易还是货物贸易仍存在较大分歧。

2．The Market Access Issue of Trading Body

Cross-border e-commerce and payment business can break through space and time limit, making the business radiation to every corner of the world, the economic and financial information and capital chain are increasingly focused on data platform. Once the trading body lacks of adequate financial strength or problems such as irregular operations, credit crisis, system failures, information leakage, will cause the risk of customers' foreign exchange funds.

2．交易主体市场准入问题

跨境电子商务及支付业务能够突破时空限制，将商务辐射到世界的每个角落，使经济金融信息和资金链日益集中在数据平台。一旦交易主体缺乏足够的资金实力或出现违规经营、信用危机、系统故障、信息泄露等问题，便会引发客户外汇资金风险。

Section Six　Payment Business Defects of Cross-Border E-Commerce（跨境电子商务支付业务管理缺陷）

1．Difficulty in Auditing the Trade Authenticity

The virtuality of e-commerce is directly responsible for the difficulty in auditing the Trade Authenticity for the Supervision Department of the Foreign Exchange when it comes to the authenticity of cross-border e-commerce transactions, the legitimacy of the money; this provides a way for both domestic and overseas abnormal funds to deal with the balance of payments through cross-border e-commerce.

1．交易真实性难以审核

电子商务的虚拟性直接导致外汇监管部门对跨境电子商务交易的真实性、支付资金的合法性难以审核，为境内外异常资金通过跨境电子商务办理收支提供了途径。

2．Difficulties of the Balance of Payments

On the one hand, through the electronic payment platform, the domestic electric business bank account is not directly involved with the cross-border capital flows, and it usually takes 7 to 10 days for the payment platform to complete the real trading fund settlement, so it is more difficult for the trading main body to implement the provisions of the declaration. On the other hand, different transaction modes of international payment declaration also produce certain effects on the declarer entities of International Balance of Payment. Payment institutions, serve as the actual remittance body of offline payment unified purchase, and can declare payment mechanism as the main body of the international balance of payments. But it is difficult for this declaration mode to reflect each transaction essence of funds, adding the difficulties of foreign exchange supervision.

2．国际收支申报存在困难

一方面，通过电子支付平台，境内外电子商务的银行账户并不直接发生跨境资金流动，且支付平台完成实质交易资金清算常需要 7～10 天，因此由交易主体办理对外收付款申报的规定较难实施。另一方面，不同的交易方式下对国际收支申报主体也产生一定的影响。线下统一购汇支付方式的实际购汇人为支付机构，可以支付机构为主体进行国际收支申报，但此种申报方式难以体现每笔交易资金实质，给外汇监管增加了难度。

Section Seven　Local Implementation Plans（地方实施方案）

Currently, local governments are positively studying and formulating implementation plans, and introducing supporting policies. For example, the cross-border e-commerce industrial park built in Xiacheng District, Hangzhou was officially opened on July 8, 2013, and the whole process of customs clearance services including customs clearance and customs inspection could be realized in the park.

With the introduction of implementation plans of local governments, new-type customs supervision model and export rebate policy will better drive the retail and export of cross-border e-commerce. It is expected that cross-border e-commerce will witness a more rapid growth in the future.

目前，各地正积极研究制订实施方案，出台配套政策。例如，杭州市在下城区建立的跨境贸易电子商务产业园于 2013 年 7 月 8 日正式启用，在园区内实现报关、报检等全流程通关服务。随着各地实施方案陆续出台，新型海关监管模式和出口退税政策将更好地带动跨境电子商务零售出口，预计未来跨境电子商务零售出口将出现更快增长。

Part B　Terminology Practice

1. **Cross-border e-commerce**: a new-type mode of trade that digitalizes and electronizes of the exhibition, negotiation and conclusion of a business of the traditional trade by Chinese production and trade enterprises through e-commerce, finally realizing the import and export of products.

2. **Network space**: a virtual reality of net address and password.

3. **B2B**: business-to-business, commerce transactions between businesses, such as between a manufacturer and a wholesaler, or between a wholesaler and a retailer.

4. **B2C**: business-to-consumer, is the type of commerce transaction in which businesses sell products or services to consumers.

5. **TOT**: terms of trade, refers to the relative price of exports in terms of imports and is defined as the ratio of export prices to import prices. It can be interpreted as the amount of import goods an economy can purchase per unit of export goods.

6. **International trade**: the exchange of capital, goods, and services across internation borders or territories, which could involve the activities of the government and individual.

7. **Globalization**: the worldwide movement toward economic, financial, trade, and communications integration.

8. **Decentralization**: the process of redistributing or dispersing functions, powers, people or things away from a central location or authority.

9. **Intangibility**: used in marketing to describe the inability to assess the value gained from engaging in an activity using any tangible evidence. It is often used to describe services where there isn't a tangible product that the customer can purchase, that can be seen, tasted or touched.

10. **Turnover**: financial ratio that measures the efficiency of a company's use of its assets in generating sales revenue.

11. **Virtual Reality (VR)**: immersive multimedia or computer-simulated life, replicates an environment that simulates physical presence in places in the real world or imagined worlds and lets the user interact in that world.

12. **Electronic money**: the money balance recorded electronically on a stored-value card. These cards have microprocessors embedded which can be loaded with a monetary value.

Part C   Useful Expressions

1. based on 基于

2. profoundly affect 深远影响

3. traditional way to trade 传统贸易模式

4. a new-type mode of trade 新型贸易模式

5. at the same time 在同一时间

6. brand competitiveness 品牌竞争力

7. realize the transformation 实现转型

8. upgrade the level of foreign trade 外贸升级

9. share the characteristics of 共享（分享）……的特征

10. digital products and services 数字化产品和服务

11. physical objects 实物

12. be given priority to 以……为主

13. due to 由于……

14. bring positive effect 带来积极的影响

15. in terms of 以……形式

16. …attract great attention from… 引起……高度重视

17. be mainly divided into… 主要划分为……

18. trading body 贸易主体

Part D   Exercise

I. Answer the following questions according to the information you have got.

1. What is the definition of "cross-border e-commerce"?

2. What is "Network space"?

3. What is B2B?

4. What is B2C?

5. What are the features of cross-border e-commerce?

6. Why is it difficult to identify the e-commerce users' identity and its geographical location?

7. What is the definition of globalization?

8. What is decentralization?

9. What are the features of China's cross-border e-commerce development?

10. Summarize the policy defects of cross-border e-commerce.

11. What is virtual reality?

12. Summarize payment business defects of cross-border e-commerce.

13. What is electronic money?

14. What is TOT?

15. What does intangibility mean?

II. Match each one on the left with its correct meaning on the right.

1. turnover　　　　A. the exchange of goods, and services across international borders

2. network space　　B. the digitalization and electronization of a business

3. E-money　　　　C. redistributing or dispersing functions away from a central location

4. terms of trade　　D. worldwide movement toward economic, financial, trade, and communications integration

5. B2B　　　　　　E. businesses sell products or services to consumers

6. B2C　　　　　　F. commerce transactions between businesses

7. globalization　　G. amount of import goods an economy can purchase

8. decentralization　H. the money balance recorded electronically on a stored-value card

9. cross-border e-commerce　　　I. a virtual reality of net address and password

10. international trade　　　　　J. financial ratio that measures the efficiency of acompany's use of its assets in generating sales revenue

1. (　　) 2. (　　) 3. (　　) 4. (　　) 5. (　　)

6. (　　) 7. (　　) 8. (　　) 9. (　　) 10. (　　)

III. Translate the following phrases into Chinese.

1. profoundly affect

2. traditional way to trade

3. a new-type mode of trade

4. at the same time

5. brand competitiveness

6. realize the transformation

7. upgrading of foreign trade

8. sharing the characteristics of

9. digital products and services

10. physical objects

11. be given priority to

12. bring positive effect

13. in terms of

14. have attracted great attention from

15. Trading Body

IV. Case study for cross-border e-commerce.

Case Description:

Tmall has established many cross-border logistics warehouses through cooperation and free trade zone in cross-border aspect. In cities like Ningbo, Shanghai, Chongqing, Hangzhou, Zhengzhou, Guangzhou, Tmall has piloted free trade zone for its cross-border e-trade, and cooperation has been done in form of the industrial park of cross-border, laying cross-border outlets across the board. By adopting these measures, Tmall hedges its risks exposure to the basic law and the legal protection, compressing delivery time of the consumers, improving the convenience of overseas direct delivery service. In other words, cross-border business is from the so-called "gray area" to the door of the "light". In 2014, according to China's cross-border e-network operators, during the shopping spree festival "double eleven", more than half of the international goods of Tmall International had been through the free trade mode into the hands of domestic consumers, so it is clear that this mode is an important pilot of cross-border e-commerce.

Question:

What sort of cross-border mode does Tmall International belong to? Please comment on this mode.

案情介绍：

天猫在跨境方面通过和自贸区的合作，在各地保税物流中心建立了各自的跨境物流仓。它在宁波、上海、重庆、杭州、郑州、广州 6 个城市试点跨境电子商务贸易保税区、产业园签约跨境合作，全面铺设跨境网点，规避了基本法律风险，同时获得了法律保障，压缩了消费者从订单到接货的时间，提高了海外直发服务的便捷性，使得跨境业务在"灰色地带"打开了"光明之门"。据中国跨境电子商务网监测显示，2014 年"双十一"，天猫国际一半以上的国际商品就是以保税模式进入国内消费者手中的，是跨境电子商务的一次重要尝试。

问题：

天猫国际属于哪种跨境模式？请对这种模式进行评论。

V. Describe one or two cases about policy defects in doing cross-border e-commerce.

VI. Please determine whether the following statements are TRUE or FALSE. Then put T for TRUE or F for FALSE in the bracket at the end of each statement.

1. Cross-border e-commerce is developed on the network. (   )

2. Network is a medium body with boundary, sharing the characteristics of globalization and decentralization. (   )

3. The positive effect brought by features of network is the greatest sharing degree of information, whilst its negative impact is that the users confront risks. (   )

4. Due to the decentralization of cross-border e-commerce and global features, it is easy to identify the e-commerce users' identity and its geographical location. (   )

5. For network, the transmission speed is irrelevant to geographical distance. (   )

6. The rapid development of cross-border e-commerce has attracted little attention from government and business circle. (   )

7. Basic pattern of trade of cross-border e-commerce in China is mainly divided into business to business (B2B) and business to consumer (B2C). (   )

8. Those orders by electronic commerce, contract, etc., while are transported by the traditional mode of transportation, are classified as trade in goods category, which does not belong   the category of the management of the GATT. (   )

VII. Translate the following sentences into English.

1. 2013 年 3 月，国家外汇管理局下发《支付机构跨境电子商务外汇支付业务试点指导意见》，决定在上海、北京、重庆、浙江、深圳等地开展试点支付机构以实现跨境电子商务外汇支付业务，目前共有 22 家支付机构获得此牌照，包括支付宝、钱宝（Globebill）、财付通等。

2. 中国政府对外汇实行严格的管制，授权外管局逐一审批贸易和投资中的外汇交易。但是跨境电子商务中交易金额小、交易频繁，如果外管局坚持以前的监管方式，就会给支付造成很大障碍。

3. 外管局颁发跨境支付牌照后，用户可以通过支付宝等第三方支付平台使用人民币进行支付，支付宝负责向境外电商支付美元、英镑、欧元、日元、韩币等当地货币，再由境外电商网站或者支付宝合作的转运公司将商品运送至国内。

4. 支付宝直接与境外商户合作，截至 2014 年 3 月，支付宝服务已覆盖 32 个国家和地区的上千家网站的购物付款，支持 15 种海外货币结算。财付通与美国运通于 2012 年 11 月 19 日宣布"财付通美国运通国际账号"正式上线。用户可以直接在境外接受美国运通卡的商户进行购物。

VIII. Multiple Choices.

1. The differences between Alibaba International Station and Alibaba Express include (　　).

A. product completion content　　　　　　B. product validity period

C. payment methods　　　　　　　　　　D. delivery methods

2. If an account is set up in AliExpress with a U.S. dollar account, which of the following payment methods is used by the buyer to pay for the payment toward the U.S. dollar account? (　　).

A. Moneybookers　　　B. PayPal　　　C. T/T　　　　D. Credit Card

3. Which of the following types can be selected for AliExpress product shipping settings? (　　).

A. Standard shipping　　　　　　　　　B. Free shipping

C. Custom shipping　　　　　　　　　　D. No delivery

4. Taobao search sorting filter rules are (　　).

A. search relevance　　　　　　　　　　B. category relevance

C. customer evaluation relevance　　　　　D. product relevance

5. In Alibaba Chinese Station, services that are not personal editions are (　　).

A. post business opportunities　　　　　　　　　　B. view buyer information

C. with a third-party certification body certification　　　D. use Wangwang

6. Which of the following description of the Alibaba Chinese station information ranking rules is incorrect? (　　)

A. The top ten in the search results page is online marketing information.

B. Setting up priority display information will be ranked before the information is not set.

C. Integrity pass individual member information is ranked before the company member.

D. The information released by the trust-pass members is prior to the information released by the regular members.

7. In Alibaba Chinese Station, which of the following certifications does not require companies to provide? (　　).

A. Corporate photo　　　　　　　　　　B. Business license

C. Mandate　　　　　　　　　　　　　D. Copy of corporate identity card

8. In Alibaba Chinese Station, keyword settings must be (　　).

A. correct, accurate and accurate　　　　B. innovative

C. unique　　　　　　　　　　　　　　D. funny

9. When the international station releases product information, which of the following brief descriptions of the product is incorrect? (   )

A. A good brief description requires that the language is concise, while highlighting the advantages of the product.

B. Brief description to write "Low price high quality".

C. Brief description no more than 5 lines and 128 characters.

D. Brief description is one of the items that must be completed.

10. Which of the following steps is correct in the international station product release? (   )

A. Select category, fill in the information, review and go online.

B. Select category, go online, fill in the information.

C. Fill in the information, review online, select the category.

D. Fill in the information, select the category, review online.

Chapter Two   Cross-Border E-Commerce Operation Mode

第二章   跨境电子商务营运方式

Part A   Text

A Brief Introduction to Cross-Border E-Commerce Operation Mode

Cross-border (foreign trade) e-commerce is, essentially, the latest innovation and practice of e-commerce in the field of international trade. E-commerce is a new type of commerce and trade mode based on Internet technology and infrastructure, taking both parties to the transaction as the main body, using electronic payment and electronic settlement as its means; it relies on the support of modern logistics industry as well.

跨境（外贸）电子商务从本质上讲，是电子商务在国际贸易领域的一个最新的创新运用与实践。电子商务是一种以互联网技术和基础设施为基础，以交易双方为主体，以电子支付和电子结算为手段，同时依靠现代物流业支撑的一种新型商务贸易模式。

From this perspective, this book defines cross-border e-commerce as an international business transaction in which the subjects of transactions belong to different countries or different regions. The subjects of transactions reach or facilitate international transactions, make payment and settlement through the e-commerce platform, followed by effecting the relevant cross-country or regional logistics support for the delivery of goods.

从这个角度看，本书对跨境电子商务的定义，是指分属不同国家或区域的交易主体通过电子商务平台达成或促成国际交易，进行支付与结算，并通过跨越国家或区域的物流支持商品送达，最终完成交易的一种国际商务活动。

Based on the direction of import and export, cross-border e-commerce can be divided into two categories:"export-oriented" cross-border e-commerce and "import-type" cross-border e-commerce. Based on transaction patterns, cross-border e-commerce can also be divided into two main categories: B2B cross-border e-commerce and B2C cross-border e-commerce.

跨境电子商务基于进出口的方向可以划分为两类："出口型"跨境电子商务和"进口型"跨境电子商务。跨境电子商务基于交易，模式可以划分为两大类：B2B 跨境电子商务和 B2C 跨境电子商务。

Section One　Platform Trade Mode of Cross-Border E-Commerce（跨境电子商务平台交易模式）

1．Background

Since entering into the 21st century, more and more domestic and overseas foreign trade enterprises hope to tap customers and conduct business with more diversified and more efficient methods as well as channels, due to the fact that the traditional marketing mode is far from satisfying with the new development of international trade trend. With the rise of "Internet" in recent years, e-commerce has been gradually emerging. The advantages of e-commerce versus traditional business models are increasingly apparent: e-commerce has made transactions more transparent by breaking the traditional trade-time constraints; e-commerce can save manpower, material and financial resources; its advantages are also supported and advocate by more and more foreign trade enterprises of all kinds. To a large extent, e-commerce has satisfied the demand of many foreign trade enterprises for the expansion of import and export business, especially the demand and expansion in overseas markets. Therefore, many traditional foreign trade companies are initiating their acts to attach importance to this latest change in the international market and gradually embark on the cross-border e-commerce path. Foreign trade companies, aiming to promote business through cross-border e-commerce, will mainly adopt two modes of operation. Namely, one is to build their own independent foreign trade business web site; the other is mainly based on third-party e-commerce platform.

1．背景

进入 21 世纪以来，越来越多的国内外外贸企业希望用更多样化、更高效的方法和渠道来挖掘客户、开展业务，因为传统的营销模式已经远远无法满足新的国际贸易发展趋势。近年来电子商务伴随着互联网的崛起而逐渐兴起，与传统商务模式相比，电子商务的优点日益显现：电子商务通过打破传统的贸易时空限制，使得交易行为变得更加透明化、简单化；电子商务能够大力节省人力、物力以及财力，其优点也越来越受到外贸企业的青睐和推崇。电子商务在很大程度上满足了许多外贸企业的进出口业务拓展需求，尤其是海外市场需求和拓展，因此，不少传统外贸公司开始重视国际市场的这种最新变化，逐渐走上跨境电子商务之路。外贸公司通过跨境电子商务拉动业务，主要会采用两种模式和运营方式，一是搭建属于自己的独立的外贸商务网站；二是主要依靠第三方电子商务平台。

2．Cross-Corder E-commerce Platform Trading Mode

Figure 2-1 illustrates the cross-border e-commerce platform transaction mode process. First of all, domestic suppliers can publish relevant product information and query the global market demand information on cross-border e-commerce platform; international buyers can also publish their product demand information and query the global market product information on cross-border e-commerce platform; if domestic suppliers and international buyers meet the same demand with each other, they may conduct initial cross-border e-commerce cooperation intention negotiation through sending business relations invitation or direct inquiry (inquiry). If they fail to reach an agreement, they shall continue to find their own cross-border partners. After the initial negotiation on the intent of cross-border e-commerce cooperation is reached, both parties will continue their detailed negotiation and in-depth consultation on the contract so as to conclude the contract ultimately. After signing the contract, they eventually enter the actual transaction mode, that is, logistics delivery, settlement and payment procedures, until the completion of the transaction is done.

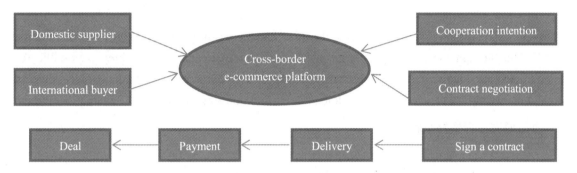

Figure 2-1　Cross-Border E-commerce Platform Transaction Mode

2. 跨境电子商务平台交易模式

图 2-1 体现了跨境电子商务平台交易模式流程。首先，国内供应商可以在跨境电子商务平台发布相关的产品信息并查询全球市场的需求信息；国际采购商也可以在跨境电子商务平台发布其相关的产品需求信息并查询全球市场的产品信息。基于这个平台，如果有国内供应商和国际采购商相互需求一致，则可以通过建立业务关系或直接的询盘（询价）进行初步跨境电子商务合作意向磋商，如未能达成一致，将继续寻找各自的跨境合作伙伴。初步跨境电子商务合作意向磋商达成一致后，双方将继续进行针对合同的详细洽谈和深入磋商，最后签订合同。签订合同后，便进入实际交易模式，即进行物流发货、结算支付等程序，直至完成交易。

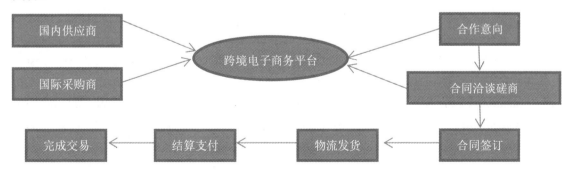

图 2-1　跨境电子商务平台交易模式图

Section Two　Advantages of Cross-Border E-Commerce Operation Mode（跨境电子商务运营模式的优势）

1. Boosting the Welfare of International Trade

The innovation of the cross-border e-commerce operation mode has led to the change of the traditional business process, together with the realization of the electronicization and digitization of international trade. On the one hand, through the cross-border e-commerce operation mode, international trade flows, instead of international trade logistics, can drastically reduce the manpower, material and financial resources consumption in the field of international trade and cut the transaction costs of international trade. On the other hand, cross-border e-commerce operation mode has broken through the time and space constraints in international trade, making it possible for international trade activities to be truly and efficiently carried out at any time and any place, thereby greatly increasing the efficiency of international trade and boosting the welfare of international trade.

1. 增进国际贸易福利

跨境电子商务运营模式的创新促使传统的商务流程发生了变化，实现了国际贸易电子化、数字化。一方面，通过跨境电子商务运营模式，国际贸易电子流代替了国际贸易实物流，可以大量减少国际贸易领域的人力、物力和财力消耗，降低了国际贸易交易成本；另一方面，跨境电子商务运营模式突破了国际贸易时间和空间上的限制，使得国际贸易活动可以真正实现在任何时间、任何地点的高效进行，从而大大提高了国际贸易效率，增进了国际贸易福利。

2. Information Symmetry

The open and global duality of cross-border e-commerce operation has created a large number of trading opportunities for cross-border e-commerce enterprises. At the same time, the cross-border e-commerce mode allows cross-border e-commerce enterprises to enter the global e-commerce trade market with similar transaction costs. The cross-border e-commerce operation mode has broken the barriers of time and space on the one hand and provided abundant and symmetrical information resources on the other hand. Moreover, this mode provides more possibilities for the reorganization and allocation of various economic resources as well as social elements, directly or indirectly affecting the layout of the global trade economy and the regional industrial structure. As a result, cross-border e-commerce SMEs are able to, just like any large enterprises, acquire the same amount of information resources and achieve "information symmetry", so as to enhance the international competitiveness of cross-border e-commerce SMEs.

2. 信息对称

跨境电子商务运营模式具有开放性和全球性双重特点，这为跨境电子商务企业创造了大量的贸易机会。同时，跨境电子商务模式使跨境电子商务企业可以通过相近的交易成本进入全球电子商务贸易市场之中。跨境电子商务运营模式一方面破除了交易时间和空间上的壁垒，另一方面，也提供了丰富对称的信息资源，为各种经济资源和社会要素的重新组合与配置提供了更多的可能，直接或间接地影响了全球贸易经济布局和区域产业结构。因此，跨境电子商务中小企业和大企业一样可以获得等量的信息资源，实现"信息对称"，从而提高跨境电子商务中小企业的国际竞争能力。

3．Interactivity

Cross-border e-commerce business mode has redefined and subverted the traditional mode of circulation. Cross-border e-commerce business mode bears a strong interaction, that is, through the Internet, cross-border business can be exchanged directly between the negotiations and the signing of the contract. The interaction is also reflected by the fact that consumers can reflect their own actual feedback suggestions on websites of cross-border businesses or businesses, and cross-border businesses or businesses can timely investigate cross-border product categories and cross-habitat quality of service, contributing to benign interaction. Cross-border e-commerce has made it possible for direct trade between producers and consumers at both ends of the cross-border e-commerce platform by virtue of reducing the intermediate links in trade, so as to largely change and subvert the way the entire world trade economy is operating.

3．互动性

跨境电子商务运营模式重新定义并颠覆了传统的流通模式。跨境电子商务运营模式具有很强的互动性，即通过互联网，跨境商家之间可以直接进行交流、谈判、合同签订。互动性还体现在消费者可以把自己的实际反馈建议反映到跨境企业或商家的网站之上，而跨境企业或者商家则可以根据消费者的反馈，及时地调查跨境产品种类及跨境服务的品质，做到良性互动。跨境电子商务通过减少贸易的中间环节，使得跨境电子商务平台两端的生产者和消费者的直接贸易成为一种现实可能，从而在很大程度上改变并颠覆了整个世界贸易经济运行的方式。

Section Three　Current Drawbacks and Limitations of Cross-Border E-Commerce Operation Mode（当前跨境电子商务运作模式的缺陷与局限性）

1．Limitations of Network of Cross-Border E-Commerce

The network of cross-border e-commerce mode of operation has its own limitations. Mainly reflected by the large gap between the goods shown online and the real goods received offline; consumers are often unable to get all the information concerning cross-border goods or services from the Internet, in particular, they are unable to get the most vivid and most direct impression of cross-border goods in the most rapid manner; In addition, web search function is not perfect, and there are some limitations on this aspect. One of the big questions that consumers face when shopping online across borders is how to seek cross-border goods that they really desire on numerous cross-border platform websites and buy them at the lowest price.

1．跨境电子商务运作网络的局限性

跨境电子商务运作模式网络本身有一定的局限性，主要体现为：网上的商品与实物的差距较大，消费者往往无法从网上得到跨境商品或服务的全部信息，尤其是无法以最快的速度获取对跨境商品的最鲜明、最直观的印象；另外，网络搜索功能不够完善，有一定的局限性。当消费者在跨境网上购物时，他们所面临的一个很大的问题就是如何在众多的跨境平台网站上寻找到自己真正想要的跨境商品，并以最低的价格买到。

2．Security of Cross-Border E-Commerce

Security of cross-border e-commerce mode is not decently guaranteed and this is mainly reflected in: how to deal with cross-border transactions in an open internet network, how to ensure the safety of data transmission, which has always been one of the most important factors affecting and restricting the development of cross-border e-commerce mode of operation. In addition, the current management of cross-border e-commerce is far from standardization. The concept of management actually covers many aspects, such as business management of cross-border e-commerce operations, cross-border technology management and cross-border service management. In particular, the consistency of the front-end and back-end of the business operation mode platform is also very crucial and important.

2．跨境电子商务的安全性

跨境电子商务运作模式交易的安全性得不到适当的保障，主要体现为：在开放的互联网网络上处理跨境交易，如何保证传输数据的安全一直以来都是影响和制约跨境电子商务运作模式发展的最重要因素之一。另外，目前对跨境电子商务的管理还远不够规范。这个管理的概念实际上涵盖了跨境电子商务运作商务管理、跨境技术管理、跨境服务管理等诸多方面，特别是跨境电子商务运作模式平台前后端的一致性也是非常关键和重要的。

3．Standardization of Cross-Border E-Commerce

Cross-border e-commerce supplier mode of operation is also facing the issue of standardization. Due to the different national conditions and cultures of diverse countries or regions across borders, there are bound to exist many differences and "heterogeneities" in the forms and means of cross-border e-commerce transactions. In the face of borderless and global cross-border trade activities, e-commerce operators shall establish a relevant mode of operation which entails a unified international standard, aiming to achieve a standardized cross-border e-commerce operation. At the same time, both cross-border logistics and distribution also confront the issue of standardization. Online consumers often encounter delayed delivery, and due to the relatively high costs of international logistics and distribution, it is imperative to form a standardized and efficient cross-border e-commerce distribution management system.

3．跨境电子商务标准化问题

跨境电子商务供应商运作模式也面临标准化的问题。由于不同国家或区域的国情和文化

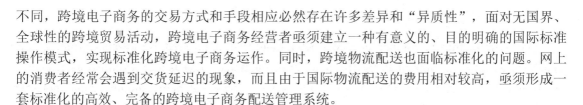

不同，跨境电子商务的交易方式和手段相应必然存在许多差异和"异质性"，面对无国界、全球性的跨境贸易活动，跨境电子商务经营者亟须建立一种有意义的、目的明确的国际标准操作模式，实现标准化跨境电子商务运作。同时，跨境物流配送也面临标准化的问题。网上的消费者经常会遇到交货延迟的现象，而且由于国际物流配送的费用相对较高，亟须形成一套标准化的高效、完备的跨境电子商务配送管理系统。

4．Legalization of Cross-Border E-Commerce

Cross-border e-commerce mode of operation is also facing the issue of legalization. Mainly reflected in the following aspects: the legal issues of electronic contracts. On the one hand, the existence of electronic contracts are easily tampered with, fabricated and so difficult to prove their authenticity and effectiveness of the problem; on the other hand, the digital seal of electronic contracts and the legal validity of signatures also urgently cry out for the existing laws to effectively regulate. Because of the existence of digital information on the computer network, the issue of intellectual property rights has become prominent in the field of intellectual property (patents, trademarks, copyrights, trade secrets, etc.).

4．跨境电子商务法制化问题

跨境电子商务运作模式还面临法制化的问题，主要体现为以下方面。电子合同的法律问题：一方面，电子合同存在容易被篡改、编造等难以证明其真实性和有效性的问题；另一方面，电子合同的数字化印章和签名的法律效力还亟须现有的法律有效地对其进行规范。除此之外，由于计算机网络上所承载的是以数字化形式存在的信息，因而，在知识产权领域（专利、商标、版权和商业秘密等），版权保护的问题就显得十分突出。

Section Four　Current Representative Operation Mode of Cross-Border E-Commerce（目前跨境电子商务具有代表性的营运模式）

1．Overseas Purchasing Cross-Border E-Commerce Mode

Overseas purchasing cross-border e-commerce mode is referred to as "Hai-Dai" in Chinese, this model is just after the "Hai-Tao" model, which is well-known and recognized by domestic consumers as a cross-border online shopping concept. The overseas purchasing cross-border e-commerce mode is defined, by this present book, as a mode in which a certain business overseas purchases goods for domestic consumers and further effect cross-border logistics and distribution, so as to enable the domestic consumer get the delivered goods.

1．海外代购跨境电子商务模式

海外代购跨境电子商务模式简称"海代"，这种模式是继"海淘"之后第二个被国内消费者所熟知的跨境网购概念。本书对海外代购跨境电子商务模式的定义，就是一种为国内消费者购买商品，并进一步通过跨境物流配送，将国内消费者所购商品送达的商业模式。

2. Drop-Ship Platform Cross-Border E-Commerce Mode

Drop-ship platform cross-border e-commerce mode can be referred to as drop-shipping mode. This book defines drop-ship platform cross-border e-commerce mode as a cross-border e-commerce platform that sends customer order information received to wholesalers or vendors, while wholesale merchants send consumers retail based on order information for related goods and services. In this drop-shipping mode, because the supplier is often a brand seller, a wholesaler or a manufacturer, in effect, the drop-shipping platform is a typical e-commerce B2C mode. It can also be understood as a third-party B2C model, such as Tmall in China.

2. 直发/直运平台跨境电子商务模式

直发/直运平台模式可以称为 drop-shipping 模式。本书对直发/直运平台模式的定义是：通过一种跨境电子商务平台，将接收到的消费者订单信息发给批发商或厂商，而批发商或厂商则根据订单信息以零售的形式对消费者发送相关货物和服务的模式。在这种直发/直运模式下，因为供货商往往就是品牌商、批发商或厂商，所以，实际上直发/直运平台跨境电子商务模式是一种典型的电子商务 B2C 模式。也可以将其理解为一种第三方 B2C 模式，如国内的天猫商城。

3. Self-Run B2C Cross-Border E-Commerce Mode

In the self-run B2C model, most cross-border e-commerce products require cross-border e-commerce platforms to fulfill their own stocking. Therefore, self-run B2C mode is the most important category in all modes. Self-run B2C model can be subdivided into two categories: self-vertical and integrated self-employed. Vertical self-supporting cross-border B2C platform refers to cross-border platform whose choice of self-cross-border category tends to focus on a particular area, such as focusing on foods, luxury items, cosmetics or clothing. The self-run cross-border category of the integrated self-run cross-border B2C platform is not limited to a specific category. Currently, representatives of the comprehensive self-run cross-border B2C platform are Amazon and No. 1 stores.

3. 自营 B2C 跨境电子商务模式

在自营的 B2C 模式下，大多数跨境电子商务商品都需要跨境电子商务平台自己备货。因此，自营的 B2C 模式是所有模式里最重要的一类。自营 B2C 模式可以细分为两大类：垂直型自营和综合型自营。垂直型自营跨境 B2C 平台是指，跨境平台在选择自营跨境品类时会集中于某个特定的范畴，如集中于食品、奢侈品、化妆品或服饰等。综合型自营跨境 B2C 平台的自营跨境品类不限于特定的范畴，目前综合型自营跨境 B2C 平台的代表是亚马逊和 1 号店。

4. Shopping Guide / Rebate Cross-Border E-Commerce Platform Mode

Shopping guide/rebate cross-border e-commerce mode is a more "straightforward" e-commerce model. This model includes two steps: drainage step and commodity trading step. Drainage step

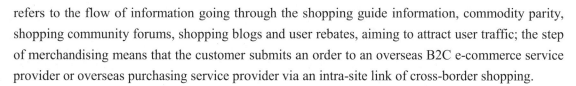

refers to the flow of information going through the shopping guide information, commodity parity, shopping community forums, shopping blogs and user rebates, aiming to attract user traffic; the step of merchandising means that the customer submits an order to an overseas B2C e-commerce service provider or overseas purchasing service provider via an intra-site link of cross-border shopping.

4. 导购/返利跨境电子商务平台模式

导购/返利跨境电子商务模式是一种更加"简单"的电商模式，这种模式包括两个步骤：引流步骤和商品交易步骤。引流步骤是指，通过导购资讯、商品比价、海购社区论坛、海购博客以及用户返利来吸引用户流量；商品交易步骤是指，消费者通过站内链接向海外 B2C 电商或者海外代购者提交订单，实现跨境购物。

5. Overseas Flash-Purchase Cross-Border E-Commerce Mode

In addition to the above four types of imported retail cross-border e-commerce modes, overseas flash-purchase cross-border e-commerce mode is a relatively unique approach, and here treats it separately as a separated cross-border e-commerce mode. As the supply chain environment for cross-border flash-purchase is more complicated than that in the domestic area, the platforms involved in cross-border flash-sale operations have only been in the pilot phase for a long time to come.

5. 海外商品闪购跨境电子商务模式

除了以上 4 种进口零售跨境电子商务模式之外，海外商品闪购是一种相对独特的做法，所以本书将其单独列为一种跨境电子商务模式。由于跨境闪购所面临的供应链环境比起境内更为复杂，所以，在很长一段时间里，涉足跨境闪购的平台都只是处于小规模试水阶段。

Part B   Terminology Practice

1. **Information asymmetry**: in contract theory and economics, information asymmetry refers to the situation in transactions where one party has more or better information than the other. This asymmetry creates an imbalance of power in transactions, which can sometimes cause the transactions to go away, a kind of market failure in the worst case. Examples of this problem are adverse selection, moral hazard, and information monopoly.

2. **Homogeneity and heterogeneity**: homogeneity and heterogeneity are concepts often used in the sciences and statistics relating to the uniformity in a substance or organism. A material or image that is homogeneous is uniform in composition or character (i.e. color, shape, size, weight, height, distribution, texture, language, income, disease, temperature, radioactivity, architectural design, etc.); one that is heterogeneous is distinctly nonuniform in one of these qualities.

3. **Supply chain**: refers to a system of organizations, people, activities, information and resources involved in moving a product or service from supplier to customer. Supply chain activities involve the transformation of natural resources, raw materials, and components into a finished

product that is delivered to the end customer.

4. **Standardization**: standardization or standardisation refers to the process of implementing and developing technical standards based on the consensus of different parties that include firms, users, interest groups, standard organizations and governments.

5. **Logistics**: generally refers to the detailed organization and implementation of a complex operation. In a general business sense, logistics is the management of the flow of things between the point of origin and the point of consumption in order to meet requirements of customers or corporations.

6. **Distribution**: in economics, distribution is the way total output, income, or wealth is distributed among individuals or among the factors of production (such as labour, land, and capital). In general theory and the national income and product accounts, each unit of output corresponds to a unit of income. One use of national accounts is for classifying factor incomes and measuring their respective shares, as in national income.

7. **Legalization**: refers to the process of removing a legal prohibition against something which is currently not legal.

8. **Export**: the term export means sending of goods or services produced in one country to another country. The seller of such goods and services is referred to as an exporter; the foreign buyer is referred to as an importer.

9. **Import**: an import is a good brought into a jurisdiction, especially across a national border, from an external source. The party bringing in the good is called an importer. An import in the receiving country is an export from the sending country.

10. **Drop-ship platform cross-border e-commerce mode**: refers to a cross-border e-commerce platform that sends customer order information to wholesalers or vendors, while wholesale merchants send consumers retail based on order information for related goods and services.

11. **Overseas purchasing cross-border e-commerce mode**: refers to a mode in which a certain business overseas purchases goods for domestic consumers and further effect cross-border logistics and distribution, so as to enable the domestic consumers get the delivered goods.

12. **E-business**: a term which can be used for any kind of business or commercial transaction that includes sharing information across the internet. Commerce constitutes the exchange of products and services between businesses, groups and individuals, which can be seen as one of the essential activities of any business.

Part C　Useful Expressions

1. from this perspective　从这个角度看
2. belong to　属于……
3. followed by　紧跟着……
4. be divided into　被分为……

5. due to the fact that 由于……

6. far from 远远不够……

7. to a large extent 很大程度上……

8. embark on 踏上……

9. it is illustrated 它说明了……

10. on the intent of 对……的意图

11. have led to 已经导致了……

12. a large number of 大量的

13. reflected by 由……反映

14. in addition 另外

15. deal with 处理

16. at the same time 与此同时

17. tamper with 篡改

18. cry out for 亟须……

Part D Exercise

I. Answer the following questions according to the information you have got.

1. What is the definition of e-business?

2. In contract theory and economics, what does information asymmetry deal with?

3. What do supply chain activities involve?

4. What is the definition of Logistics?

5. In economics, what does distribution refer to?

6. What is the definition of drop-ship platform cross-border e-commerce mode?

7. What is the definition of overseas purchasing cross-border e-commerce mode?

II. Match each one on the left with its correct meaning on the right.

1. Export   A. the way total output or income is allocated among individuals

2. Import   B. detailed organization and implementation of a complex operation

3. E-business   C. business transaction that includes sharing information across the internet

4. Logistics   D. a goods brought into a jurisdiction, especially across a national border, from an external source

5. Distribution   E. sending of goods or services produced in one country to another country

1. (   ) 2. (   ) 3. (   ) 4. (   ) 5. (   )

III. Translate the following terms and phrases into Chinese.

1. cross-border e-commerce operation mode   2. latest innovation

3. modern logistics industry   4. domestic and overseas

5. foreign trade enterprise   6. tap customer

7. conduct business   8. traditional marketing mode

9. third-party e-commerce platform　　10. signing the contract

11. the welfare of international trade　　12. electronization

13. information symmetry　　14. cross-border e-commerce SMEs

15. international competitiveness　　16. drawbacks and limitations

17.data transmission

IV. Case study for cross-border e-commerce.

Case Description:

Alibaba International Station creates integrated services through multiple channels. In 2018, Alibaba's new trade festival business conference,with the theme of "Commercial and Business Excellence", was held at the Hangzhou Future Technology International Conference Center. As the first major promotion event of the international station in 2018, it will not only be able to test the warm and cold of the cross-border B2B business in 2018, but also make it more clear the core layout of the international station in the next few years. Alibaba International aims to help the entire supplier on the platform, complete the end-to-end online international trade service, realize the "Global Buy, Global Sell" strategy, and help suppliers to, by means of Ali's payment, finance, or business categories, provide deterministic services in the buyers quadrant.

Question:

Based on the above case of Alibaba International Station, please review the future development trend of cross-border e-commerce.

案情介绍：

阿里巴巴国际站通过多元化渠道打造综合服务。2018 年，以"品商兼优买卖全球"为主题的阿里巴巴新贸易节日商家大会在杭州未来科技国际会议中心召开。作为 2018 年国际站的首个大型促销活动，它不仅试水了 2018 年跨境 B2B 业务的冷暖，同时也使国际站未来几年的核心布局更清晰化。阿里巴巴国际站着眼于帮助平台上的供应商完成端到端的在线化国际贸易服务，实现"全球买，全球卖"的策略，并且帮助供应商通过阿里的支付、金融，或是商业类产品为买家提供确定性的服务。

问题：

通过以上阿里巴巴国际站的案例，评论跨境电子商务今后的发展趋势。

V. Describe one or two cases about the latest platform cross-border e-commerce mode.

VI. Please determine whether the following statements are TRUE or FALSE. Then put T for TRUE or F for FALSE in the bracket at the end of each statement.

1. The purchase information on Alibaba.com's international website is particularly suitable for buyers who cannot find suitable products on the website. (　　)

2. For members of Alibaba China Suppliers, the product image must be in JPG format; the size of each image cannot exceed 200K. (　　)

3. In the international station, the completeness of the product attribute filling is conducive to making it easier for buyers to search. (　　)

4. In the international station, the so-called five-star website refers to the 100% utilization rate of the window products on the homepage, the products are professionally grouped, the TM remains online, the company column is fully utilized, and there is a rich company image display. (　　)

5. For members of Alibaba International Station, the product pictures provided should not put too many products in the same picture, otherwise the product details cannot be shown forfeited. (　　)

6. In the corporate website design of the international station, customers can freely upload BANNER pictures in a format of 700×780. (　　)

7. Uploading product images in AliExpress can be directly selected from Alibaba international station. (　　)

8. AliExpress can accept both RMB and US dollars, but you need to open a US dollar account. (　　)

9. CNFM, a free buyer for the international station, can directly become an AliExpress seller. (　　)

10. With the Alipay account to quickly register the AliExpress account, you do not need to fill in the Alipay account. (　　)

VII. Translate the following sentences into English.

1. 进入 21 世纪以来，越来越多的国内外外贸企业希望用更多样化、更高效的方法和渠道来挖掘客户、开展业务，因为传统的营销模式已经远远无法满足新的国际贸易发展趋势。伴随着互联网的崛起，近年来电子商务逐渐兴起。

2. 跨境电子商务运营模式突破了国际贸易时间和空间上的限制，使得国际贸易活动可以在任何时间、任何地点高效进行，从而大大提高了国际贸易效率，增加了国际贸易福利。

3. 跨境电子商务运营模式重新定义并颠覆了传统的流通模式。跨境电子商务运营模式具有很强的互动性，即通过互联网，跨境商家之间可以直接进行交流、谈判、合同签订。互动性还体现在消费者可以把自己的实际反馈建议反映到跨境企业或商家的网站上，跨境企业或者商家可以根据消费者的反馈，及时调查跨境产品种类及跨境服务的品质，做到良性互动。跨境电子商务通过减少贸易的中间环节，使得跨境电子商务平台两端的生产者和消费者的直接贸易成为一种现实可能，从而在很大程度上改变了整个世界经济贸易运行的方式。

4. 跨境电子商务运作模式还面临法制化的问题，主要体现为电子合同的法律问题和知识产权问题。电子合同的法律问题：一方面，电子合同存在容易被篡改、编造等难以证明其真实性和有效性的问题；另一方面，电子合同的数字化印章和签名的法律效力还亟须现有的法律有效地对其进行规范。除此之外，由于计算机网络上所承载的是以数字化形式存在的信息，因而，在知识产权领域（专利、商标、版权和商业秘密等），版权保护的问题就显得十分突出。

5. 在直发/直运模式下，因为供货商往往就是品牌商、批发商或厂商，所以，实际上直发/直运平台跨境电子商务模式是一种典型的电子商务 B2C 模式。也可以将其理解为一种第三方 B2C 模式，如国内的天猫商城。

VIII. Multiple Choices.

1. After Alibaba.com's products are uploaded, Alibaba staff will conduct the audit. General audit time is (   ) hours.

A.6   B.12   C.24   D.48

2. As for Alibaba International Station, which of the following product category releases has the lowest CTR? (   ).

A. Apparel>Pants, Trousers & Jeans

B. Apparel>Baby Clothing>Baby Pants, Trousers & Jeans

C. Apparel>Children's Clothing>Children's Pants, Trousers & Jeans

D. Apparel>others

3. Alibaba international station home page enter keywords. The search bar that cannot be searched is (   ).

A. Product (Product Information)   B. Suppliers (Supplier Information)

C. Promotion (promotion information)   D. Buyers (buyer information)

4. AliExpress's personal authentication management can be authenticated by (   ) below.

A. Alipay user authentication, Taobao user authentication, Alibaba user authentication

B. Alipay user authentication, bank account real name authentication, Alibaba Chinese station user authentication

C. Alipay user authentication, personal real name authentication, bank account real name authentication

D. Alipay user authentication, Alibaba Chinese station user authentication, personal real name authentication

5. Escrow currently supports the maximum transaction amount for single orders below (   ).

A. USD 5 000 (Total Product Price plus Total Freight)

B. USD 8 000 (Total Product Price plus Total Freight)

C. USD 10 000 (Total Product Price plus Total Freight)

D. USD 15 000 (Total Product Price plus Total Freight)

6. Which of the following is incorrect for an AliExpress bank account? (   ).

A. Personal Dollar Account   B. Company Dollar Account

C. Alipay   D. Personal RMB Account

7. Keywords, as a station promotion tool for each product, how many word counts can be set up to a maximum extent? (   ).

A. 100   B. 200   C. 300   D. 400

8. At the international station, in order to lift product ranking, by increasing exposure, we should (   ).

A. fill product information as complete as possible

B. according to product characteristics, put a piece of information into related categories and publish multiple supply and demand information

C. according to the different habits of customers in different regions, set different keywords

D. detailed description should be as detailed as possible, fully introduce the product's specifications and models, and increase the credibility of information to increase exposure

9. At the international station, which of the following statements about product optimization is correct? (　　)

A. Eye-catching product titles can directly increase the feedback rate.

B. Appropriate, beautiful pictures can increase product click-through rate.

C. A brief description of the equivalent slogan can significantly increase the product's click through rate.

D. Detailed description should be as detailed as possible, fully introduce the product's specifications and models, and increase the credibility of information to increase the feedback rate.

10. At the international station, the following statements about Alibaba's international window products are (　　).

A. if the information quality factors are the same, window products are more easily found by customers

B. window products will be placed in front of ordinary products

C. showcase products appear directly on the company homepage

D. the maximum number of window products is 20

Chapter Three   An Overview of Third-Party Cross-Border E-commerce Platform

第三章   第三方跨境电子商务平台概述

Part A   Text

A Brief Introduction to Third-Party Cross-Border E-Commerce Platform

Third-party cross-border e-commerce platforms generally refer to a kind of cross-border e-commerce operation mode in which services are rendered to those providers and demanders that are independent of cross-border products or cross-border services, mainly through network service platforms and in accordance with specific e-commerce transaction and e-commerce service standards.

第三方跨境电子商务平台，一般泛指独立于跨境产品或跨境服务的提供者和需求者，主要通过网络服务平台，并按照特定的电子商务交易与电子商务服务规范，为跨境贸易的买卖双方提供服务的一种跨境电子商务运营模式。

The service content of the third-party cross-border e-commerce platform may include, but not limited to, "publishing and searching of supply and demand information, establishment of transactions, payment, and logistics". At present, the representative third-party cross-border e-commerce platforms in China are: Alibaba's AliExpress, Dunhuang Network, China Manufacturing Network and so on.

第三方跨境电子商务平台的服务内容可以包括但不限于供求信息发布与搜索、交易的确立、支付、物流。目前国内有代表性的第三方跨境电子商务平台有阿里巴巴速卖通、敦煌网、中国制造网等。

Section One   Features of Third-Party Cross-Border E-Commerce Platform （第三方跨境电子商务平台的特点）

1．Independence

The third-party cross-border e-commerce platform is neither a trade buyer nor a trade seller, but rather, exists as a platform for cross-border e-commerce transactions. Like the trading market in physical trading, it is actually an intermediary trading market in the online world.

1．独立性

第三方跨境电子商务平台既不是贸易买家，也不是贸易卖家，而是作为跨境电子商务交易的一个平台存在，如同实体买卖中的交易市场一样，它实际上是网络世界的中介交易市场。

2．Relying on the Network

With the development of e-commerce business and international trade, third-party cross-border e-commerce platform has emerged; like traditional e-commerce, it relies on the network to play its intermediary trading market role.

2．依托网络

第三方跨境电子商务平台是随着电子商务和国际贸易的发展而出现的，和传统的电子商务一样，它必须依托于网络才能发挥其中介交易市场的作用。

3．Specialization

As a service platform for trading markets, third-party cross-border e-commerce platforms require more professional business support technologies, including order management, payment security and logistics management, so as to achieve the objective of providing safe and convenient services for both cross-border e-commerce buyers and sellers.

3．专业化

作为交易市场服务平台，第三方跨境电子商务平台需要更加专业的商务贸易支撑技术，包括对订单管理、支付安全和物流管理等技术支撑，实现其为跨境电子商务买卖双方提供安全便捷服务的宗旨。

Section Two　Profit Mode of Third-Party Cross-Border E-Commerce Platform（第三方跨境电子商务平台的盈利模式）

1．Membership Fee Profit Mode

In the form of receiving membership fee or registering as a member, third-party cross-border e-commerce platforms achieve profitamenberbility through the online store rental, cross-border company certification, and cross-border product information recommendation.

1．会员费盈利模式

第三方跨境电子商务平台以收取会员费或注册成为会员的形式，通过网上店铺出租、跨境公司认证、跨境产品信息推荐等方式实现盈利。

2．Advertising Fee Profit Model

Third-party cross-border e-commerce platforms make money through various types of advertising fees, including text ads, such as keywords, or embedding different-color text in text-linked information articles, image ads and dynamic advertising flash. At the same time, ad Networks that share ads on well-known cross-border e-commerce sites are also an important channel for profitable advertising. Mail shot and commercial survey delivery are also commonly used tools.

2．广告费盈利模式

第三方跨境电子商务平台通过各类广告费实现盈利，其中包括文字广告，如关键字，或者是在文字链接资讯文章中嵌入不同颜色的文字、图片广告和动态广告 flash 等。同时，广告联盟分享投放知名跨境电子商务网站上的广告，也是一个重要的广告费实现盈利渠道。邮件广告和商业调查投放也是常用的手段。

3．Search / PPC Profit Mode

Third-party cross-border e-commerce platform makes its margins through a variety of keywords PPC rankings for profitability. In fact, keywords PPC rankings refer to the keywords rankings by customers search. In addition, the hot words link the cross-border shops or a cross-border business site is also a commonly used search / bid ranking means.

3．搜索/竞价排名盈利模式

第三方跨境电子商务平台通过各类关键词竞价排名进行收费盈利，关键词竞价排名即客户通过搜索关键词得到的排名。另外，热点词汇直达跨境商铺或跨境企业网站也是常用的搜索/竞价排名手段。

4．Value-Added Service Profit Mode

Third-party cross-border e-commerce platforms also make margins and profits by offering various value-added services, including corporate certification, independent domain names, search engine optimization and ezine downloads. The platform also provides a variety of information and reporting services, such as industry data analysis reports, industry development reports, customer messages, cutting-edge messaging services and mail services, web site data analysis reports, as well as experts online information.

4．增值服务盈利模式

第三方跨境电子商务平台还通过提供各种增值服务来盈利，包括企业认证、独立域名、搜索引擎优化和电子杂志下载等。平台还提供各种信息和报告服务，如行业数据分析报告、行业发展报告、客户留言、前沿资讯短信服务和邮件服务、网站数据分析报告以及专家在线咨询等。

5．Offline Service Profit Mode

Third-party cross-border e-commerce platforms also make money by offering a variety of offline physical services，including cross-border e-commerce network marketing planning training, cross-border e-commerce product exhibitions, cross-border e-commerce industry associations, cross-border e-commerce seminars and summit forums, etc. In addition, some periodicals are embedded with ads or industry information to achieve profitability.

5．线下服务盈利模式

第三方跨境电子商务平台还通过提供各种线下实体服务来盈利，包括跨境电子商务网络营销策划培训、跨境电子商务产品展会、跨境电子商务行业商会、跨境电子商务研讨会和高峰论坛等。另外，还在某些期刊内通过行业资讯、植入广告等来实现盈利。

6．Business Cooperation Profit Mode

Third-party cross-border e-commerce platforms also make money by cooperating with governments, industry associations, businesses and the media in cross-border countries or regions. In addition, third-party cross-border e-commerce platform can also cooperate with other websites, such as advertising networks (Baidu Union, Google Alliance).

6．商务合作盈利模式

第三方跨境电子商务平台还通过与跨境国家或区域的政府、行业协会、企业和媒体等合作实现盈利。另外，第三方跨境电子商务平台还可以与其他的网站进行合作，如广告联盟（百度联盟、谷歌联盟）等。

7．Trading Profit Charging Mode

Third-party cross-border e-commerce platforms also make profits through various trading links such as online brokerage, transaction commissions, payment services, online auctions and cross-border logistics services, etc.

7．交易环节收费盈利模式

第三方跨境电子商务平台还通过各种交易环节进行收费盈利，如网上业务中介、交易佣金、支付服务、网上拍卖以及跨境物流服务等。

Section Three　Classification and Brief Introduction to Third-Party Cross-Border E-Commerce Platforms（第三方跨境电子商务平台分类与简介）

1．B2B Cross-Border E-Commerce Platform

B2B (Business-to-Business) is carried out between cross-border businesses and enterprises. It is mainly based on general information dissemination and transaction matching, serving as the business bridge for the establishment of cross-border trade. At present, cross-border e-commerce mainstream platform mode is B-B-C rather than B2C. That is, cross-border e-commerce = cross-border commerce (B2B) + localized e-commerce (B2C, B2B), traditional enterprises are increasingly turning to conduct small orders after they switch to cross-border e-commerce. Small orders at present are with three kinds of solutions: online wholesale + overseas warehouse mode; online supply distribution mode; operation agent.

1．B2B 跨境电子商务平台

B2B（Business-to-Business）是在跨境企业与企业之间进行的，一般以信息发布与交易撮合为主，主要是建立跨境商家之间贸易的桥梁。跨境电子商务主流平台模式不是 B2C，而是 B-B-C，即跨境电子商务=跨境贸易（B2B）+本地化电商（B2C、B2B），传统企业转向跨境电商后，越来越趋向做小订单。小订单现有 3 种解决方案：在线批发+海外仓模式；在线货源分销模式；代运营。

In essence, B2B cross-border e-commerce is a commerce platform for the dissemination and management of cross-border e-commerce information. With this cross-border platform, cross-border product information and cross-border company information can be rapidly released globally. Therefore, B2B cross-border e-commerce platform is ideal for small and medium enterprises to do online promotion. In addition to e-commerce platforms such as China Manufacturing Network, Alibaba, Global Sources and other cross-border commercial activities conducted through third-party cross-border e-commerce website platforms, there are also e-commerce B2B platforms directly operated by enterprises such as Dunhuang Network.

B2B 跨境电子商务本质上是一个跨境电子贸易信息发布与管理的商务平台，借助这样的跨境平台可以快速将跨境商品信息和跨境公司信息发布到全球。因此，B2B 跨境电子商务平台非常适合中小企业做网上推广。除了如中国制造网、阿里巴巴、环球资源等通过第三方跨境电子商务网站平台进行跨境商业活动的电商平台外，也有企业之间直接进行商业活动的电子商务 B2B 平台，如敦煌网等。

2．B2C Cross-Border E-Commerce Platform

B2C (Business-to-Customer) refers to e-commerce transactions between cross-border merchants and customers. Cross-border consumers purchase cross-border goods and services frequently, and in small quantities, from cross-border vendors through the Internet. This mode, also known as online retailing, treats itself as an electronic retail because it resembles the actual sales process. This platforms offer everything ranging from flowers and books to computers and cars to consumer goods and services. For example: Dangdang, Amazon online bookstore.

2．B2C 跨境电子商务平台

B2C（Business-to-Customer）指的是跨境商家与顾客之间的电子商务交易，跨境消费者通过网络向跨境厂商小批量、频繁地购买跨境商品或服务。这种模式又称为网上零售，因为它类似于实际中的销售过程，所以通常被看作是一种电子化的零售形式，如提供从鲜花、书籍到计算机、汽车等各种消费商品和服务。例如当当网、亚马逊网上书城。

Cross-border businesses provide cross-border consumers with a new cross-border shopping environment via the Internet cross-border online stores where consumers experience cross-border online shopping and cross-border payments. This mode saves customers and businesses a great deal of time and space, greatly improving the transaction efficiency. Major B2C cross-border

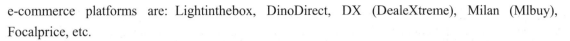

e-commerce platforms are: Lightinthebox, DinoDirect, DX (DealeXtreme), Milan (Mlbuy), Focalprice, etc.

跨境企业通过互联网为跨境消费者提供了一个新型的跨境购物环境——跨境网上商店，消费者通过网络实现跨境购物、跨境支付。这种模式节省了客户和企业的时间和空间，大大提高了交易效率。目前主要的 B2C 跨境电子商务平台有兰亭集势（Lightinthebox）、大龙网（DinoDirect）、DX（DealeXtreme）、米兰网（Mlbuy）、Focalprice 等。

3．Profile of main B2B, B2C, C2C Cross-Border E-Commerce Platforms

Lightinthebox was on the line in year 2007, and in its early period, it focused on the electronic products, mainly with B2B small wholesale trade. In early 2009, Lightinthebox set off on the line wedding product series, with the sales of that year hit nearly 30 million US dollars. Lightinthebox attaches great importance to the operation of social marketing tools such as SNS and BBS. It is based on leading online marketing technologies such as Google Marketing, Facebook, Twitter, Linkedin and other social networking communities marketing.

3．主要 B2B、B2C、C2C 跨境电子商务平台简介

兰亭集势于 2007 年上线，早期主营电子产品，以 B2B 小额外贸批发为主。2009 年初，兰亭集势上线婚纱产品线，当年销售近 3 千万美元。兰亭集势非常重视 SNS、BBS 等社会化营销工具的运营，立足领先精准的网络营销技术，如谷歌营销、Facebook、Twitter、Linkedin 等社会化网络社区营销。

Established in 2006, DX (dealextreme.com)'s main business scope is the main electronic products and 3C gadgets, such as U disk, cell phone case. DX enjoys a very well-known brand image in South America. From 2008 to 2009, with soar of the small foreign trade market brought by the financial crisis, DX has witnessed a high growth. With the explosive growth of DX, it became the largest foreign trade B2C and the leader in 3C electronic products.

DX（dealextreme.com）于 2006 年成立，主营电子产品和 3C 小配件，如 U 盘、手机壳等，在南美有非常知名的品牌形象。2008—2009 年，金融危机带来小额外贸市场高增长，DX 借势爆发，一跃成为最大的 B2C 跨境电子商务平台，是 3C 电子产品领域的龙头老大。

Mlbuy is a first-class domestic apparel trade B2C operator and it was officially launched in 2008. DinoDirect's main trading items are "colorful fast-moving consumer goods closely related to family life", including communications-related electronic technology products, small household appliances, accessories, clothing, auto parts electronics, outdoor products and handicrafts.

米兰网是国内一流的服饰外贸 B2C 运营商，于 2008 年正式上线运营。大龙网（DinoDirect）的主要贸易对象为跟家庭生活息息相关的多姿多彩的快速消费品，具体包括通信类电子科技产品、小家电类、饰品、服装、汽车配件电子产品、户外用品、手工艺品。

In addition to C2C, eBay's B2C and B2B transactions are also quite active. There is a wholesale zone for each category, with access to 26 countries through the global navigation at the bottom of its homepage. eBay does not provide warehousing and logistics services; it just recommended the sellers third-party cross-border logistics services. eBay began as an auction site and more as a social e-commerce website. The advantage of eBay is with PayPal, a global one-stop payment, is very attractive to small and medium-sized sellers. Therefore, eBay boasts its wider global buyer coverage.

除 C2C 外，eBay 的 B2C 和 B2B 交易也相当活跃，每一个分类都有一个批发专区，通过首页底部的全球站导航，可以进入 26 个国家发布批发信息。eBay 不提供仓储物流服务，仅为卖家推荐第三方跨境物流服务。eBay 以拍卖网站起家，更多的是一种社交型电子商务网站，eBay 的优势在于 PayPal（全球最大的在线支付平台），这种全球性的一站式支付对中小卖家具有很大的吸引力，所以 eBay 的全球买家覆盖面较广。

Started with B2C, Amazon is specialized in supply chain management and cost control, especially its global system of warehouse logistics system; Amazon is more popular in the United States market.

Amazon 以 B2C 起家，擅长供应链管理和成本控制，尤其是其全球化的系统仓储物流体系在美国市场比较受欢迎。

AliExpress is the global trading platform created by Alibaba group, and thus it is called the "international Edition Taobao" by the majority of sellers. Launched in April 2010, after rapid development in recent years, AliExpress has now covered overseas buyers in more than 220 countries and regions, the daily flow of overseas buyers has reached more than 50 million, with the highest peak reached 100 million; AliExpress has become the world's largest cross-border trading platform.

全球速卖通是阿里巴巴旗下面向全球市场打造的在线交易平台，被广大卖家称为"国际版淘宝"。速卖通于 2010 年 4 月上线，经过近几年的迅猛发展，目前已经覆盖 220 多个国家和地区的海外买家，每天海外买家的流量已经超过 5 000 万，最高峰值达到 1 亿。速卖通已经成为全球最大的跨境交易平台。

Part B   Terminology Practice

1. **Profit**: in economics, profit in the accounting sense of the excess of revenue over cost is the sum of two components: normal profit and economic profit. Normal profit is the profit that is necessary to just cover the opportunity costs of the owner-manager or of the firm's investors. In the absence of this much profit, these parties would withdraw their time and funds from the firm and use them to better advantage elsewhere. In contrast, economic profit, sometimes called excess profit, is profit in excess of what is required to cover the opportunity costs.

2. **Profitability index**: also known as profit investment ratio (PIR) and value investment ratio (VIR), is the ratio of payoff to investment of a proposed project. It is a useful tool for ranking projects because it allows you to quantify the amount of value created per unit of investment.

3. **B2B**: Business-to-Business (B2B or, in some countries, B to B) refers to a situation where one business makes a commercial transaction with another. This typically occurs when a business

re-sells goods and services produced by others.

4. **B2C**: Business-to-Consumer, is the type of commerce transaction in which businesses sell products or services to consumers. Traditionally, this could refers to individuals shopping for clothes for themselves at the mall, diners eating in a restaurant, or subscribing to pay-per-view TV at home. More recently, the term B2C refers to the online selling of products, or e-tailing, in which manufacturers or retailers sell their products to consumers over the Internet.

5. **M-Commerce**: Mobile e-commerce (m-commerce) is a term that describes online sales transactions that use wireless electronic devices such as hand-held computers, mobile phones or laptops. These wireless devices interact with computer networks that have the ability to conduct online merchandise purchases. Any type of cash exchange is referred to as an e-commerce transaction.

6. **POS**: Point of Sale (POS) refers to the physical location at which goods or services are purchased and transaction data is captured through electronic cash registers or other electronic devices such as magnetic card readers, optical and bar code scanners or some combination of these.

7. **C2C**: Customer to Customer (C2C) markets provide an innovative way to allow customers to interact with each other. Traditional markets require business to customer relationships, in which a customer goes to the business in order to purchase a product or service. In customer to customer markets, the business facilitates an environment where customers can sell goods or services to each other.

8. **O2O**: Online to Offline is a phrase (commonly abbreviated to O2O) that is used in digital marketing to describe systems enticing consumers within a digital environment to make purchases of goods or services from physical businesses.

9. **C2B**: Consumer-to-Business (C2B) is a business mode in which consumers (individuals) create value and businesses consume that value. For example, when a consumer writes reviews or when a consumer gives a useful idea for new product development then that consumer is creating value for the business if the business adopts the input.

10. **B2G**: Business-to-Government (B2G) is a derivative of B2B marketing and is often referred to as a market definition of "public sector marketing" which encompasses marketing products and services to various government levels through integrated marketing communications techniques such as strategic public relations, branding, marketing communications (Marcom), advertising, and web-based communications.

Part C　Useful Expressions

1. be rendered to　被呈现

2. in accordance with　与……一致

3. include, but not limited to 包括但不限于……

4. rely on 依靠……

5. in the form of 以……形式

6. various types of 各式各样

7. be carried out 被执行

8. in essence 本质上

9. ranging from 从……到……

10. established in 创建于……

11. bring by 由……导致

12. be officially launched 正式发布

13. recommend sb sth 向……推荐……

14. global buyer coverage 全球买家覆盖面

15. the majority of 大部分

Part D   Exercise

I. Answer the following questions according to the information you have got.

1. What is a "B2B" mode?

2. What is a "B2C" mode?

3. What does "Mobile e-commerce" stand for?

4. What is the difference between "B2B " and "B2C" mode?

5. What is the difference between "C2C" and "C2B" mode?

6. What is POS?

7. What does O2O stand for?

8. What is a "B2G" mode?

II. Match each one on the left with its correct meaning on the right.

1. E-commerce	A. a measure of the benefit provided by goods or service to an economic agent
2. Digital economy	B. a transaction of buying or selling online
3. PayPal	C. an economy that is based on digital computing technologies
4. Profit maximization	D. other things being equal, a firm will attempt to maximize its profits.
5. B2B	E. businesses sell products or services to consumers
6. B2C	F. commerce transactions between businesses
7. economic value	G. a payment processor for online vendors

1. (   )   2. (   )   3. (   )   4. (   )   5. (   )   6. (   )   7. (   )

III. Translate the following terms and phrases into Chinese.

1. Search / PPC profit mode   2. value-added service

3. offline service   4. include, but not limited to

5. in the form of   6. in essence

7. a great deal of	8. be officially launched
9. recommend sb sth	10. global buyer coverage
11. supply chain management	12. cost control
13. AliExpress	14. small and medium-sized sellers
15. auction site	

IV. Case study for cross-border e-commerce.

Case Description:

On January 17, 2018, Huading Corp. formally announced the completion of the merger and acquisition of Tongtuo Technology. Through the issuance of shares and the payment of cash, 100% equity of Tongtuo Technology was purchased for a consideration of 2.9 billion yuan and a total of approximately 1.257 billion yuan in supporting financing. Tongtuo Technology Co., Ltd. is a cross-border e-commerce company based on the "Extensive Supply Chain, Universal Channel" mode. It is committed to providing China's high-quality supply chain products, through eBay, Amazon, AliExpress, Dunhuang.com, Wish, and its own websites, to the rest of the world. Its main products include game accessories, computer accessories, mobile phone accessories, home appliances, health and beauty, auto parts, photographic equipments, audio and video, apparel, toys, outdoor and other dozens of categories.

Question:

Based on the above cases, please review the strategic significance of the acquisition of Huading Corp.

案情介绍：

2018 年 1 月 17 日，华鼎股份正式宣布完成并购通拓科技。通过发行股份及支付现金方式购买通拓科技 100%的股权，交易对价 29 亿元，同时拟配套融资约 12.57 亿元。通拓科技是一家基于"泛供应链、泛渠道"模式经营的跨境电子商务公司，致力于把中国优质供应链产品通过 eBay、亚马逊、速卖通、敦煌网、Wish、自有网站等多种渠道销售到世界各地。其主营产品包括游戏配件、计算机配件、手机配件、家居、健康美容、汽车配件、摄影器材、影音视频、服饰、玩具、户外等数十个品类。

问题：

根据以上案例，评述华鼎股份并购通拓科技的战略意义。

V. Describe one or two cases about third-party cross-border e-commerce platform.

VI. Please determine whether the following statements are TRUE or FALSE. Then put T for TRUE or F for FALSE in the bracket at the end of each statement.

1. In the international stations, the completeness of the product attribute filling is conducive to making it easier for buyers to search. (   )

2. In the international stations, the so-called five-star website refers to the 100% utilization of window products on the homepage, the professional grouping of products, the maintenance of TM

online, the full utilization of company columns, and the richness of corporate image display. (　　)

3. For members of Alibaba International Station, do not put too many products in the same picture in the product pictures provided, otherwise the product details cannot be shown forfeited. (　　)

4. In the corporate website design of the international station, customers can freely upload BANNER pictures in a format of 700×780. (　　)

5. Uploading product images at AliExpress can be selected directly from the Alibaba international station.(　　)

6. AliExpress can accept RMB or USD, but you need to open a USD account. (　　)

7. The international station free buyer CNFM can directly become an AliExpress seller. (　　)

8. With the Alipay account to quickly register AliExpress account, you do not need to fill in the Alipay account. (　　)

9. AliExpress products can be shipped by sea. (　　)

10. Taobao train is a promotional tool tailored for Taobao sellers by Taobao. It is a service for accurate promotion of goods through keyword bidding and pay-per-click.(　　)

VII. Translate the following sentences into English.

1. 第三方跨境电子商务平台，一般泛指独立于跨境产品或跨境服务的提供者和需求者，主要通过网络服务平台，并按照特定的电子商务交易与电子商务服务规范，为跨境贸易的买卖双方提供服务的一种跨境电子商务运营模式。

2. 第三方跨境电子商务平台的服务内容可以包括但不限于供求信息发布与搜索、交易的确立、支付、物流。目前国内有代表性的第三方跨境电子商务平台有阿里巴巴速卖通、敦煌网、中国制造网等。

3. 专业化。作为交易市场服务平台，第三方跨境电子商务平台需要更加专业的商务贸易支撑技术，包括对订单管理、支付安全和物流管理等技术支撑，实现其为跨境电子商务买卖双方提供安全便捷服务的宗旨。

4. 增值服务盈利模式。第三方跨境电子商务平台还通过提供各种增值服务来盈利，包括企业认证、独立域名、搜索引擎优化和电子杂志下载等。平台还提供各种信息和报告服务，如行业数据分析报告、行业发展报告、客户留言、前沿资讯短信服务和邮件服务、网站数据分析报告以及专家在线咨询等。

5. 线下服务盈利模式。第三方跨境电子商务平台还通过提供各种线下实体服务来盈利，包括跨境电子商务网络营销策划培训、跨境电子商务产品展会、跨境电子商务行业商会、跨境电子商务研讨会和高峰论坛等。另外，还在某些期刊内通过行业资讯、植入广告等来实现盈利。

VIII. Multiple Choices.

1. Among the Alibaba Chinese stations, which of the following are the advantages of high quality supply information? (　　).

A. The star reaches 3 stars or more than 3 stars

B. Set the exact category

C. The title of the message contains only one product name

D. The information shows the picture

2. In the Alibaba Chinese station, as for the function of Wang Pu, which of the following description is correct? (　　).

A. Customer feedback system　　　　　B. Website browsing analysis

C. Information distribution system　　　D. Product display system

3. The differences between the Enterprise Edition and the Personal Edition in Alibaba Chinese Station are (　　).

A. check buyer contact information　　　B. ranking

C. certification cycle　　　　　　　　　D. price

4. At the international station, what should members of the Alibaba International Station note the following when publishing commercial information? (　　).

A. The title is concise and clear, highlighting the relevant characteristics of the product

B. Keyword is the name of the product in the industry that is conventional or generic

C. Detailed description should be as detailed as possible, fully introduce the product's specifications and models to increase the credibility of the information

D. Match a suitable picture to make the product more intuitive

5. According to operating statistics in Alibaba International Station, the average exposure of Alibaba International's window products is 8 times that of ordinary products. Which of the following sorting operations for setting up the showcase products are correct? (　　).

A. You can sort products by dragging products under the Manage Window Products page

B. You can right-click on the product link and select "Sort" from the shortcut menu

C. Automatic sorting by initials can be achieved

D. You can change the window number to sort the top left window

6. At Alibaba International Station, the wedding dress keywords can be set to (　　).

A. 2011 New Stye Wedding Dress　　　B. Wedding Dress

C. Dress　　　　　　　　　　　　　　　D. Lace Edged Wedding Dress

7. How can we get the window recommendation on the AliExpress website? (　　).

A. Upgrade of the seller's grade

B. Participate in AliExpress's irregular activities

C. Purchase window

D. Become a supplier and send 10 window recommendations

8. In AliExpress, the quality of the product release standard includes the (　　).

A. title professional

B. timely stocking, no more than 3 days

C. the price range is divided into more than 4

D. rich pictures, detailed description of more than 5 pictures

9. The logistics methods that can be selected in the AliExpress shipping settings are (   ).

A. Shipping   B. EMS   C. UPS   D. SF

10. In Taobao, the conditions that are not part of the consumer protection service program are
(   ).

A. taobao registered users

B. do not open stores on other platforms

C. shop credits must be above a drill

D. user sellers rate above 97% (including 97%)

Chapter Four   International Trade Online Trading Platform

第四章   国际贸易在线交易平台

Part A   Text

Background of Emerging International Online Trade

At present, the traditional export business on a global scale is facing an increasingly serious dilemma. The development of international trade increasingly presents a new trend of continuous trade flow reduction and the gradual decline of the bulk foreign trade. This trend has directly contributed to the rapid rise of the small volume of foreign trade in international trade.

当前，全球范围内的传统外贸出口业务面临日益严峻的考验。国际贸易发展日益呈现贸易流程不断缩短而大宗外贸逐步衰退的新趋势。这种趋势直接促使了国际贸易小宗外贸交易的快速崛起。

Affected by this, B2B international trade platform revenue, on both of the world's major countries and regions levels, has gradually declined, while the small B2C platform or B2B international trade platform has enjoyed a rapid growth. Against this background, many enterprises have launched online trading platforms for international trade on line with the global trend of international trade, especially cross-border e-commerce platforms. On the one hand, these new e-commerce platforms can effectively compete with the small-scale foreign trade platforms, restricting the continued infiltration of the small-scale foreign trade platforms on its market share. On the other hand, it will also help increase the satisfaction of suppliers in various countries and regions in the existing trading platforms.

受此影响，全球各国和区域的大宗 B2B 国际贸易平台的营业收入出现日益下滑的态势，而与此同时，小宗 B2C 平台或国际贸易 B2B 平台快速成长。在此大背景之下，许多企业推出了符合全球国际贸易发展趋势的国际贸易在线交易平台，特别是跨境电子商务平台，这些新型的电子商务平台一方面可以有效地与小宗外贸平台竞争，对抗和制约小宗外贸平台对其市场份额的不断蚕食，另一方面也有助于提高现有交易平台上各国和区域的供应商会员的满意度。

This chapter uses the example of an AliExpress trade to introduce the actual operation flow and principles of the online trading platform for international trade.

本章以全球速卖通为例，介绍国际贸易在线交易平台的实际运营流程和原理。

Section One   AliExpress Platform Profile（阿里巴巴速卖通平台简介）

Officially launched in April 2010, AliExpress is Alibaba's only online trading platform created for the global market; it is, by the majority of sellers, called "International Edition Taobao". AliExpress is oriented at the overseas buyers, executing secured transactions through Alipay international accounts, and using the international express delivery. AliExpress is the world's third-largest English online shopping site.

全球速卖通（AliExpress）于 2010 年 4 月正式上线，是阿里巴巴旗下唯一面向全球市场打造的在线交易平台，被广大卖家称为"国际版淘宝"。全球速卖通面向海外买家，通过支付宝国际账户进行担保交易，使用国际快递发货，是全球第三大英文在线购物网站。

AliExpress is to help small and medium-sized enterprises to contact terminal wholesale and retail outlets, with small quantities and more batches of fast sales, expanding profit margins and aiming to create the integration of orders, payment, logistics into one of the foreign trade online trading platform.

全球速卖通是阿里巴巴帮助中小企业接触终端批发零售商，小批量、多批次快速销售，拓展利润空间而全力打造的融合订单、支付、物流于一体的外贸在线交易平台。

After the sale of AliExpress in 2010, after several years of rapid development, now AliExpress has covered daily buyers more than 220 countries and regions overseas, and its overseas traffic has flowed more than 38 million, leading to its position as the world's largest foreign trade online transactions platform. In 2013, the global AliExpress website set sail, with its potential being equivalent to Taobao's in 2005.

速卖通在 2010 年上线后，经过几年的迅猛发展，目前已经覆盖 220 多个国家和地区的海外买家，每天海外买家的流量超过 3 800 万，已经成为全球最大的外贸在线交易平台。2013 年全球速卖通网站全面起航，潜力相当于 2005 年的淘宝。

As a part of Alibaba.com, AliExpress serves as a popular global consumer marketplace. AliExpress is, in effect, a wholesale marketplace established and rendered by Alibaba.com, the world's largest B2B online marketplace. Launched in April 2010, AliExpress (www.aliexpress.com) is a global retail marketplace, of which target is oriented at worldwide consumers, many of which are situated in Russia, the United States and Brazil.

作为阿里巴巴的一部分，速卖通是一个全球消费者市场。实际上，速卖通是全球最大的 B2B 在线交易平台，它是由 Alibaba.com 建立并维持日常运营的批发市场。速卖通（www.aliexpress.com）于 2010 年 4 月推出，它是一个全球性的零售市场，其目标是面向世界各地的消费者，其中许多来自俄罗斯、美国和巴西。

The platform enables consumers from around the world to buy or purchase directly from wholesalers and manufacturers in China and possess access to an overwhelmingly great variety of commodities at wholesale prices. AliExpress brings worldwide consumers products at wholesale prices on even the smallest orders.

该平台使来自世界各地的消费者可以直接从中国的批发商和制造商处购买或采购，并以批发价格获得绝大多数种类的商品。即使是最小的订单，速卖通也能以批发价格向全球消费者提供产品。

AliExpress renders minimum orders as low as 1 item, buyers' protection and express delivery with full tracking. AliExpress currently hosts thousands of diverse categories of commodities from a wide range of industries, including the following: Apparel & Accessories, Automobiles & Motorcycles, Mobile Phones, Computer Hardware & Software, Electronics, Health & Beauty, Lights & Lighting, Luggage, Bags & Cases, Security & Protection, Shoes & Accessories, Watches & Jewelry and Wedding Supplies.

速卖通提供买家保障和快递全程跟踪，最低订单数量低至 1 件。目前速卖通拥有数以千计的各类商品，包括服装和配件，汽车和摩托车，手机，计算机硬件和软件，电子产品，健康和美容，灯具和照明，行李箱，箱包，安全和防护，鞋类和配件，手表和珠宝，以及婚礼用品。

As shown in Figure 4-1, AliExpress is actually a third-party cross-border e-commerce platform that serves as an intermediary bridge linking buyers and sellers around the world. Among the global buyers are, but not limited to, small wholesale buyers around the world, as well as end-consumer groups; global sellers include, but are not limited to, foreign trade companies, foreign trade-oriented manufacturing enterprises, and foreign trade SOHO groups. During this process, in addition to playing the role of an intermediary bridge, AliExpress also brings together "third-rate" information flow, logistics and capital flow, and at the same time, realizes the collection of big data. Among them, the information flow includes cross-border products information, customer credit rating system; logistics related to logistics and express delivery companies such as DHL, UPS, EMS and TNT; cash flow involves a series of payment instruments such as Credit card, Alipay and Western Union.

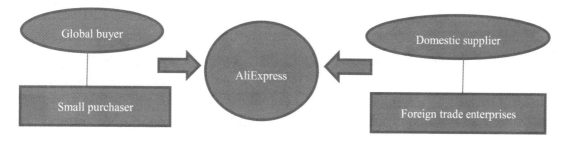

Figure 4-1　Flow Diagram of AliExpress

如图 4-1 所示，阿里全球速卖通实际上是一个第三方跨境电子商务平台，起着联结全球买家与卖家的中介桥梁作用。其中的全球买家包括但不限于全球各地的小额批发采购商，以及终端消费者群体；全球卖家包括但不限于外贸公司、外贸导向型生产企业，以及外贸 SOHO 群体。阿里全球速卖通在这一流程中，除了发挥中介桥梁作用之外，还汇集了"三流"，即信息流、物流和资金流，同时实现了大数据的收集。其中，信息流包括跨境商品信息、客户信用评级体系等；物流涉及如 DHL、UPS、EMS 和 TNT 等物流快递企业；资金流涉及一系列的支付工具，如 Credit card、Alipay 和 Western Union 等。

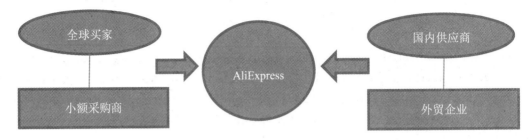

图 4-1　速卖通流程示意图

Section Two　Global Positioning of AliExpress（全球速卖通的定位）

AliExpress' business orientation is to serve as a cross-border platform that helps SMEs to deal online with individual consumers directly and globally. The function of the AliExpress consists of goods display, customer orders, online payment and cross-border logistics as a whole. To achieve the purpose of expanding profit margins, a small batch and multi-batch rapid sales approach has been adopted. As a result, AliExpress has shaped its core strengths, namely, small orders, big market; low costs, high security.

全球速卖通的企业定位是作为一个帮助中小企业直接与全球的个人消费者在线交易的跨境平台。全球速卖通的功能集商品展示、客户下单、在线支付和跨境物流于一体。以小批量、多批次快速销售的方式达到拓展利润空间的目的。因此，全球速卖通塑造了自身的核心优势，即：小订单，大市场；低成本，高安全。

In this unique positioning, AliExpress and Taobao are different in that Taobao's positioning is mainly for domestic sellers and mainly via domestic express delivery; AliExpress' positioning is mainly for overseas buyers, through Alipay International Account to execute secured transactions and ship with international courier. In addition, AliExpress International and Alibaba International Online are also significantly different in that Alibaba International is a platform for suppliers to release and display the information; buyers at the International station are to purchase samples or make foreign trade trial orders, just as buying things in the free market, where the prices of their products are a result of buyers and sellers' negotiation and final confirmation; while the AliExpress is as an online trading platform, requiring its sellers indicate the price, be able to support third-party guarantee payment and international express delivery, so as to suit and support the international express delivery of small orders, similar to the procurement in the supermarket.

在这种独特定位之下，全球速卖通与淘宝有着不同点，淘宝的定位主要是面向国内卖家，通过国内快递发货；而速卖通的定位主要是面向海外买家，通过支付宝国际账户进行担保交易，并使用国际快递发货。另外，全球速卖通和阿里巴巴国际站在进行在线交易方面也有着明显的不同，阿里巴巴国际站是一个让供应商完成信息的发布和展示的平台，买家在国际站上采购样品或外贸试单，就如同在自由市场上购买东西，其产品价格必须得到买卖双方商议和最终确认，之后其订单才能够继续进行。而全球速卖通则是一个在线交易平台，要求其卖家必须标明价格，同时要能够支持第三方担保支付以及国际快递发货，以适合和支持国际快递的中小订单交易，类似于在超市采购。

Section Three　Buyers and Sellers on AliExpress Platform（全球速卖通平台的买家和卖家）

Buyers of the AliExpress platform can be subdivided into two main groups of buyers, namely, those online retailers on platforms, such as eBay and Amazon.com, as well as offline small and medium sized retailers. The majority of sellers on the AliExpress platform are existing Chinese suppliers on Alibaba.com platforms, and those sellers can be subdivided into three major categories of sellers, that is, foreign trade manufacturing enterprises, foreign trade companies and SOHO owners of foreign trade. Such groups of people are also likely to come from C2C platforms such as eBay, dhgate.com, tradetang.com and Taobao, etc. Among these sellers, they are mainly small and medium-sized foreign trade companies and SOHO owners of foreign trade. Some powerful foreign trade production-oriented enterprises are of relatively small proportion.

全球速卖通平台的买家可以细分为两大类主要购买人群，线上的是在诸如 eBay、Amazon.com 等平台上的零售商；线下的主要包括一些实体店中的中小零售商。全球速卖通平台上的卖家大部分是 Alibaba.com 现有平台上的中国供应商会员。此类卖家可以细分为三大类主要卖家群，即外贸生产型企业、外贸公司以及外贸 SOHO 一族，这类人群同时也很有可能是 eBay、dhgate.com、tradetang.com 以及淘宝等各类 C2C 平台上做生意的卖家。在这几类卖家中，主要以中小型的外贸公司以及外贸 SOHO 一族为主，一些有实力的外贸生产型企业参与的比例相对较小。

Section Four　Global AliExpress Platform Channels（全球速卖通平台渠道）

Currently, because AliExpress platform is just a sub-channel of Alibaba.com, and thus its buyers base mainly comes from Alibaba.com. On the one hand, the Global AliExpress Platform attracts overseas international cross-border buyers to the platform through web site alliances, licensing e-mail marketing, searching engine optimization and paid searching engine marketing. On the other hand, the main seller base of the AliExpress platform comes from the existing stock customers on the Alibaba.com platform, namely the existing domestic Chinese suppliers. In addition, AliExpress also appeals domestic sellers to the global AliExpress platform through penetrating into competitors , as well as online and offline expansion.

目前，因为全球速卖通平台只是 Alibaba.com 的一个子频道，所以其买家人群主要还是来源于 Alibaba.com。一方面，全球速卖通平台通过网站联盟、许可电子邮件营销、搜索引擎优化以及付费搜索引擎推广等方式把海外的跨境买家吸引到全球速卖通的平台上。另一方面，全球速卖通平台的主要卖家人群来源于 Alibaba.com 平台上的现有存量客户，即现有的中国国内供应商。除此之外，全球速卖通平台还通过深入对手内部，线上、线下拓展等方式把国内卖家吸引到全球速卖通平台上。

Section Five　AliExpress Profit Mode（全球速卖通盈利模式）

The profit mode of AliExpress platform comes from its platform charges; the main income can be grouped into two categories.

全球速卖通平台的盈利模式来源于平台收费，主要收入可以分为两大类。

1．Membership Fee

Annual platform membership fee shall be paid to join the current AliExpress platform.

1．会员费

目前要加入全球速卖通平台需要首先按年缴纳平台会员费。

2．Trading Commission

Alibaba charges for each successful transaction on the AliExpress platform, according to their different payment methods, with a certain percentage of the corresponding total transaction amount of unequal transaction commissions. Among them, wire transfer, Alipay and other cross-border online payment methods are allowed. For example, cross-border sellers conduct transactions by Alipay; commission charged by Alibaba tends to be more favorable during the discount period; the commission is basically equal to the total price of the product plus a certain percentage of freight.

2．交易佣金

阿里巴巴对于速卖通平台上的每笔成功交易，根据其不同的支付方式，在相应的交易总额中收取一定比例的不等额交易佣金。其中，支持电汇、支付宝以及其他跨国在线支付方式。比如，跨境卖家采用支付宝进行交易，阿里巴巴在优惠期内收取的佣金会比较优惠，佣金基本等于产品总价加上一定比例的运费。

Section Six　Marketable Products（适销产品）

Products sold on the AliExpress platform must firstly be suitable for sale over the Internet and be suitable for shipping by air courier. These products basically bear the following characteristics.

在全球速卖通平台上销售的商品首先必须适宜通过网络销售并且适合通过航空快递运输。这些商品基本具备下面的特点。

（1）Smaller, mainly to facilitate delivery by courier, reduce international logistics costs.

（1）体积较小，主要是方便以快递方式运输，降低国际物流成本。

（2）Higher value-added, the value of a single piece of goods over the freight is not suitable for a single sale, but can go with package sale, so as to reduce the logistics costs proportion.

（2）附加值较高，一件货物的价值超过运费则不适合单件销售，可以打包出售，从而降低物流成本占比。

（3）Uniqueness, decent online transaction goods need to be unique, in order to constantly stimulate the buyers' purchase.

（3）具备独特性，在线交易业绩佳的商品需要独具特色，才能不断刺激买家购买。

（4）More reasonable price: if the online transaction price is higher than the local market price of the product, it fails to attract buyers online to place orders.

（4）价格较合理：在线交易价格若高于产品在当地的市场价，就无法吸引买家在线下单。

Part B　Terminology Practice

1. **Electronic Trading Platform**: in economics, an electronic trading platform known as an online trading platform, is a computer software program that can be used to place orders for economic products over a network with an economic intermediary.

2. **Revenue**: in general usage, revenue is income received by an organization in the form of cash or cash equivalents.

3. **Economic growth**: it is the increase in the inflation-adjusted market value of the goods and services produced by an economy over time. It is conventionally measured as the percent rate of increase in real gross domestic product, or real GDP.

4. **Enterprise**: is an organizational entity and legal entity made up of an association of people, be they natural, legal, or a mixture of both who share a common purpose and unite in order to focus their various talents and organize their collectively available skills or resources to achieve specific declared goals and are involved in the provision of goods and services to consumers.

5. **Entrepreneurship**: this refers to the practice of starting new organizations, particularly new businesses.

6. **Marketplace**: a market, or marketplace, is a location where people regularly gather for the purchase and sale of provisions, livestock, and other goods.

7. **Intermediary entity**: refers to those enterprises or businesses designed to bridge the gap between companies which work for profits and other nonprofit organizations which work for public interest.

8. **SOHO**: refers to the modern concept of "small office home office".

9. **Payment**: is the trade of value from one party (such as a person or company) to another for goods, or services, or to fulfill a legal obligation.

10. **Business orientation**: refers to perspectives including the decision-making perspective, market intelligence perspective, culturally based behavioral perspective, strategic perspective and customer orientation perspective.

Part C　Useful Expressions

1. directly contributed to... 直接促使了······

2. affected by 受······影响

3. a rapid growth 快速成长

4. in line with 符合

5. compete with 与······竞争

6. on the one hand...on the other hand... 一方面······另一方面······

7. be oriented at 面向······

8. small and medium-sized enterprises 中小企业

9. terminal wholesale and retail outlets 终端批发和零售网点

10. in effect 实际上

11. minimum orders 最低订单

12. a wide range of 大范围的

13. a series of 一系列的

14. serve as 作为

15. core strength 核心力量

16. position as... 定位······

17. be subdivided into 细分为

18. profit mode 盈利模式

19. tend to be 倾向于

20. be suitable for 适合······

Part D　Exercise

I. Answer the following questions according to the information you have got.

1. What is electronic trading platform?

2. What is economic growth? And how to measure it?

3. What is the definition of "marketplace"?

4. Based on the conditions for marketable products taught in this lesson, what are the products that may be eligible for sale at AliExpress?

5. What does "SOHO" mean?

6. What does business orientation mean?

II. Match each one on the left with its correct meaning on the right.

1. contributed to　　A. business

2. a rapid growth　　B. bridge

3. in effect　　　　C. a location where people gather for the purchase and sale of goods

4. a wide range of　　　　D. small office home office

5. serve as　　　　　　　E. be likely to

6. tend to　　　　　　　F. function as

7. SOHO　　　　　　　G. a great variety of

8. Marketplace　　　　　H. actually

9. Intermediary　　　　　I. a skyrocket

10. enterprise　　　　　　J. lead to

1. (　　) 2. (　　) 3. (　　) 4. (　　) 5. (　　)

6. (　　) 7. (　　) 8. (　　) 9. (　　) 10. (　　)

III. Translate the following terms and phrases into Chinese.

1. directly contributed to　　　　　　2. affected by

3. a rapid growth　　　　　　　　　　4. in line with

5. compete with　　　　　　　　　　6. on the one hand…on the other hand…

7. is oriented at　　　　　　　　　　8. small and medium-sized enterprises

9. terminal wholesale and retail outlets　　10. in effect

11. minimum orders　　　　　　　　　12. a wide range of

13. a series of　　　　　　　　　　　14. serve as

15. core strength　　　　　　　　　　16. positioning

17. be subdivided into　　　　　　　　18. profit mode

19. tend to be　　　　　　　　　　　20. be suitable for

IV. Case study for cross-border e-commerce.

Case Description:

Amazon has set up its warehouses in Shanghai free trade zone so as to use the free trade mode (that is, the bonded stock), to market goods in China, and this mode is still in progress.

According to the Chinese cross-border e-network operators, No.1 Store also imported goods by Shanghai free trade zone of bonded import entry mode or overseas direct mail, and thus goods can be ready for the overseas import to Shanghai free trade zone in advance. In addition, Wal-Mart, the strategic investor of No. 1 store, has carried out its resources integration in retail market, which will bring advantage in the international market for No.1 Store's on-line shopping business.

On January 9, 2015, the dominant cross-border B2C e-commerce site "Sunfeng overseas online shopping" was launched. Products involved are from the United States, Germany, the Netherlands, Australia, New Zealand, Japan, South Korea and other overseas online shopping hot countries. "Sunfeng overseas online shopping" provides product localization, the renminbi, Chinese customer service team support and other services, providing a key order flow experience. Currently online goods are involved with maternal and infant, food, articles for daily use, etc. The goods can be delivered within 5 working days or so.

Questions:

What kind of cross-border mode does Amazon/No.1 Store/"Sunfeng overseas online shopping" belong to? What are the main advantages and disadvantages of this mode?

案情介绍：

亚马逊在上海自贸区设立仓库，以自贸模式（即保税备货）将商品销往中国，这种模式目前还在推进中。

1 号店是通过上海自贸区的保税进口模式或海外直邮模式入境，可以提前将海外商品进口至上海自贸区备货。除此之外，1 号店的战略投资方沃尔玛在国际市场的零售和采购资源整合优势将利好"1 号海购"业务。

2015 年 1 月 9 日，顺丰主导的跨境 B2C 电商网站"顺丰海淘"正式上线。提供的产品涉及美国、德国、荷兰、澳大利亚、新西兰、日本、韩国等海淘热门国家。"顺丰海淘"提供商品定位、人民币支付、中文客服团队支持等服务，以及一键下单体验。目前上线的商品锁定在母婴、食品、生活用品等种类。货物可在 5 个工作日左右送达。

问题：

亚马逊海外购、1 号海购、顺丰海淘属于什么跨境模式？这种模式有何主要优缺点？

V. Describe one or two cases about the latest development of AliExpress.

VI. Please determine whether the following statements are TRUE or FALSE. Then put T for TRUE or F for FALSE in the bracket at the end of each statement.

1. The development of international trade increasingly presents a new trend of continuous trade flow reduction and the gradual decline of the bulk foreign trade. (   )

2. New e-commerce platforms can effectively compete with the big-scale foreign trade platform , restricting the continued infiltration of the big-scale foreign trade platform on its market share. (   )

3. Officially launched in April 2011, AliExpress is Alibaba's only online trading platform created for the global market. (   )

4. AliExpress is oriented at the overseas sellers, executing secured transactions through Alipay Chinese accounts. (   )

5. AliExpress is to help small and medium-sized enterprises to contact terminal wholesale and retail outlets. (   )

VII. Translate the following sentences into English.

1. 全球速卖通于 2010 年 4 月正式上线，是阿里巴巴旗下唯一面向全球市场打造的在线交易平台，被广大卖家称为"国际版淘宝"。全球速卖通面向海外买家，通过支付宝国际账户进行担保交易，并使用国际快递发货。全球速卖通是全球第三大英文在线购物网站。

2. 全球速卖通是阿里巴巴帮助中小企业接触终端批发零售商，小批量、多批次快速销售，拓展利润空间而全力打造的融合订单、支付、物流于一体的外贸在线交易平台。

3. 全球速卖通的企业定位是作为一个帮助中小企业直接与全球的个人消费者在线交易的跨境平台。全球速卖通的功能集商品展示、客户下单、在线支付和跨境物流多种功能于一体，以小批量、多批次快速销售的方式达到拓展利润空间的目的。因此，全球速卖通塑造了自身的核心优势，即：小订单，大市场；低成本，高安全。

4. 全球速卖通平台的买家可以细分为两大类主要购买人群，线上的是在诸如 eBay、Amazon.com 等平台上的零售商；线下的主要包括一些实体店中的中小零售商。全球速卖通平台上的卖家大部分是 Alibaba.com 现有平台上的中国供应商会员。此类卖家可以细分为三大类主要卖家群，即外贸生产型企业、外贸公司以及外贸 SOHO 一族，这类人群同时也很有可能是 eBay、dhgate.com、tradetang.com 以及淘宝等各类在 C2C 平台上做生意的卖家。在这几类卖家中，主要以中小型的外贸公司以及外贸 SOHO 一族为主，一些有实力的外贸生产型企业参与的比例相对较小。

5. 交易佣金。阿里巴巴对于速卖通平台上的每笔成功交易，根据其不同的支付方式，在相应的交易总额中收取一定比例的不等额交易佣金。其中，支持电汇、支付宝以及其他跨国在线支付方式。比如，跨境卖家采用支付宝进行交易，阿里巴巴在优惠期内收取的佣金会比较优惠，佣金基本等于产品总价加上一定比例的运费。

VIII. Multiple Choices.

1. AliExpress buyer's website is (   ).

   A. http://daxue.aliexpress.com/   B. www.aliexpress.com

   C. www.alibaba.com   D. seller.aliexpress.com

2. What are the payment methods for Russian buyers? (   ).

   A. VISA   B. Master card   C. Webmoney   D. QIWI

3. What kinds of languages can be displayed in AliExpress products information? (   ).

   A. Chinese   B. Portuguese   C. English   D. Russian

4. How is AliExpress billed? (   ).

   A. Charge according to the number of products

   B. 5% commission based on transaction amount

   C. Charges based on participating platform activities

   D. Registration is not charged

5. What methods can be used for AliExpress website login? (   ).

   A. AliExpress username   B. Registered email

   C. Registering your phone   D. AliExpress account number

6. What is correct about the product category? (   )

   A. You must select category before you can enter the product release page.

   B. Category is important in product sequencing.

   C. Wrong category selection affects exposure.

   D. Wrong category selection will be punished by the platform.

7. Which of the following should be included in a complete heading? (   ).

   A. Product Name   B. Product material   C. Services   D. Logistics advantages

8. What are the two options for the product's effective period? (   ).

   A. 14 days   B. 7 days   C. 30 days   D. 60 days

9. What are the structure of shop products? (   ).

   A. Explosion   B. Profits   C. Drainage   D. Long-tail

Chapter Five   Cross-Border E-Commerce Inquiry

第五章   跨境电子商务询盘

Part A   Text

A Brief Introduction to Inquiry

What is an inquiry? Inquiry (Enquiry) is, in fact, a request for information on price, trade terms, etc. An importer may send out an inquiry to an exporter, inviting a quotation or an offer for the goods he wishes to buy or simply asking for some general information about these goods.

什么是询盘？实际上，询盘（询价）是关于价格、贸易条款等信息的请求。进口商可以向出口商发出询价，邀请他对想要购买的商品进行报价或报盘，或者简单地询问有关这些商品的一般信息。

Cross-border e-commerce inquiry works as a channel for a cross-border e-commerce platform leading buyers and suppliers to communicate; buyers, by means of the cross-border e-commerce search platform, are able to find favorite products and click on the details of the page to leave a message in the form of mail, sent to the supplier's primary account / sub-account of the corporate email, and displayed at the inquiry.

跨境电子商务询盘是跨境电子商务平台的买家和供应商沟通交流的渠道，买家在跨境电子商务搜索平台搜索到心仪的产品后点击详情页面进行留言，留言信息以邮件形式发送至供应商主账号/子账号的企业邮箱，并展示在询盘处。

When a business intends to import, he may send out an inquiry to an exporter, inviting a quotation or an offer for the goods he wishes to buy or simply asking for some general information about these goods. The exporter, on receiving the inquiry, will make a reply to it. In this way, the negotiation is getting started.

当一个企业打算进口时，他可以向出口商发出询价，邀请他对想要购买的货物进行报价或报盘，或只是要求提供关于这些货物的一般信息。出口商在接到询价后，会做出答复。这样，商务接洽就开始了。

According to the content or purpose, an inquiry may be either a general inquiry or a specific inquiry. If the importer wants to have a general information of the products or commodities, which the exporter is in a position to supply, he may ask the exporter to send him a catalogue, a brochure, a price list and samples. This is a general inquiry. If the importer intends to purchase a certain product or commodity, he may ask the exporter to make an offer or a quotation on this product. Such kind of inquiry is called a specific inquiry.

根据内容或目的，询盘可以是一般询盘或具体询盘。如果进口商想知道出口商可以提供的产品或商品的一般信息，他可以要求出口商给他发送目录、小册子、价目表和样品。这是一个一般询盘。如果进口商打算购买某种产品或商品，他可以要求出口商提供该产品的报价或报盘。这种查询被称为具体询盘。

Section One　Inquiry Reply Process of Cross-Border E-Commerce Platform（跨境电子商务平台回复询盘流程）

This section takes Alibaba International Station as an example to introduce the cross-border e-commerce platform's inquiry reply process.

本节以阿里巴巴国际站为例，介绍跨境电子商务平台回复询盘流程。

(1) Inquiry Location: My Alibaba-My shortcut to enter the inquiry or opportunity management center for inquiry.

（1）询盘位置：通过"我的阿里巴巴"—"我的快捷入口"进入询盘或商机管理中心进行询盘。

(2) All RFQs: Click on All RFQs at the RFQ to list all the RFQs received by all the buyers for this LMH. If you are the owner of the account, you can log in to see all the inquiry information received in the sub-account.

（2）所有询价单：在询盘处点击所有询价单，就会列出该登录账号所收到的所有买家发送的询盘。如果是企业主账号登录，就能查看所有子账号收到的询盘信息。

(3) Check the inquiry: Click the inquiry to check the inquiry information, the left side shows the contact information and relevant information of the buyer's account. The right side shows the product information viewed and consulted by the buyer. Click to jump to the product details page.

（3）查看询盘：点开询盘查看询盘信息，左侧显示买家账号的联系方式和相关信息，右侧显示买家所查看和咨询的产品信息，点击可跳转到产品详情页。

(4) Generate quotations: click to generate quotations, distribution set the MOQ, payment methods, product prices, product specifications and other information.

（4）生成报价单：点击生成报价单，设置最小起订量、支付方式、产品价格、产品规格等信息。

(5) Order Now: Click Generate Quote and the buyer receives your reply to see the Order Now button. No quotation is generated: after the reply inquiry, the buyer only sees the text reply, without the Order Now button, the inquiry status is following up. Generated Quotation: Generate Quotation Reply to Inquiry. The buyer can see the Order Now button, which is quoted. The Order Now button, in a sense, can be considered to encourage buyers to place orders. The quotation usage of the inquiry quotation will be counted by the system as the quotation rate of the online quotation. In the Product Management and Supplier Diagnosis Optimization department, the usage rate of the online quotation of the shop and the usage rate of the excellent online quotation of the supplier may be checked. The

best inquiry is to generate quotations to promote the buyer orders, but also to enhance the accumulation of online data.

（5）立即下单：点击生成报价单后买家收到你的回复能看到"立即下单"按钮。未生成报价单时，回复询盘后买家只看到文字回复，无"立即下单"按钮，该询盘状态为跟进中。已生成报价单时，生成报价单后回复询盘买家能看到"立即下单"按钮，该询盘状态为已报价。"立即下单"按钮某种意义上也能促使买家下单。询盘的生成报价单使用率会被系统统计为线上报价单使用率，在"产品管理"—"供应商诊断优化"处可查看店铺线上报价单使用率和优秀供应商线上报价单使用率情况，最好对每一次的询盘都生成一个报价单记录，提高买家的下单率，也能提升线上数据积累。

Section Two　Inquiry Letter（询盘信）

An inquiry can be made not only to one party alone but also to several parties at the same time. In this way the inquiry can make a comparison between the terms of sales stated in the incoming offers and decide on which offer is the most advantageous. Then he can choose to trade with the one who has quoted or offered the best terms.

询盘不仅可以对一方进行询问，还可以同时对多方进行询问。通过这种方式，询盘可以比较收到的报价中所述的销售条款，并决定哪个报价最有利。然后，可以选择与提供最佳条款者进行贸易。

An inquiry is a letter written by a buyer to a prospective seller asking about the specification, quality, quantity of supply, prices, etc. of goods he wants to buy. In actual practice today an inquiry can be sent by fax or telex or e-mail in addition to a letter.

询盘信是买家写给准卖家的信，询问对方想要购买的商品的规格、质量、供货量、价格等。在实际操作中，除了一封信以外，还可以通过传真、电传或电子邮件发送询问。

Section Three　Decent Specimen Letters（正式的信件样本）

The following letters are definitely good and decent examples for learners to master the skill of writing a letter for an inquiry and a reply. It is well demonstrated by the following letters that an inquiry can usually be divided into three parts. In the first part, tell our supplier how we obtain his name and why we write the letter to him. In the second part, introduce our own business, including the goods we need, the quantity we want, the terms of trade we prefer and so on. In the third one, state the response we hope for a prompt reply to receive. End our letter with a complementary close.

下面的信件对于学习者掌握写信询盘和回复信的技巧来说，是一个好的例子。通过以下信件可以很好地证明，询盘通常可以分为三部分。第一部分告诉供应商我们如何获得他的名字，以及为什么我们写信给他。第二部分介绍自己的业务，包括需要的货物、想要的数量、喜欢的贸易条件等。第三部分说明我们希望得到及时的答复。用敬语结束信函。

Specimen Letter 1

Inquiry

Dear Sir,

We are one of the leading importers of sweaters in Korea. We have seen your products showed at the Canton Fair.

At present, we are in the market for your sweater, Item No.GE-0756. Will you please quote the lowest price CIF Pusan, inclusive of our 5% commission, stating the earliest date of shipment and terms of payment? We would find it the most helpful if you could provide us with the samples of different colors.

Should your price be found competitive and delivery date acceptable, we intend to place a large order with you.

An early reply will be appreciated.

Yours faithfully,

Comments

This is a perfect example letter of inquiry for you to get acquainted with the general form. In the whole process of trade negotiation, inquiry is one of the basic steps for traders to reach business conclusions. Clearly captioned letters by virtue mean hopes for successful businesses. Therefore, the tidiness, clarity, courtesy and the relativity of the letters as well as their captions or subjects are always important directions for readers to make decision.

样信 1

询价

亲爱的先生：

我们是韩国主要的毛衣进口商之一。我们之前在广交会上看到了您的产品展示。

目前，我们对您编号为 GE-0756 的毛衣有购买意向。请您报最低釜山到岸价格，包括我们 5%的佣金，并告知我方最早的装运日期和付款条件。希望您能为我们提供不同颜色的样品。

如果您的价格具有竞争力并且交货日期可以接受，我们打算向您发出大的订单。

早日回复，不胜感激。

谨启

评论

这是了解一般形式询盘的一个范例。在贸易谈判的全过程中，询价是交易者达成商业合同的基本步骤之一。表达明确、措辞优美的信函是交易成功的希望。因此，此类信件的整齐、清晰、礼貌和主题，对于信函的阅读者所做出的决定发挥着重要的影响。

Specimen Letter 2

Reply

Dear Sir,

Thank you for your inquiry of May 18th, 2015 and we are pleased to send you our quotation for the goods you required as follows:

    Commodity: Women's sweater in assorted colors, Item No.GE-0756

    Size: Large (L), Medium (M), Small (S)

    Maximum Export Quantity: 100 dozen per color

    Price: US $ 40.00 per dozen, CIFC 5% Pusan

    Shipment: within 25 days after receipt of L/C

    Payment: be irrevocable L/C at sight

You are cordially invited to take advantage of this attractive offer. We are anticipating a large order from Japan, and that will cause a sharp rise in price.

We look forward to receiving your first order.

                         Yours faithfully,

Comments

This letter demonstrates how to write a reply letter in a proper, decent and perfect business manner. Reply with a quotation is clearly shown in this letter as well as the skill to invite a business deal in the future.

样信 2

回复

亲爱的先生：

感谢您于 2015 年 5 月 18 日的询盘，我们很乐意向您发送您所需货物的报价，具体如下：

    商品：各色女装毛衣，商品编号：GE-0756

    尺寸：大（L），中（M），小（S）

    最大出口数量：每种颜色 100 打

    价格：每打 40.00 美元，CIFC 釜山 5%

    装运：收到信用证后 25 天内

    付款方式：不可撤销信用证

诚挚地邀请您接受这个有吸引力的报价。我们预计来自日本的大订单将导致价格大幅上涨。

我们期待收到您的第一个订单。

                         谨启

评论

这封信展示了如何以适当、体面和完美的商业方式写回信。这封信中清楚地显示了报价的回复以及未来邀请对方进行商业交易的技巧。

Section Four　AliTM Inquiry Letter Sample（AliTM 询盘信件样本）

Sample letter after the buyer's bid

买家出价后的样信

1. Dear, thank you for your order! Yet it brought to our attention that your payment hasn't been received.

The total amount shall be: Item $___ + Shipping $___ = Total $___.

If you got any problem on payment, please feel free to contact us to help you, thanks!

1．亲，谢谢您的订单！但我们还没有收到您的付款。

付款总金额为：货物$ ___ +运费$ ___ =总计$ ___ 。

如果您在付款时遇到任何问题，请随时与我们联系以便帮助您，谢谢！

2．Dear, thank you for your support! We will send out the package as soon as possible after your payment.

2．亲，谢谢您的支持！付款后我们会尽快发出包裹。

3．Dear, there are only 5 days left to get 8% off, please kindly finish your payment as earlier as possible, many thanks.

3．亲，现在离享受8%的折扣只剩5天了，请尽早完成付款，非常感谢。

4．Dear, please finish your payment today, then you still have the chance to get a free present (only for the first 20 customers).

4．亲，请您今天完成付款，然后您还有机会获得一个免费的礼物（只限前20名顾客）。

Sample letter after the buyer's payment
买家付款后的样信

1．Hi Dear,

Thanks for your order and payment. Your item will be sent out in 3 working days as promised. After doing so, we will send you a notification letter with tracking No. 1234. By the way, please confirm your address, post code and phone number updated.

Any special requirements please reply within 24 hours, thanks!

1．嗨，亲，

感谢您的订单和付款。您的物品将按承诺在 3 个工作日内寄出。我们会寄给您一封追踪号码为1234的通知信。请确认您的地址、邮政编码和电话号码。

如有特殊要求，请在24小时内回复，谢谢！

2．Hi Dear,

Your credit card has not been approved by AliExpress, if you want the item now, we have prepared for you and you can place a new order. Besides, you can pay via Western Union, TT payment or try other means as well. Other than that, please contact with the Ali initiatively!

Warmest regards!

2．嗨，亲，

您的信用卡尚未经过AliExpress的批准，如果您现在需要这个货物，我们已经为您准备好了，您可以下一个新的订单。此外，您可以通过西联汇款、TT付款或尝试其他方式。除此之外，请主动与阿里联系！

温馨问候！

Sample letter after the seller's delivery
卖家发货后的样信

1．Hi Dear,

We have sent out your package, which is estimated to arrive in 5-7 days in normal conditions. If not, please feel free to contact us.

Tracking number: ABC1234

Tracking website:www.abc.com(Information will be shown on the website in 1-2 working days)

Thanks again for your great purchase, sincerely hope our item and customer service can offer you a pleasant and satisfactory buying experience.

1．嗨，亲，

我们已经发出了您的包裹，估计在正常情况下 5～7 天到达。如果没有收到，请随时与我们联系。

追踪号码：ABC1234

跟踪网站：www.abc.com（信息将在 1～2 个工作日内显示在网站上）

再次感谢您的购买，衷心希望我们的物品和客户服务能为您提供愉快和满意的购物体验。

2．Dear friend,

Your package has been sent out, the tracking No. is GDUT123 via DHL, please keep an eye on it, hoping you satisfied with it and wishing to conduct more business with you in the near future. Best wishes!

2．亲爱的朋友，

您的包裹已经通过 DHL 寄出，追踪号码是 GDUT123，请留意查收，希望您满意，希望在不久的将来能与您开展更多的业务。

3．Dear customer,

We have already sent the goods out today, and we can receive the tracking number in 8 hours, we'll send you the relevant message as soon as we receive it.

3．尊敬的客户，

我们已经将货物寄出，我们可以在 8 小时内收到追踪号码，我们会尽快给您发送相关信息。

Sample letter after the goods' arrival
货物到达后的样信

1．Hi Dear,

We have checked on tracking website learning that you have already received your order! Is it arrived in good condition without any breakage?

If you are satisfied with your purchase and our service, it would be highly appreciated that you give us five-star feedbacks and leave positive comments on your experience with us!

And if you got any problem, please contact us directly for assistance, instead of submitting a refund request. We aim to solve all problems in an efficient manner, thank you!

1. 嗨，亲，

我们通过跟踪网站了解到您已经收到货物了，货物是否完好无损地到达了？

如果您对您购买的货物和我们的服务感到满意，希望您给我们五星级的反馈，并对您的经历留下积极的评论，我们将非常感谢！

如果您有任何问题，请直接联系我们寻求帮助，而不要提交退款申请。我们的目标是以高效的方式解决所有问题，谢谢！

2. Hi Dear,

Your positive comments are highly appreciated. Your encouragement is bound to keep us moving forward. Besides, if you email back some photos to show us what the item looks, you can obtain free coupons or discount price on your next purchase. Many thanks and hope that we'll have the honor with more chances to serve you.

2. 嗨，亲，

非常感谢您的正面评论。您的鼓励必然会使我们前进。此外，如果您通过电子邮件发回一些您收到的货物的照片，您可以在下次购买时获得免费优惠券或折扣价格。非常感谢，希望我们将有更多的机会为您服务。

Section Five　Writing Template for Inquiry（询盘写作模板）

Based on the above examples of specific letters, the writing template for inquiry can be summarized as follows for reference.

基于上述具体询盘信件的例子，可以将询盘信件的写作模式进行归纳，以供参考。

1. General Inquiry(一般询盘)

We are very much interested in importing（产品名称）from you since you are（对方身份）. We would be grateful if you could let us have detailed information about（产品名称）and send us samples of your complete product range as well.

We have been（我方身份）for（公司历史年限）and have（销售渠道）. We are in great need of （产品名称）in our production. Our credit standing has been AAA rated since（起始年）.

If business terms are satisfactory, we'll place regular orders with you.

2. Reply to the General Inquiry（回复一般询盘）

We are glad to learn that you are interested in our（产品名称）. Attached please find（附件信息）. As you requested, we have sent you samples of our complete range（邮寄方式）.

We are one of the（公司性质）, specializing in（经营范围）. All our products are manufactured（产品优势）. We（公司优势）. We will allow a（折扣幅度）discount for your orders. For（欲知信息）, please（获知信息途径）.

We look forward to your trial order.

3．Specific Inquiry（具体询盘）

We are（公司性质）. We have obtained your name and address from（信息来源）and we are very interested in（产品名称）.

We'd like to have an（产品数量）quotation of the said products,（价格术语）.We'd like you to tell us about（其他欲知事项）. If（下订单前提条件）, we will place an order with you.

We would await your reply.

Section Six　Useful Sentences for Inquiry（询盘常用句子）

1. Heavy enquiries witness the quality of our products.
大量询盘证明我们产品质量过硬。

2. As soon as the price picks up, enquiries will revive.
一旦价格回升，询盘将恢复活跃。

3. Enquiries for carpets are getting more numerous.
对地毯的询盘日益增加。

4. Enquiries are so large that we can only than allot you 200 cases.
询盘如此之多，我们只能分给你们 200 箱货。

5. Enquiries are dwindling.
询盘正在减少。

6. Enquiries are dried up.
询盘正在绝迹。

7. They promised to transfer their future enquiries to Chinese Corporations.
他们答应将以后的询盘转给中国公司。

8. Generally speaking, inquiries are made by the buyers.
询盘一般由买方发出。

9. Mr. Baker is sent to Beijing to make an inquiry at China National Textiles Corporation.
贝克先生来北京向中国纺织公司进行询价。

10. We regret that the goods you inquire about are not available.
很遗憾，你们所询的货物现在无货。

11. In the import and export business, we often make inquiries at foreign suppliers.
在进出口贸易中，我们常向外商询价。

12. To make an inquiry about our oranges, a representative of the Japanese company paid us a visit.
为了对我们的橙子询价，那家日本公司派了一名代表访问了我们。

13. We cannot take care of your inquiry at present.
我们现在无力顾及你方的询盘。

14. Your inquiry is too vague to enable us to reply you.
你们的询盘不明确，我们无法答复。

15. Now that we've already made an inquiry about your articles, will you please reply as soon as possible?

既然我们已经对你们的产品询价，可否尽快给予答复？

16. China National Silk Corporation received the inquiry sheet sent by a British company.

中国丝绸公司收到了英国一家公司的询价单。

17. Thank you for your inquiry.

谢谢你们的询价。

18. May I have an idea of your prices?

可以了解一下你们的价格吗？

19. Can you give me an indication of price?

你能给我一个估价吗？

20. Please let us know your lowest possible prices for the relevant goods.

请告知你们有关商品的最低价。

21. If your prices are favorable, I can place the order right away.

如果你们的价格优惠，我们可以马上订货。

22. When can I have your firm CIF prices, Mr. Li?

李先生，什么时候能得到你们到岸价格的实盘？

23. We'd rather have you quote us FOB prices.

我们希望你们报离岸价格。

24. Would you tell us your best prices CIF Hamburg for the chairs.

请告知你方椅子到汉堡的到岸价格的最低价。

25. Will you please tell the quantity you require so as to enable us to sort out the offers?

为了便于我方报价，可以告诉我们你们所需的数量吗？

26. We'd like to know what you can offer as well as your sales conditions.

我们想了解你们能供应什么，以及你们的销售条件。

27. How long does it usually take you to make delivery?

你们通常要多久才能交货？

28. Could you make prompt delivery?

可以即期交货吗？

29. Would you accept delivery spread over a period of time?

不知你们能不能接受在一段时间里分批交货？

30. Could you tell me which kind of payment terms you'll choose?

能否告知你们将采用哪种付款方式？

31. Will you please tell us the earliest possible date you can make shipment?

你能否告知我们最早的装船日期？

32. Do you take special orders?

你们接受特殊订货吗？

33. Could you please send us a catalog of your rubber boots together with terms of payment?

你能给我们寄来一份胶靴的目录，连同告诉我们付款方式吗？

34．He inquired about the varieties, specifications and price, and so on.

他询问了品种、花色和价格等情况。

35．We have inquired of Manager Zhang about the varieties, quality and price of tea.

我们向张经理询问了茶叶的品种、质量、价格等问题。

36．Our buyers asked for your price list or catalogue.

我们的买主想索求你方的价格单或目录。

37．Prices quoted should include insurance and freight to Vancouver.

所报价格需包括到温哥华的保险和运费。

38．I would like to have your lowest quotations CIF Vancouver.

请报温哥华到岸价的最低价格。

39．Will you please send us your catalogue together with a detailed offer?

请把你们的产品目录和详细报价寄给我们好吗？

40．We would appreciate your sending us the latest samples with their best prices.

请把贵公司的最新样品寄给我们并附上最优惠的价格，不胜感激。

41．Your ad. in today's *China Daily* interests us and we will be glad to receive samples with your prices.

我们对你们刊登在今天《中国日报》上的广告很感兴趣。我们将很高兴收到你方的样品及报价。

42．Will you please inform us of the prices at which you can supply?

请告知我们贵方能供货的价格。

43．If your prices are reasonable, we may place a large order with you.

若贵方价格合理，我们可能向你们大量订货。

44．If your quality is good and the price is suitable for our market, we would consider signing a long-term contract with you.

若你方商品质量好且价格适合我方市场的话，我们愿考虑与你方签署一项长期合同。

45．As there is a growing demand for this article, we have to ask you for a special discount.

鉴于我方市场对此货的需求日增，务必请你们考虑给予特别折扣。

46．We would appreciate your letting us know what discount you can grant if we give you a long-term regular order.

若我方向你们长期订货，请告知能给予多少折扣，不胜感激。

47．Please quote your lowest price CIF Seattle for each of the following items, including our 5% commission.

请就下列每项货物向我方报到西雅图的最低到岸价格，其中包括我们5%的佣金。

48．Please keep us informed of the latest quotation for the following items.

请告知我方下列货物的最新价格。

49．Mr. Smith is making an inquiry for green tea.

史密斯先生正在对绿茶进行询价。

50. Now that we have already made an inquiry on your articles, will you please make an offer before the end of this month?

既然我们已经对你们的产品进行了询价，请在月底前报价。

51. As a rule, we deliver all our orders within 3 months after receipt of the covering letters of credit.

一般来说，在收到相关信用证后 3 个月内我们就全部交货。

52. Please quote us your price for 100 units of Item 6 in your catalog.

请给我们提供你们产品目录上 100 组 6 号产品的报价。

53. Those items are in the greatest demand in foreign markets.

那些产品在国外市场上的需求量很大。

54. Would you please quote me your prices for the goods?

你能报给我这些商品的价格吗？

55. We have quoted this price based on careful calculations.

这个报价是我们在精打细算的基础上得出来的。

56. A five-percent commission will certainly help you in pushing your sales.

5%的佣金肯定会有助于你们的销售。

57. From other suppliers, we get a higher commission rate for the business in this line.

对这类产品的交易，我们从其他供货者那里可得到更高的佣金。

58. We will give you back a 5% commission by check.

我们将用支票支付你方 5%的佣金。

59. You may invoice the goods at contract price minus 3% commission.

你们可以按合同价格减去 3%的佣金开发票。

60. The commission shall be paid either by means of goods covered under this contract or by check.

佣金可用合同项下的货物支付，也可用支票支付。

Part B   Terminology Practice

1. **Credit inquiry**: an inquiry into the reputability of a business house and its ability to meet financial commitments.

2. **Profit margin**: the difference between what it costs to make something and its net price, (real price) off which discount is not allowed.

3. **Inquiry (Enquiry)**: a request for information on price, trade terms, etc. An importer may send out an inquiry to an exporter, inviting a quotation or an offer for the goods he wishes to buy or simply asking for some general information about these goods.

4. **Commission**: a form of payment to an agent for services rendered.

5. **Distribution channels**: the means by which goods are distributed.

6. **End-user**: the ultimate user for whom a machine, product, or service is designed.

7. **Middlemen**: dealers (such as agents, merchant brokers, wholesalers, etc.) who are neither producers nor consumers, but buy from the one or sell to the other, or to other middlemen or act as agents between producers, and consumers.

8. **Mail order**: a system of direct selling through the post. Catalogues are sent to potential customers, who order goods to be sent to them.

Part C　Useful Expressions

1. to inquire about　对······询价

2. be in the market for　在市场上觅购某物；想买进

3. to keep inquiry in mind　记住询盘

4. to conclude a business transaction　达成贸易交易

5. to reach an agreement　达成协议

6. to do business in a moderate way　做生意稳重

7. to make a deal　做一笔交易

8. to trade with　和······进行贸易

9. to make an inquiry　发出询盘；向······询价

10. specific inquiry　具体询盘

Part D　Exercise

I. Fill in the blanks with proper prepositions.

1. We have a potential buyer interested ＿＿＿ Green Bean of Shandong origin and shall appreciate an offer ＿＿＿ you ＿＿＿ 100 metric tons ＿＿＿ August delivery.

2. As this inquiry is quite substantial, we hope you will make an offer ＿＿＿ your most favorable price.

3. Please let us have ＿＿＿ airmail a set ＿＿＿ samples ＿＿＿ "Youth" Fountain Pen together ＿＿＿ your best offer.

4. We shall appreciate an offer ＿＿＿ you ＿＿＿ 10 metric tons ＿＿＿ prompt shipment.

5. Please let us know how many tons ＿＿＿ the seeds you are able to offer ＿＿＿ delivery September.

6. We are ＿＿＿ a position to place a substantial order ＿＿＿ you if your price is favorable.

7. Please state the packing and send us ＿＿＿ airmail samples representing your current stocks.

8. We have so far bought these goods ＿＿＿ other sources, but we now propose to cover our requirements ＿＿＿ your corporation, because we learn that you are able to offer large quantities ＿＿＿ attractive prices.

9. We have an inquiry ＿＿＿ Groundnut Kernels and shall be pleased if you will quote us your lowest price ＿＿＿ DES basis, stating the quantity available.

10. We wish to know ＿＿＿ what price per gross you are able to deliver quantities ＿＿＿ "Great Wall"

Pencils.

II. Translate the followings sentences into English.

1. 我们得知你们是中国缝纫机制造商，请告知你方能否供应脚踏式、五斗"蝴蝶"牌、"标准"牌各 300 台。

2. 我方拟购 400 辆你公司经营的"五羊"牌自行车，请电开最优惠 DEQ 汉堡价，包括给我方的 5% 的佣金。

3. 请报标题商品最低价。报盘时，请说明包装情况及最早装运期，并请寄商品说明书。

4. 上月你方代表来访时，出示了一些新的纺织品样品，现是否可供？

5. 我们另邮寄样品一批，深信一旦你们有机会查看样品，定会承认该货品质优良，价格合理。

6. 所附价格单和图解目录将给你提供有关最感兴趣的型号的具体情况。

7. 从你方在《电器》（Electrics）上刊登的广告，得知你们出口半导体收音机（Transistor），望寄插图目录和价目表，并详告你们的条款。

8. 从 ABC 公司得知你方能供应水果和干果（Fruits and Nuts），请报最优惠的成本加运输费到汉堡（Hamburg）价。报价时，请说明包装情况及最早交货期。

9. 你公司在《农业》（Agriculture）9 月号上所刊登的阿特拉斯除草剂（the Atas Weed Killer）广告，我们很感兴趣，现请告知该商品的详细情况并请寄样品。

10. 我方一客户已获得价值 4 万美元的各种电线（Wires）的进口许可证，请报最低价、最优折扣和交货期。

11. 现悉你公司在市场上投放一种电动打字机（Electric Typewriter），请告详细情况，以便向你方订购。

12. 我们还想了解各种商品的每种颜色和花样的最低出口起售量。

III. Compose a letter of inquiry with the following particulars.

1. The addressee: Messrs. Arthur Grey & Son, 19 Cheapside, London, E. C. 2.

2. You have the addressee' name and address from China Council for the Promotion of International Trade.

3. You wish to buy 100 sets of Automatic Dishwasher.

4. State clearly price terms, payment terms, time of shipment, packing conditions, etc.

5. Ask for illustrated catalogues.

IV. Please draw a letter of general inquiry asking for all the information you need.

V. Write a specific inquiry according to the following.

1. The name of the commodity you want

a certain kind of Household Electrical Appliance（某种家用电器）

2. You ask for the

a. specification　　　　　b. sample books　　　　　c. pricelist

d. payment terms　　　　e. delivery date　　　　　f. other information you need

VI. When making the first inquiry, the inquiry often asks for general information concerning the products in question. The following materials are generally requested for.

a. sample   b. booklet/brochure   c. pattern

d. catalogue   e. price-list   f. pro forma invoice

Now choose a suitable term to be used in each of the following sentences.

1. Under separate cover, we are sending you our _____ No. 6 together with our price-list. It contains illustrations and descriptions of the large varieties of our goods made in Japan.

2. We enclose our _____, and trust that the prices quoted will lead to business.

3. We take pleasure in sending you a _____, containing a detailed description of the construction and working of this engine.

4. We have duly received your wine _____, which have been tested and found satisfactory.

5. In reply to your inquiry of May 3, we are sending you _____ of our newly finished pure cotton shirts, and have pleasure in quoting you as follows.

6.Will you please airmail us the soonest possible your _____ for 2,000 sets of printing machines with prices CIF Osaka, so that we can make you an offer and obtain the necessary import licence.

VII. Multiple Choices.

1. We feel sure that they will be glad to furnish you ( ) any information you require.

A.for   B.at   C.on   D.with

2. We look forward to ( ) your catalogue and price list for women's sweater.

A.receive   B.receiving   C.received   D.being received

3. Quotations and samples will be sent ( ) receipt of your specific enquiries.

A.for   B.upon   C.with   D.to

4. As this article falls ( ) the scope of our business activities, we take this opportunity to express our wish to conduct some transactions with you in the near future.

A.with   B.in   C.within   D.at

5. We assure you ( ) our full cooperation.

A.for   B.at   C.with   D.of

6. We thank you for your letter dated May 6 ( ) our silk blouses of various styles.

A.inquiry for   B.inquiring for   C.inquired for   D.inquire for

7. They are seriously considering ( ) a complete plant for the production of cutting tools.

A.import   B.importing   C.to import   D.imported

8. Will you please send us your prices for the items ( ) below.

A.listing   B.being listed   C.to list   D.listed

9. If you can supply us the goods immediately, we shall ( ) to place a prompt trial order.

A.preparing   B.be preparing   C.prepare   D.be prepared

10. These leather handbags are fully illustrated in the catalogue and are ( ) the same high quality as our gloves.

A.for   B.of   C.to   D.in

VIII. Fill in the blanks.

Dear Sirs,

Re: Sample Cost

We really appreciate your ____(1)____ cooperation during the past several years. We think we have developed a beneficial trade ____(2)____ your area ____(3)____ the basis of equality and mutual benefit. We hope that we will reach a bigger turnover ____(4)____ the coming years.

As ____(5)____ the new samples of our products, our statistics showed that we had a very heavy burden ____(6)____ sample cost. As you know, during the past years we always supplied small quantity ____(7)____ samples to our customers free ____(8)____ charge. We not only had to pay the samples' cost, but also pay for the postage ____(9)____ express couriers, such as UPS, FedEx. However, our profit is getting smaller and smaller owing ____(10)____ the uprising prices of raw materials. ____(11)____ such circumstance, we find it is getting difficult to run business in this way. In order to solve this problem ____(12)____ a reasonable way, we hope our customer could help to share the cost ____(13)____ paying the postage. So could you please inform us your account number of UPS or FedEx or other express ____(14)____ return? So that we could send samples by your account number, while we will supply the samples free of charge in normal small quantity ____(15)____ before.

We hope that our request will gain your approval.

Yours sincerely,

Chapter Six　Cross-Border E-Commerce Market Theory

第六章　跨境电子商务市场理论

Part A　Text

A Brief Introduction to Cross-Border E-Commerce Market

Cross-border e-commerce markets are growing at noticeable rates. Cross-border e-commerce market is expected to grow by leaps and bounds in the near future. Traditional markets are only expected a tiny growth during the same time. Nowadays , brick and mortar retailers are struggling because of online retailer's ability to offer lower prices and higher efficiency. Many larger retailers are able to maintain a presence offline and online by linking physical and online offerings.

跨境电子商务市场正在以明显的速度增长。预计跨境电子商务市场将在未来实现跨越式发展。传统市场预计在同一时间内出现小幅的增长。如今，由于网上零售商能够提供更低的价格和更高的效率，实体零售商正在苦苦挣扎。许多大型零售商可以通过链接实体和在线产品实现线下线上联机销售。

Cross-border e-commerce allows customers to overcome geographical barriers and allows them to purchase products anytime and from anywhere. Online and traditional markets have different strategies for conducting business. Traditional retailers offer fewer assortments of products because of shelf space where, online retailers often hold no inventory but send customer orders directly to the manufacture. The pricing strategies are also different for traditional and online retailers. Traditional retailers base their prices on store traffic and the cost to keep inventory. Online retailers base prices on the speed of delivery.

跨境电子商务使客户能够克服地理障碍，并允许他们随时随地购买产品。在线和传统市场有不同的开展业务的策略。传统零售商由于货架空间而提供较少的产品种类，在线零售商经常不存货，而是直接将客户订单发送给制造商。传统和网上零售商的定价策略也不同。传统的零售商以商店流量和保持库存的成本为基础。在线零售商的价格则按照交货速度而定。

There are two ways for marketers to conduct business through cross-border e-commerce: fully online or online along with a brick and mortar store. Cross-border online marketers can offer lower prices, greater product selection, and high efficiency rates. Many customers prefer online markets if the products can be delivered quickly at relatively low price. However, online retailers cannot offer the physical experience that traditional retailers can. It can be difficult to judge the quality of a product without the physical experience, which may cause customers to experience product or seller uncertainty. Another issue regarding the e-commerce online market is concerns about the security of online transactions. Many customers remain loyal to well-known retailers because of this issue.

营销人员通过跨境电子商务进行交易的方式有两种：完全通过线上销售或与线下实体店结合。跨境在线营销人员可以提供更低的价格、更多的产品选择和更高的效率。如果能够以较低的价格快速交付产品，许多客户更喜欢在线市场。但是，网上零售商无法提供传统零售商可以获得的实体体验。如果没有实体经验，就很难判断产品的质量，这可能会导致客户或零售商对产品产生不确定性。关于电子商务的另一个问题是网上交易的安全性。由于这个问题，许多顾客仍然忠于知名的零售商。

Section One　Market Competition of Cross-Border E-Commerce（跨境电子商务的市场竞争格局）

Market participants of B2C export cross-border e-commerce can be divided into two types, namely, platform-based e-commerce market participants and self-service e-commerce market participants. From the cross-border e-commerce market competition pattern, platform-based e-commerce industry concentration is relatively high; Amazon, eBay, AliExpress and other international giants occupy a considerable market share; Amazon platform business revenue is on 100 billion yuan level; eBay, AliExpress sales revenue in 2016 have reached 62.1 billion yuan, 5.5 billion yuan individually.

出口 B2C 跨境电子商务行业市场参与者可以分为平台型电商市场参与者和自营型电商市场参与者两种。从跨境电子商务市场竞争格局来看，平台型电商行业集中度相对较高，亚马逊、eBay、速卖通等国际巨头占据相当大的市场份额，亚马逊平台业务收入已是千亿元人民币级别，eBay、速卖通 2016 年收入规模分别达 621 亿元、55 亿元。

Self-run e-supplier industry concentration is more fragmented, and can be divided into two types: self-built platform and third-party platform, of which Global Purchasing, being the B2C self-employed e-commerce export leader, conducts e-commerce via its self-built platform; Lanting, which has entered the market at an earlier stage, has hit the current revenue scale of 2 billion yuan. Relying on its platform, third-party platform for cross-border exports B2C companies sell their products, with the edge of the segmentation of the goods to enlarge its market share. In a word, the overall view of market competition of cross-border e-commerce is still with the pattern of the development of the topography.

自营型电商的行业集中度较分散，又可以分为自建平台型和第三方平台型两类。其中，跨境通旗下的环球易购作为出口 B2C 自营型电商龙头，通过自建平台进行跨境出口销售。此外，自建平台型电商中，进入行业时间较早的兰亭集势目前收入规模 20 亿元左右；第三方平台型跨境出口 B2C 企业依托第三方平台销售产品，精于在细分品类中做大市场占有率，整体来看仍然呈现各抱地势的发展格局。

Section Two　Market Strategy of Cross-Border E-Commerce（跨境电子商务的市场战略）

The market strategy of cross-border e-commerce lies in breaking the drawbacks of multi-level general trade and low efficiency. The market strategy of cross-border e-commerce can be reached by reducing the layers of intermediate channels, reducing costs and optimizing resource allocation. Under the general trade mode, the costs of information gathering in cross-border trade and logistics costs account for a large proportion of the total costs. For the exporting enterprises, too many intermediate links (including traders, large and small distributors, etc.) cut into their profit margins. As for overseas consumers, due to a longer supply chain of cross-border trade, on the one hand, there is a time lag between production and sales, resulting in a poor product timeliness; on the other hand , due to the presence of more middlemen, cost-efficiency suffers. Figure 6-1 compares the process differences between cross-border e-commerce and general trading patterns.

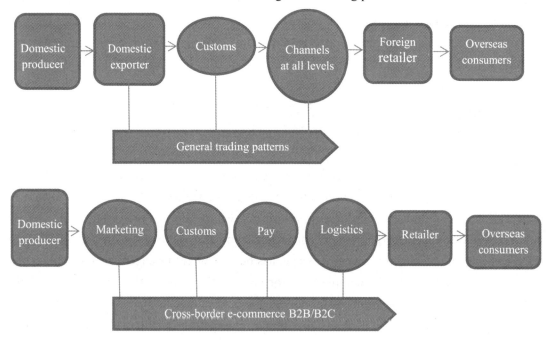

Figure 6-1　Comparisons of the Process Differences between Cross-Border E-Commerce and General Trading Patterns

　　跨境电子商务的市场战略在于打破了一般贸易多层级、效率低的弊端。通过削减中间渠道提效率、降低成本、优化资源配置，实现跨境电子商务的市场战略。在一般贸易方式下，跨国贸易发生的信息搜集成本、物流成本在总成本中所占比重较大。对出口企业而言，由于中间环节（包括贸易商、大小经销商等）过多导致其利润率较低。对于海外消费者而言，由于跨境贸易供应链条较长，一方面存在产品从产到销的时间滞后性，产品时效性差；另一方面由于存在较多中间商，产品性价比大打折扣。图 6-1 对比了跨境电子商务与一般贸易模式的流程区别。

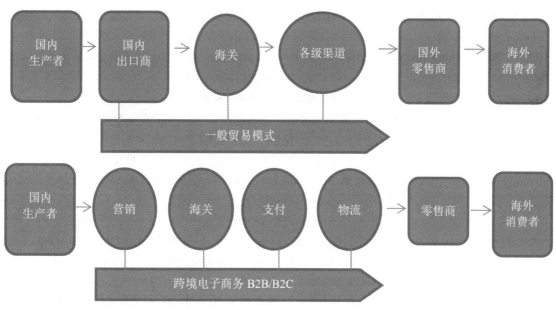

图 6-1　跨境电子商务与一般贸易模式的流程对比图

Cross-border e-commerce market strategy relies on Internet technologies to make the information between supply and demand richer and more symmetrical, so as to enhance the efficiency of information exchange and bring trade gains to both supply and demand sides. For suppliers, cross-border e-commerce (especially cross-border B2C e-commerce) has the effect of lowering costs. On the one hand, it can shorten the flow of circulation and break the monopolistic strikes of importers, exporters, wholesalers, distributors and retailers in the domestic and overseas channels under the traditional foreign trade mode and directly bridge the gap with downstream consumers, by doing so, costs of goods circulation are lessened, besides, product cost-effectiveness and attractiveness are both upgraded; on the other hand, suppliers can independently grasp the marketing channels, which not only help enterprises to create their own brands, getting rid of the plight of low-end foundry and value chain, but also improve supply chain management and channel management efficiency by relying on the data analysis of terminal sales, production, sales, etc.

可见，跨境电子商务市场战略依托于互联网技术，使供需之间的信息更加丰富而对称，有助于提升信息交流效率，可为供需双方带来贸易利得。对于供应商来说，跨境电子商务（特别是跨境 B2C 类电商）有着提效降本的作用。一方面能够缩短流通环节，打破传统外贸模式下国内外渠道中进出口商、批发商、分销商和零售商的层层垄断盘剥，与下游消费者之间直接搭建桥梁，减少商品流转成本，提升产品性价比与吸引力；另一方面，供应商能够自主掌握营销渠道，既有利于企业创建自主品牌，摆脱代工和价值链低端的困境，还可以依托对终端销售的数据分析，合理规划采购、生产、销售等，提升供应链管理和渠道管理效率。

Section Three　Trade Ecosphere of Cross-Border E-Commerce（跨境电子商务贸易生态圈）

For SMEs, the cross-border e-commerce platform provides logistics, customs clearance and payment services to domestic suppliers nationwide, which has greatly improved the previous mode in which SMEs are at a disadvantage position in the business owing to their small scale. SMEs are provided services in various aspects such as design, production, logistics, marketing and finance under the platform provided by cross-border e-commerce and relying on the platform's global cross-border trade ecosystem to facilitate their foreign trade business development.

对于中小企业来讲，跨境电子商务平台统一为各国国内的供应商提供物流、通关、支付服务，极大地改善了在以往的模式中，中小企业因为自身规模较小而在对外贸易业务流程中处于不利地位的情况。中小企业依托平台形成的全球跨境贸易生态圈，在跨境电子商务提供的平台支持下获得设计、生产、物流、营销、金融等各个方面的服务，有利于中小企业对外贸易业务的开展。

For consumers, cross-border e-commerce offers more diverse and better shopping choices and experiences. The value it provides lies in the abundance of products and a substantial increase in the number of available products small and medium-sized supplier companies can participate in exports on their own, leading to a more competitive market structure, where product updates in a faster manner, and the market demand is reflected more quickly, so as to lift the products' cost-effectiveness.

跨境电子商务为消费者提供了更加多样化和更好的购物选择与体验。它提供的价值在于可用产品数量大幅增加——中小型供应商可以通过自主参与出口，使得电子商务市场格局更具竞争性，跨境产品更新速度加快，能够更快地反映跨境市场的需求，从而提高产品的性价比。

Cross-border e-commerce trade activities in the form of "Internet plus foreign trade" can reduce the intermediate links and ensure the matching degree and symmetry of information between supply and demand sides well. At the same time, the sustainable and healthy development of the cross-border e-commerce trade ecosystem also requires related supporting services. Among them, the payment services are related to transaction security, the cost of logistics services and the efficiency of customs clearance services. These links are closely linked and developed together. Mutual support, such as synergies, can promote the healthy development of cross-border e-commerce trade.

以"互联网+外贸"的形式开展的跨境电子商务贸易活动，可以缩减中间环节，很好地保证供求双方的匹配程度和信息对称。同时，跨境电子商务贸易生态圈的可持续健康发展还需要相关的配套服务支持。其中，支付服务关乎交易安全，物流服务关乎成本，通关服务关乎效率。这些环节环环相扣，共同发展，相互支持，如产生协同效应，就能促进跨境电子商务贸易的健康发展。

Section Four   Long-Tail Market Theory（长尾市场理论）

The concept of long-tail was first proposed by Chris Anderson in 2004. The concept of "long-tail" is used to describe the business and economic modes of websites such as Amazon and Netflix. It is also one of the market theories for cross-border e-commerce.

长尾这一概念最早由 Chris Anderson 在 2004 年提出，用"长尾"这一形象说法和图形来描述诸如亚马逊和 Netflix 之类网站的商业和经济模式，也是跨境电子商务市场理论之一。

According to the long tail market theory, the long tail market refers to those markets where demand is poor or products that are not sold well. The essence of the long tail market is that the long tail products appear to be small and insignificant, yet they are able to add up to a large extent. This is in line with the characteristics of the cross-border e-commerce market. In this sense, the long-tail innovation is not really about finding or tapping into a new market, but rather relying entirely on long-tail effects through changes in marketing.

As it is shown by Figure 6-2, there is an inverted U-shaped function relationship between consumer's stimulus obtained from the external market environment and consumer's emotion response to the stimulus.

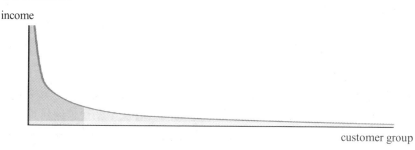

Figure 6-2　Long-Tail Market

根据长尾市场理论，长尾市场指的是那些需求不旺，或者是销量不佳的产品所共同构成的一种市场类型。长尾市场的本质就在于，长尾产品看似很小，微不足道，但却能够积少成多，聚沙成塔，这与跨境电子商务市场的特征不谋而合。从这个角度上说，长尾的革新，实际上并不是在于发现或挖掘一个新的市场，而是完全依托于通过市场营销方式的变革来达到长尾效应。

如图 6-2 所示，从外部市场环境获得的消费者刺激与消费者对刺激的情绪反应之间存在倒 U 型函数关系。

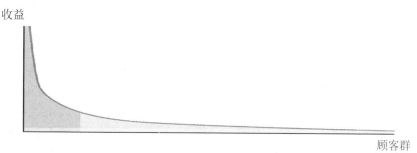

图 6-2　长尾市场

According to the long tail market theory, each individual consumer has a specific, relatively stable sense of self-comfort stimulation point, which is the most appropriate consumer stimulus level. There is an inverted U-shaped function relationship between consumer 's stimulus obtained from the external market environment and consumer's emotion response to the stimulus. At the apex of the function locates the consumer's optimal level of stimulation. When the level of stimulation provided by the external market environment is below the optimal level of stimulation for the consumer, the consumer tends to seek novel, unique and sophisticated experiential exploration to increase the level of stimulation. Consumers treat participating in the acquisition of long-tailed markets as an experiential discovery that increases their level of excitement from the novelty, uniqueness and sophistication of the innovation process that brings them to the point where most appropriate stimulation point locates. Therefore, the whole process of consumers participating in the product supply chain is also the process by which consumers gain experience value.

根据长尾市场理论，每一个个体消费者都有一个特定的、相对稳定的、自我感觉舒适的刺激点，这个刺激点就是所谓的消费者的"最适宜刺激水平"。消费者从外部市场环境获得的刺激与消费者对该刺激所做出的情感反应之间呈现出一种倒 U 型的函数关系。该倒 U 型的函数的顶点，就是消费者的"最适宜刺激水平"，而当外部市场环境提供的刺激水平低于消费者的这一水平时，消费者就会寻求一些新奇、独特和复杂化的体验探索行为来提升刺激水平。消费者将参与长尾市场产品获取的过程视为一种"体验式"探索活动，并从创新过程带给他们的新奇、独特和复杂的体验中提升刺激水平，使之更接近自己的"最适宜刺激水平"。因此，消费者参与整个产品供应链的过程实际上也是消费者从中获得体验价值提升的过程。

Long-tail market theory provides a theoretical framework for cross-border e-commerce market strategy, that is, cross-border e-commerce businesses, through development, can help consumers find the information of the products or services they need, and reduce the search costs of consumers , so as to explore "Long-tail market" potential demand, extending cross-border e-commerce market "long-tail".

长尾市场理论为跨境电子商务市场战略提供了一个理论框架，即跨境电子商务商家通过开发能够帮助消费者找出所需要的产品或服务信息，并减少消费者的搜寻成本，从而发掘"长尾市场"上的潜在需求，延展跨境电子商务市场的"长尾"。

Section Five　Cross-Border E-Commerce Long-Tail Effect（跨境电子商务的长尾效应）

In an XY coordinate system, the corresponding sales revenue is represented by the letter Y, and the products or services corresponding to different brands in the same industry are represented by the letter X, then such a market pattern generally appears. Among them, some of the top brands occupy most of the market, compared to the smaller majority of the other majority of small brands. Thus, in the same industry, a number of dominant market brands are accounted for a large area of the "red sea" market share; the rest of the small brands occupy the long "blue tail" .This long-tail effect also confirms what "80/20 law" said, 20% of the brand are accounted for 80% of the market.

在一个 XY 的坐标系里面，以字母 Y 表示对应销售收入，以字母 X 表示对应同一产业中的不同品牌的产品或服务，那么，一般会出现这样的市场格局情况，其中，名列前茅的若干个品牌占据市场的大部分，而相比之下，其他多数的小品牌占据较小部分。于是，在同一产业中，若干个主导市场的品牌占据了市场份额中大面积的"红海"，其余的小品牌占据了长长的"蓝尾"。这种长尾效应也印证了"二八法则"所说的20%的品牌占据了80%的市场。

Long-tail effects point out that, in fact, every consumer tastes deviate from the mainstream, and the more consumers find out, the more consumers realize they need more choices. In this way, the physical world is a world of scarcity. On this basis, the long-tail effect explains that the emergence of cross-border e-commerce companies, such as Amazon, have overturned the traditional perception that cross-border e-commerce enterprises can provide more choices at a lower cost and with shorter intermediate links. In this way, as consumers focus more and more on forgotten things, they find themselves more likely to choose. And if Internet merchants can capture these forgotten corners, there will be a bigger market than the traditional mainstream market with huge potential. This is what Chris calls the long tail effect, and as long as the channels for storage and distribution are large enough, the "long-tails" of non-mainstream elements, which account for 80%, will make up more than just a 20% share but more, even more than a half.

长尾效应指出，事实上，每一名消费者的品位都会与主流有所偏离，并且当消费者发现得越多，消费者就越能体会到他们需要更多的选择。这样，现实的世界是一个短缺的世界。在这个基础上，长尾效应解释了如Amazon等跨境电子商务企业的出现推翻了传统的认知，即跨境电子商务企业可以以较低的成本提供更多的选择，同时还可以缩短中间环节。这样，当消费者越来越多地关注那些被遗忘的事物时，他们会发现自己有了更多的选择余地。而如果互联网商家能够捕捉到这些被遗忘的角落，就会发掘出比传统主流市场更大的市场潜力。这就是Chris所谓的长尾效应，只要存储的空间足够大和流通的渠道足够多，占80%的非主流元素所形成的"长尾"不仅仅占20%的份额，而是可能达到更多，甚至超过一半。

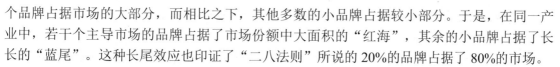

Part B　Terminology Practice

1. **Brick and Mortar**: B&M refers to a physical presence of an organization or business in a building or other structure. This term is usually used to contrast with a transitory business or an Internet-only presence, such as fully online shops. The term brick and mortar business is often used to refer to a company that possesses or leases retail stores, factory production facilities, or warehouses for its operations. More specifically, in the jargon of e-commerce businesses in the 2000s, brick-and-mortar businesses are companies that have a physical presence (e.g., a retail shop in a building) and offer face-to-face customer experiences.

2. **Retailer**: refers to those retail markets and shops, which have a very ancient history, involving the process of selling consumer goods or services to customers through multiple channels of distribution to earn a profit.

3. **Market strategy**: refers to a long-term, forward-looking approach to planning with the fundamental goal achieving a sustainable competitive advantage. The term also refers to those strategic processes, which basically involve analyses of the company's strategic initial situation prior

to the formulation, evaluation and selection of market-oriented competitive position that contributes to the corporate objectives.

4. **Market entry strategy**: refers to the planned method and approach of delivering goods or services to a brand new target market and distributing them there. When importing or exporting services, it refers to establishing and managing contacts in an alien region or a foreign country.

5. **Target market**: refers to a group of customers within a business's serviceable available market that the business has decided to aim its marketing efforts towards. Target market includes consumers who exhibit similar features and characteristics (such as gender, age, venue, income, and lifestyle) and are considered more likely to purchase a certain brand's product or service.

6. **Market segmentation**: refers to the process of dividing a broad and wide consumer or business market into sub-groups of consumers (thereby as segments) in light of some sort of shared and common features or characteristics.

7. **Customer physical experience (CPX)**: in e-commerce, this term refers to the product of an interaction between an e-commerce enterprise and a customer over the duration of their business relations. This interaction is basically made up of three elements: the customer journey, the brand links the customer interacts with, and the environments the customer experiences during their shopping and purchasing experience.

8. **Wholesaling**: refers to the distributing process in which the sale of goods or merchandise is done to retailers; to industrial, commercial, institutional, or other professional business users; or to other related subordinated services. In general, it is the sale of goods to anyone other than an individual standard consumer.

9. **Long tail**: in statistics and business, it refers to the portion of the distribution owning a large number of occurrences far from the "head" or central part of the distribution. The distribution may involve popularities, random numbers of occurrences of events with quite a variety of probabilities, etc.

10. **80/20 law**: this law states that, for numerous events, approximately 80% of the effects come from 20% of the causes. Management consultant Joseph M. Juran suggested the principle and named it after Italian economist Vilfredo Pareto showed that roughly 80% of the land in Italy was owned by 20% or so of the population, and thus it is also known as Pareto principle.

Part C   Useful Expressions

1. grow at noticeable rate 以明显的速度增长

2. grow by leaps and bounds 跨越式发展

3. be divided into 被分为……

4. account for 占……比例

5. result in 导致……

6. rely on 依赖……

7. at a disadvantage position 处于弱势

8. in the form of 以……形式

9. at the same time 同时

10. is not really about 不在于……

11. but rather 而是……

12. is represented by 由……表示

Part D　Exercise

I. Answer the following questions according to the information you have got.

1. What is the definition of "market strategy"?

2. What does the abbreviation B&M stand for and what does it indicate?

3. What is the difference between retailer and wholesaler?

4. What does the abbreviation CPX stand for in e-commerce?

5. What is the definition of "target market"?

6. What is the definition of "market segmentation"?

7. What is the definition of "long-tail"?

8. What is 80/20 law and what does it state?

9. What is self-comfort stimulation point?

10. What is the theoretical framework for cross-border e-commerce market strategy and why?

11. What is the long-tail effect?

12. How does the long-tail effect theory explain the emergence of cross-border e-commerce companies?

II. Match each one on the left with its correct meaning on the right.

1. B&M	A. the product of an interaction between an e-commerce enterprise and a customer over the duration of their business relations
2. Retailer	B. 80/20 law
3. Target market	C. because of
4. CPX	D. refers to a group of customers within a business's serviceable available market that the business aims its marketing efforts towards
5. B2G	E. businesses sell products or services to consumers
6. B2C	F. commerce transactions between businesses and government
7. Wholesaling	G. the portion of the distribution owning a large number of occurrences far from the "head" or central part of the distribution
8. Long-tail	H. distributing process in which the sale of goods or merchandise is done to retailers
9. Pareto principle	I. companies that have a physical presence
10. due to	J. selling consumer goods or services to customers through multiple channels of distribution to earn a profit

1. (　　) 2. (　　) 3. (　　) 4. (　　) 5. (　　)

6. (　　) 7. (　　) 8. (　　) 9. (　　) 10. (　　)

III. Translate the following terms and phrases into Chinese.

1. brick and mortar retailer
2. online retailer
3. overcome geographical barriers
4. pricing strategy
5. speed of delivery
6. keep inventory
7. conduct business
8. physical experience
9. self-run e-supplier
10. Trade Ecosphere
11. the abundance of products
12. cost-effectiveness
13. Internet plus foreign trade
14. long-tail market theory
15. the most appropriate consumer stimulus level
16. grow at noticeable rate
17. grow by leaps and bounds
18. be divided into
19. lies in
20. account for
21. result in
22. rely on
23. at a disadvantage position
24. in the form of
25. at the same time
26. is not really about
27. but rather
28. is represented by

IV. Case study for cross-border e-commerce.

Case Description:

In September 2014, Vipshop "Global Sales" channel was launched at its home page, at the same time, the formal express import "global sales" business overseas was open for the very first time. Vipshop "Global Sales" mode has adopted the highest level in the customs management mode, namely "Three-document Consistency" standards, leading to the results that the customer order information can be automatically generated, by which order, waybill, payment list can be produced simultaneously for the customs verification, and real-time synchronization is formed and conveyed to the e-business platform suppliers, logistics transportation, credit payment system, forming a closed circuit of the whole four chains of integrated management system.

Questions:

What sort of cross-border mode does Vipshop "Global Sales" belong to? What advantages does this mode have?

案情介绍:

2014 年 9 月，唯品会的"全球特卖"频道亮相网站首页，快递进门"全球特卖"业务正式对外开放。唯品会"全球特卖"全程采用海关管理模式中级别最高的"三单对接"标准，"三单对接"实现了将消费者下单信息自动生成用于海关核查备案的订单、运单及支付单，并实时同步给电商平台供货方、物流转运方、信用支付系统三方，形成四位一体的闭合全链条管理体系。

问题:

唯品会的"全球特卖"属于哪类跨境模式？该模式有何优点？

V. Please try to find out some latest cases about market strategies in doing cross-border e-commerce.

VI. Please determine whether the following statements are TRUE or FALSE. Then put T for TRUE or F for FALSE in the bracket at the end of each statement.

1. Nowadays, brick and mortar retailers are struggling because of online retailer's ability to offer higher prices high and cheaper efficiency.(   )

2. Cross-border e-commerce allows customers to overcome geographical barriers and allows them to purchase products anytime and from anywhere. (   )

3. Online and traditional markets have the same strategies for conducting business. (   )

4. There are two ways for marketers to conduct business through cross-border e-commerce: fully online or online along with a brick and mortar store. (   )

5. Market participants of C2C export cross-border e-commerce can be divided into two types, namely, platform-based e-commerce market participants and self-service e-commerce market participants. (   )

VII. Translate the following sentences into English.

1. 长尾市场理论为跨境电子商务市场战略提供了一个理论框架，即跨境电子商务商家通过开发能够帮助消费者找出所需要的产品或服务信息，并减少消费者的搜寻成本，从而发掘"长尾市场"上的潜在需求，延展跨境电子商务市场的"长尾"。

2. 消费者从外部市场环境获得的刺激与消费者对该刺激所做出的情感反应之间呈现出一种倒 U 型的函数关系。该倒 U 型函数的顶点，就是消费者的"最适宜刺激水平"，而当外部市场环境提供的刺激水平低于消费者的这一水平时，消费者就会寻求一些新奇、独特和复杂化的体验探索行为来提升刺激水平。

3. 根据长尾市场理论，长尾市场指的是那些需求不旺，或者是销量不佳的产品所共同构成的一种市场类型。长尾市场的本质就在于，长尾产品看似很小，微不足道，但却能够积少成多，聚沙成塔，这与跨境电子商务市场的特征不谋而合。

4. 长尾的革新，实际上并不是在于发现或挖掘一个新的市场，而是完全依托于通过市场营销方式的变革来达到长尾效应。

5. 以"互联网+外贸"的形式开展的跨境电子商务贸易活动，可以缩减中间环节，很好地保证供求双方的匹配程度和信息对称。同时，跨境电子商务贸易生态圈的可持续健康发展还需要相关的配套服务支持，其中，支付服务关乎交易安全，物流服务关乎成本，通关服务关乎效率。

6. 可见，跨境电子商务市场战略依托于互联网技术，使供需之间的信息更加丰富而对称，有助于提升信息交流效率，可为供需双方带来贸易利得。

7. 跨境电子商务的市场战略在于打破了一般贸易多层级、效率低的弊端。通过削减中间渠道提升效率、降低成本、优化资源配置，实现跨境电子商务的市场战略。

8. 出口 B2C 跨境电子商务行业市场参与者可以分为平台型电商市场参与者和自营型电商市场参与者两种。

VIII. Multiple Choices.

1. What logistics methods are included in the special line logistics? (   ).

A. Middle East Line　　　B. Special Line-YW　　　C. Russian Air　　　　　D. ePacket

2. What is the correct description of the online shipment operation?(   ).

A. The seller does not need to pay for shipping

B. The seller needs to deliver to the logistics provider

C. Some regional logistics providers can come to collect

D. Sellers outside the collection area need to ship to the domestic warehouse

3. What is the correct statement about custom shipping settings? (   ).

A. Set custom shipping can choose to set by weight

B. You can choose whether to ship according to the country

C. Set custom shipping can choose to set according to the quantity

D. You can choose whether to ship according to region

4. What kinds of logistics methods are included in postal logistics? (   ).

A. ePacket   B. Hong Kong Post Air Mail

C. EMS   D. China Post Air Mail

5. What is the difference between online delivery and offline delivery?(   ).

A. Online shipping costs are paid online with Alipay

B. The price of online delivery is lower than the market price

C. The online logistics provider is a platform certified high-quality logistics provider

D. Online shipment support online complaint claims, more protection

6. If you do not make any changes, what is the platform's default committed arrival times? (   ).

A. China Post and Hong Kong Airlines Air Bags default for Brazil for 39 days

B. EMS, E-mail Post default time 27 days

C. China Post, Hong Kong Airlines Size Pack for Russia Default 60 days

D. The default time for commercial express delivery (DHL, UPS, FEDEX, TNT) is 23 days

7. What kinds of logistics methods are included in commercial express delivery? (   ).

A. DHL   B. Fedex IP   C. TNT   D. UPS Express Saver

8. What are the risks of using China Post air parcels? (   ).

A. High packet loss rate   B. Longer shipping cycle

C. High prices   D. Incomplete cargo tracking information

9. What is the correct statement about AliExpress shipping? (   ).

A. The seller must use the logistics method selected by the buyer

B. Sellers can choose to send goods online

C. The seller can contact the logistics provider

D. Sellers must ship within their own delivery time

10. How many days are promised delivery time of EMS in novice freight template? (   ).

A. 39 days   B. 27 days   C. 14 days   D. 60 days

Chapter Seven　Commodities Display & Products Quality

第七章　商品展示和产品质量

Part A　Text

A Brief Introduction to Cross-Border E-Commerce Commodity Launch and Display

New product release of cross-border e-commerce company is a very important step. Early pre-steps such as product development, testing, positioning, pricing, and even the future growth largely depends on the release of new products. Nowadays, cross-border e-commerce product launches and product display need to integrate a variety of resources and platforms, not only includes the traditional media, but also need to take into account the new social media, as well as those online marketing tools. If cross-border e-commerce enterprises want to get a better communication effect, they must clearly depict the value of new products out to showcase the unique selling points and appeal points.

跨境电子商务企业新产品的发布是一个非常重要的步骤。前期的产品研发、测试、定位、定价，甚至未来的成长很大程度上都要依赖于新产品的发布。现在跨境电子商务新产品的发布和商品展示需要整合多种资源和平台，不仅仅包含之前的传统媒体，还需要加入新的社会化媒体、在线营销工具等。跨境电子商务企业想要获得更好的传播效果，就必须清楚地把新产品的价值描述出来，展示商品独特的卖点和诉求点。

The quality of cross-border e-commerce products is an indispensable part of cross-border international trade. Whether physical or intangible trade, the goods sold have their own quality, and the quality determines the market share of goods and market prices. Therefore, the quality of the sales contract is the most important terms, and also the basis for signing the contract. Goods are the basis for international trade, and all goods show a certain quality. Therefore, the quality of goods is not only the main condition for the contracts for the sale of international goods by cross-border e-commerce, but also the first thing that needs to be agreed upon when conducting cross-border negotiations between importers and exporters of e-commerce.

跨境电子商务企业商品的品质是跨境国际贸易不可缺少的部分。无论是有形贸易还是无形贸易，所销售的货物都有其自身的品质，并且该品质决定着该商品的市场占有率和市场价格。因此，品质是销售合同中最主要的条款，也是签订合同的基础。商品是进行国际贸易的基础，而所有商品都表现出一定的品质。因此，商品的品质不仅仅是跨境电子商务国际货物销售合同的主要条件，同时也是跨境电子商务进出口商进行交易磋商时首先要取得一致意见的事项。

Section One   Suggestions for Product Display of Cross-Border E-Commerce（跨境电子商务商品展示建议）

For the launch of new products in the cross-border e-commerce platform, it is carried out mainly based on SEO concepts and principles. Search Engine Optimization (SEO), which is the core to build search engine friendly website or landing page. Publishing a new product requires attention to the requirements of search engine optimization and the performance of the new product's landing page, which is a photo, description, or video of the landing page. Make sure the page is a well-defined metadata, title tag, caption, unique URL, and a clear, concise meta-description of the new product. Specific suggestions are as follows.

在跨境电子商务平台发布新产品主要是基于 SEO 理念和原则，即搜索引擎优化（Search Engine Optimization，SEO），其核心是构建搜索引擎友好型的网站或者登陆页（landing page）。发布新产品需要关注搜索引擎优化的要求和新产品登陆页的性能，即登陆页的照片、描述或视频，确保页面具有定义良好的编码、标题标签、标题文字、唯一确定的网址和有关新产品清晰简洁的元数据描述。具体可以按照以下的产品发布建议。

1. Category

First, the release of products is to pinpoint product categories, some products' category is clear, and some is not. When businesses are not sure what category their own products belong to, the core keywords can be applied to search at Ali Home page by looking at the natural rankings, on which category the leading peer products rank, and searching for several times. If all those searching results are the same particular category, then it is.

1．类目

首先，发布产品要找准产品类目，有的产品类目清晰明了，有的不然，当不确定自身的产品到底属于哪个类目时，就用核心的关键词去阿里首页搜索，看看自然排名下，排在前面的同类产品放在了哪个类目里面，多搜索几次，如果都是此类目，那就是该产品类目了。

2. Title/Caption of the Product

Now the title/caption of the product has more weight than the keywords, and the words in each keyword must be included in the title. And the main key words shall be placed on the far right of the title. For example: the main keyword is ABC BACKPACK, the title is high quality wholesale price transparent ABC BACKPACK. The title generally can not be too long, 60-80 characters is recommended.

2．产品标题

现在产品标题的权重大于关键词，每一个关键词里面的词都要包含在标题里面，并且主推的第一关键词要放在标题的最右边。例如：主关键词是 ABC BACKPACK，标题为 high quality wholesale price transparent ABC BACKPACK。标题一般不能太长，60～80 个字符为佳。

3. Keywords

Cross-border e-commerce platform provides three general recommendations to be filled in all keywords, resources offered by Ali tend to be valuable. Generally speaking, the first fill keyword shall be the "main push", sitting on the right of the title. These three keywords can not be imaginary, but shall be of search hot.

3. 关键词

跨境电子商务平台提供的 3 个关键词，一般建议要全部填上，阿里提供的资源往往很有价值。一般第一个填的关键词作为主推，放在标题右边。这 3 个关键词不能是虚构的，必须是具备一定搜索热度的。

4. Product Picture

Generally speaking, the main 6 pictures shall all be filled, the general picture shall be of no watermark, so the customer experience can be improved. The main map and the details of the map are to be made by the recommended size. Product images can be named with different keywords. Product attributes: highly recommended all fill-in.

4. 产品图片

一般来说，主图的 6 张图片都要放满，而且图片一般是没有水印的，这样可以提高客户的体验度。主图、详情图根据建议的尺寸来定。产品图片可以用不同的关键词命名。产品属性：强烈建议全部填满。

5. Custom Attributes

Custom attributes highly recommended all fill-in. Make sure to fill in the main keyword in the first line of customattributes on the right. Transaction Information: completely fill-in. And fill in the main keywords in the supplementary information below the MOQ. Logistics Information: completely fill-in. Moreover, fill in the main keywords in the supplementary information below the supply capacity. Insert a primary keyword in the regular package. Featured services: whether the product sample is supported.

5. 自定义属性

自定义属性强烈建议全部填满。自定义属性的右边第一行，一定要填写主关键词。交易信息要填写完整。并且，在最小起订量下面的补充信息里面填写主关键词。物流信息要填写完整。并且，在供货能力下面的补充信息里面填写主关键词。常规包装里面插入一个主关键词。特色服务：可以看看产品是否支持索样。

6. Product Details

Intelligent editing is generally suggested and recommended while normal editing can also be used. Details page layout of the content should be reasonable, not messy. Content uploads require tidiness and uniformity. In the product details page, code shall be adopted and applied. If a series of pictures are to be placed in a row in product details, and especially when several pictures cluster together, insert a title/caption between the pictures, by which the keyword density can be increased. For online wholesale products, as the final guide, some guiding hints for the customers shall be added on the details page which can push the buyers to contact.

6．产品详情

一般建议使用智能编辑，也可以使用普通编辑。详情页版面的内容要合理，不能杂乱。上传产品的内容要求整洁和统一。在产品详情页，应采用并正确应用代码。产品详情里面如果连续放置很多图片，当多张图片在一起时，在图片与图片中间放一个标题，这样可以增加关键词密度。对于在线批发的产品，详情页里面可以放一些引导买家联系你的语言，作为最后的引导。

Section Two　Cross-Border E-Commerce AliExpress Platform Product Release Tips（跨境电子商务全球速卖通平台产品发布技巧）

1．Image Upload Skills

1．图片上传技巧

(1) In order to facilitate the unified management of the picture, the seller, when naming the picture, should ensure that is in line with the same product number. In general, each product should have at least 5 or more product images.

（1）为了便于对图片进行统一管理，卖家在对图片命名时，应该保证与产品编号一致。一般来讲，每个产品都应该拥有至少 5 张以上的产品图。

(2) To ensure the clarity of the picture, it is best to fully reflect the product material, appearance, performance and so on. When taking pictures, try to show the product from a variety of different perspectives.

（2）要保证图片的清晰度，最好能充分体现产品的材质、外观、性能等。拍摄图片时，尽量从多种不同的角度来对产品进行展示。

(3) Pictures and products are to be consistent. If there is serious color or surface discrepancy between online pictures and the offline goods, a large number of consumer complaints are following.

（3）图片与产品要保持一致，如果存在严重的色差或表面差异，很容易被大量的消费者投诉。

(4) Product attributes such as product name, material, color, appearance, size, quality, packaging and serial number can all become important factors influencing consumer decision-making. Therefore, all the related factors and pictures should be as perfect as possible.

（4）产品名称、材质、颜色、外观、尺寸、质量、包装及编号等产品属性，都能成为影响消费者决策的重要因素，所有相关的因素和图片都要尽可能地完美。

(5) Pictures shall not be repeatedly used. It is suggested to browse the pictures provided by AliExpress bank, so as to ensure no duplicate problems occur.

（5）图片不要重复使用，建议浏览速卖通银行提供的图片，以确保不会出现重复的问题。

(6) Pictures can be dealt with via PS and other tools for the existence of the watermark pictures, so as to avoid other stores' URLs and watermarks.

（6）可以通过 PS 等工具对存在水印的图片进行处理，从而避免其他店铺的网址以及水印。

(7) When upload pictures, you can refer to eBay and other foreign shopping sites in the same product sellers concerning how to set the picture.

（7）上传图片时，可以参考 eBay 等国外购物网站中同类产品的卖家如何设置图片。

(8) To avoid outdated and inappropriate pictures. At present, AliExpress platform overseas users are mainly in Europe and the United States, Australia and Russia, hence it is suggested to understand their preferences and culture.

（8）避免出现不合时宜的图片，目前，速卖通平台的用户主要是欧美、澳大利亚以及俄罗斯的海外群体，因此建议要了解他们的喜好和文化。

(9) After you have uploaded the pictures on the AliExpress platform, you also need to upload the goods pictures to Alibaba International Station.

（9）在速卖通平台上传完图片后，还要将这些图片上传到阿里巴巴国际站中。

(10) There are also some tips for uploading the pictures. First upload the vertical and horizontal sizes, then upload the front view, section view and background view, and then upload the package diagram, the back view with the barcode, the card map, and carton chart and so on.

（10）图片的上传顺序也有一定的技巧，首先要上传横竖各一张尺寸，接着上传正面图、剖面图以及背景图，然后依次上传包装图、附带条形码的背面图、卡片图以及纸箱图等。

2. Skills for Searching Hotness

2. 搜索热度的确定渠道技巧

(1) The hot words in the data steward.
（1）数据管家里面的热搜词。

(2) Hot search terms in the industry perspective.
（2）行业视角里面的热搜词。

(3) Visitor marketing guest search term.
（3）访客营销客人搜索词。

(4) Inquiry, RFQ guest's search term.
（4）询盘、RFQ 客人的搜索词。

(5) A drop-down box suggestion that appears when releasing a product, and so on.
（5）发布产品时出现的下拉框推荐词，等等。

3．Product Keyword Setting Skills

3．产品关键词的设置技巧

(1) Keywords need to bear a close relationship with the product.

（1）关键词需要确保与产品存在着密切的联系。

(2) It is best to combine the popular words of the moment.

（2）最好能结合当下比较流行的热门词汇。

(3) Keywords should be consistent with overseas users' search habits.

（3）关键词要与海外用户的搜索习惯保持一致。

(4) Ensure that the keywords have enough exposure, in addition to the title of the product, but also can use the product description, set custom attributes and product details page and other ways to highlight the product keywords.

（4）确保关键词有足够的曝光度，除了产品标题以外，还可以借助产品的简要描述、设置自定义属性以及产品详情页等方式来对产品关键词进行强调。

(5) Keyword optimization, through a variety of ways and channels to obtain product-related keywords, so as to provide better keywords to provide an important reference.

（5）关键词优化。通过多种方式以及渠道来获取与产品相关的关键词，从而为指定效果更佳的关键词提供重要参考。

Section Three　Methods of Stipulating Quality of Commodity（货物品质的表示方法）

The quality of commodity is the combination of the intrinsic quality and outside form or shape of the commodity, such as modeling, structure, color, luster, chemical composition, mechanical performance, biological features, etc. The qualities of different commodities can be expressed in different ways. The methods of stipulating quality of commodity depend on the quality, character and the customary usage in practice. In international trade, there are two ways to indicate the quality of the goods either by description or by sample.

商品的品质是商品的外观形态和内在质量的综合，如造型、结构、颜色、光泽、化学成分、机械性能和生物化学特征等。不同种类的商品可以用不同的方法表示品质。确定商品品质的方法主要取决于商品的性质、特点及其在国际贸易中长期以来形成的习惯做法。在国际贸易中，表示商品品质的方法可分为用文字说明和用样品展示两个大类。

1．Sale by Description

In the international trade, mostly the goods are sold by the method of sale by specification, grade or standard except some special cases. This method may be further classified into the following types.

1. 凭文字说明买卖

在国际货物买卖业务中，除某些特殊情况外，大部分货物是按规格、等级或标准进行销售的。具体可以分为以下几种。

(1) Sale by specification, grade or standard. The specification of the goods refers to certain main indicators which indicate the quality of the goods, such as composition, content, purity, size, length, thickness, etc. Sale by specification is a sales way of convenience and accuracy. So in practice it is most widely used. Goods with different quality should have different standards, and for those with different application there are also different standards.

The grade of the goods refers to the classifications of the commodity of one kind which is indicated by words, numbers or symbols. The classifications are usually decided by different qualities, weights, compositions, appearances, properties, etc. For example, Chinese raw silk is sold by standard and its standard consists of 12 grades: 6A, 5A, 4A, 3A, 2A, A, B, C, D, E, F, and G. In practice, we often have Special Grade, First Grade, Second Grade, Large, Medium, Small, etc.

When the method of sale by grade is used, the quality clause in business is simplified. The quality of the goods can be known by simply stating its grade. However, the seller and the buyer should reach a consensus on the grades. When the goods are sold by grade, it is ok when the grade of goods is stated clearly. However, different countries have their own different grades to illustrate the goods, so when the buyer and the seller cannot understand each other's grade standard, it is better for both parties to stipulate which grade should be accepted in great details. For example, in the U.S.A., there is "American Industrial Materials Inspection Association Standards (ASTM)", in Germany there is "German Industrial Standards (DIN)", in UK there is "The British Standard Association Standards(BS)", in Japan there is "Japanese Industry Standard (JIS)". When the goods are dealt with this term, the goods delivered by the seller should be in exact conformity with the stipulations such as grade, specifications and standard in the contract. Otherwise the buyer has the right to ask for reducing the price difference, or will refuse to take the goods, even to cancel the contact and declare for compensation.

（1）凭规格、等级、标准买卖。规格是指表达商品质量的一些主要指标，如成分、含量、纯度、大小、长度、厚度等。凭规格买卖比较方便、准确，在国际货物买卖中应用最广。商品不同，表示商品品质的指标亦不同；商品的用途不同，要求的品质指标也会有所不同。

等级是指对同类商品按照规格中若干主要指标的差异，用文字、数字或符号所做的分类。凭等级买卖只需说明其级别，即可明确买卖货物的品质。例如，中国生丝就是按标准销售的，共分 12 个等级：6A、5A、4A、3A、2A、A、B、C、D、E、F、G。实际业务中，常有特级、一级、二级、大号、中号、小号等。

当采用凭等级买卖的方式时，就简化了交易中表示品质的条款。只要说明其等级，就可了解所要买卖商品的品质。然而，买卖双方必须对等级有共同的认识。凭等级买卖时，只需说明商品的等级，即可明确商品的品质。由于不同国家等级的划分原则各不同，如果双方不熟悉等级内容，则最好列明每一等级的具体规格。例如，在美国就有"美国工业材料检验协会标准", 在德国有"德国工业品标准", 在英国有"英国标准协会标准", 日本有"日本工业标准", 等等。凡按这类方式成交时, 卖方所交货物必须与合同规定的规格、等级、标准相符。否则, 买方有权要求扣减品质差价, 甚至可以拒收货物、撤销合同并要求赔偿损失。

The standard refers to the specifications or grades which are stipulated and announced (laid down and proclaimed) in a unified way by the government department or commercial organization of a country such as the chamber of commerce, etc.

It is worthy to note that the standard of a commodity is subject to change or amendment and a new standard often takes place of the old one. So, in case of sales by standard, it is important and necessary to mention in the terms also the name of the publication, in which the standard of the commodity appears.

e.g.: Tetracycline HCL Tablets (Sugar Coated) 250mg. B.P. 1973

B.P. = British Pharmacopoeia

标准是指政府机关或商业团体, 如商业协会等统一制定和公布（已确定并宣布）的规格或等级。

值得注意的是, 某种商品的标准或等级经常会进行变动和修改, 新的标准常常代替旧的标准。因此, 如果按标准买卖, 就必须注明是按照哪个版本的标准, 并标明援用标准的版本年份。

例如: 四环素糖衣片, 250mg, 1973 年英国药典

B.P.=英国药典

For those agricultural and by-products that are easy to change in quality and difficult to stipulate the standard, the following ways would be preferred:① Fair Average Quality (F.A.Q.); ② Good Merchantable Quality (G.M.Q.).

对于某些品质变化较大而难以规定统一标准的农副产品, 通常采用以下两种方法来表示其品质: ① 良好平均品质; ② 上好可销售品质。

In the international agricultural and by-product market, there is a commonly adopted standard, i.e., fair average quality (F.A.Q.). According to the explanation of some countries, F.A.Q. refers to the average quality level of the export commodity within a certain period of time. This kind of standard is quite ambiguous. In fact, it does not represent any fixed, accurate specification.

For example:

Chinese Groundnut, 2009 crop, F.A.Q.

Moisture : (max.) 13%

Admixture: (max.) 5%

Oil content: (min.) 44%

良好平均品质是国际农副产品市场通用的标准。据有些国家解释, 良好平均品质指出口商品在一定期限内的平均质量水平。这种解释模棱两可, 事实上它不代表任何固定的、准确的规格。

例如:

中国花生仁, 2009 年产, 良好平均品质

水分：（最高）13%

杂质：（最高）5%

含油量：（最低）44%

For the trading of wood and aquatic products, good merchantable quality (G.M.Q.) is employed to indicate the quality. G.M.Q. means the goods is free from defects and is good enough for use or consumption. G.M.Q. is usually not supplement with specifications and when disputes arise because of the quality of the goods, exporters will have to be invited to make the arbitration.

在买卖木材和水产品时，可以采用上好可销品质表示货物的品质。上好可销品质是指卖方必须保证其交付的货物品质良好，适合销售，在成交时无须以其他方式证明商品的品质。但如果出现由于货物的质量引发的争议，卖方必须被邀请进行仲裁。

ISO 9000 series standards are the international quality assurance standards formulated by the International Standard Organization (ISO) to meet the need for international trade development, which can function as international pass to the world market. While ISO 14000 "Environmental Management" series standards are environmental management standards for standardizing enterprise environmental behavior, controlling and reducing the damage or environmental contamination caused by production process. ISO 14000 certificate means that the products produced are in accordance with the requirements of international environmental trend. The enterprises with ISO 14000 certificate can be called a green enterprise, whose products can be referred to as environmental products. The products with these two certificates are of great competition capabilities.

With the development of technology and the change of situations, the standard of a commodity is always subject to change or amendment and a new standard often takes the place of the old one. Therefore, the standard of the same commodity formulated by a country usually has several editions with some different contents. So in the contract, the standards based on which copy should be specified very clearly.

ISO 9000 系列标准是国际标准化组织为适应国际贸易发展的需要而制定的国际品质保证标准，ISO 9000 证书具有国际通行证的作用。ISO 14000 环境管理系列标准是国际标准化组织为规范企业的环境行为，控制和减少企业在生产经营过程中对环境造成的破坏而制定的环境管理标准。ISO 14000 证书是表明产品符合国际环保潮流的环保证书，符合 ISO 14000 系列标准的企业称为绿色企业，其生产的产品经认可成为环保产品。两证齐全的产品在国际市场上具有较强的竞争力。

随着技术的发展和情况的变化，某种商品的标准经常要进行变动和修改，新的标准规则常常代替旧的标准。因此，某个国家颁布的同一商品标准通常有几个内容不尽相同的版本。在合同中，应该明确说明应采用哪个版本的标准。

(2) Sale by brand name or trade mark.Brand name or trade mark is based on high quality, which is used by the manufacturers todistinguish their high quality goods with the others of the like. Brand is the name of the goods, while trade mark is the tag. They are related to each other closely. As to the goods whose quality is stable, reputation is sound and with which the customers are quite familiar,

we may sell it by brand name or trade mark. For example, "Maxam Dental Cream" "Haier Air Conditioner" "Toyota Automobile", etc. Since these goods with the same brand name or trade mark possess the same quality and their quality remains unified and unchanged, their brand names or trademarks are often used to indicate the quality of these goods. Such a method is called sale by brand name or trade mark.

（2）凭牌号或商标买卖。牌号或商标都是以品质为基础的，是生产者或销售者用以区别其他同类商品的一种标志。牌号是商标的名称，商标是牌号的标记，两者不能脱离对方而单独存在。用牌号或商标表示品质，一般都是在国际市场上有良好信誉、品质稳定的商品，被广大客户所喜爱，因而可以凭牌号或商标买卖。例如，"美加净牙膏""海尔空调""丰田汽车"等。由于这些同一牌名或商标的商品具有相同的品质，且品质统一、稳定，所以这些牌名或商标经常用来表示商品的品质。这种方法称为凭牌名或商标买卖。

(3) Sale by name of origin.Some goods, just like some agricultural products and by-products subject to the influence of nature and traditional production techniques, are well known by their origins for their excellent quality all over the world. As to these products, the origins may well indicate their qualities. These goods can be sold by name of origin.

e.g.: Longjing Green Tea

Jingdezhen Chinaware

（3）凭产地名卖。有些货物，特别是农副产品，受产地自然条件和传统的生产技术影响较大，一些历史较长、条件较好地区的产品，由于品质优良并具有一定的特色，产地名称也成为该项产品品质的重要标志。这类产品可凭产地名进行买卖，如龙井茶、景德镇瓷器。

(4) Sale by description and illustration.The quality of some commodities, such as large-sized machines technological instruments, electric machines, etc. can not be simply indicated by quality indexes, instead it is quite necessary to explain in detail the structure, material, performance as well as method of operation. Thus, the specific descriptions of products are required to indicate the quality of the goods. If necessary, pictures, photos, etc. must also be provided.

（4）凭说明书和图样买卖。有些商品如大型机电、仪器产品，无法用几个简单的指标来表示其品质，必须用说明书详细地说明其结构、用材、运转性能及操作方法。如果有必要，还要提供图片和照片等。

2. Sale by Sample

Sale by sample refers to the transaction method which is done by the sample agreed by both the buyer and the seller.

The sample refers to the article which can be used to represent the quality of the whole lot. In merchandising, a sample is a small quantity of a product, often taken out from a whole lot or specially designed and processed, that is given to encourage prospective customers to buy the product. The transaction that is concluded on the basis of the sample representing the quality of the whole lot can be called sales by sample. This method is used when the transaction is hard to conclude by standard, grade or words, such as some certain arts and crafts products, garmenture, local specialty, light industrial products, etc.

Sale by sample includes 3 cases, i.e., sale by the seller's sample, sale by the buyer's sample and sale by the counter sample.

2. 凭样品买卖

凭样品买卖是指买卖双方约定以样品作为交货品质依据的买卖方式。

所谓样品就是指能够代表一整批货物质量的实物，通常是指从一批货物中抽取出来或由生产和使用部门设计加工出来的能够代表出售货物品质的少量实物，用于向客户推广自己的产品。凡以样品表示商品品质并以此作为交货依据的，称为凭样品买卖。凭样品买卖的方法一般适用于难以标准化、规格化，难以用文字说明其品质的商品，如部分工艺品、服装、土特产品、轻工产品等。

凭样品买卖主要有凭卖方样品、凭买方样品和凭对等样品 3 种成交方式。

(1) Sale by the seller's sample. Seller's samples are the samples which are usually sent by the seller to the buyer, which is also called original sample.

In this case, the seller shall supply a representative sample which will possess the moderate quality among a large quantity of the physical goods, and at the same time keep a duplicate sample, which shall be in quality as or on the whole as the same as the standard sample. The sample dispatched and the duplicate sample/file sample kept shall have the same article number so as to make it convenient for delivery, verification when handling quality disputes or future transactions.

（1）凭卖方样品买卖。凭卖方样品买卖是指由卖方向买方提供货物的样品，即原样。

如果采用凭卖方样品买卖，通常卖方要提供能够代表一整批货物质量的实物，同时，卖方要自留与这些样品质量一致的复样。一般来说，发出的样品和复样具有相同的编号，以备交货或处理品质纠纷时做核对之用。

(2) Sale by the buyer's sample.

① In this case, the seller shall first take into consideration the availability of the new material and the possibility of providing the processing technology.

② In order to take the initiative, the seller may reproduce the buyer's sample, i.e., counter sample, and send it back to the buyer as a type sample. After the buyer confirms the counter sample, sale by the buyer's sample is changed into sale by the seller's counter sample.

③ The two parties shall stipulate that in case the buyer's sample results in any disputes of infringement of industrial property, the seller will have nothing to do with it.

（2）凭买方样品买卖。

① 如果按这种方式交易，卖方首先要考虑的是新材料的可用性和提供加工技术的可能性。

② 有时为了采取主动，卖方按买方来样复制，并回寄给买方确认，经确认后作为交货品质依据的样品，即对等样品。这种做法实际是把交易的性质由"凭买方样品买卖"转变为"凭卖方样品买卖"。

③ 买卖双方应在合同中明确指出如果买方样品出现了工业产权侵权，卖方不承担责任。

(3) Sale by the counter sample. Samples can be also provided by the buyer. They are given as the quality standard for the goods to be produced and delivered by the seller. Under such circumstances, to avoid future disputes over the quality of the goods, the seller usually first duplicates the samples and then sends the duplicate to the buyer for confirmation. This sample is called counter sample.

（3）凭对等样品买卖。样品可以由买方提供，作为卖方生产和交货的产品质量标准。在这种情况下，为了避免将来发生有关商品质量方面的纠纷，卖方通常会复制样品，然后将复制样品寄给买方确认。这个样品就是对等样品。

In international trade practice, if sale by samples adopted, the followings should be paid attention to:

① We should try to do the business by "sale by the seller's sample".

② When the seller sends out the sample, it is better that the seller will keep the "original" or "duplicate" sample so as to make it convenient for verification when handling quality disputes or future transactions.

③ If the transaction is done by "sale by the buyer's sample", we should pay attention to the fact that whether the sample of the buyer has something to do with the problems of politics, society and religion, such as color, pattern and design. We should also take into consideration the availability of the new material and the possibility of providing the processing technology in order to avoid the unnecessary trouble in delivery. For the sake of caution, the import and export enterprises usually make it clear as in the remarks in the contract that "For any cotton price goods produced with the designs, trade marks, brands and/or stampings provided by the buyers, should there be any dispute arising from infringement upon the third party's industrial property right, it is the buyer to be held responsibility for it.

④ When we get the sample of the buyer, it is better to make it as counter sample.

⑤ Whether it is sale by buyer's sample or by seller's sample, if it is difficult to keep the goods contracted in strict accordance with the sample, the seller should write some flexible terms in the sales contract as follows:

* Shipment shall be similar to the sample;

* Quality to be about equal to the sample;

* Quality to be nearly same as the sample.

⑥ Whether it is sale by buyer's sample or by seller's sample, if it is necessary, sometimes "sealed sample" can be adopted.

在国际贸易中，如采用凭样品销售的方式，应注意做好以下工作：

① 应争取凭卖方样品成交。

② 卖方寄出样品（原样）时应留存"原样"或"复样"，以便于在处理质量纠纷或将来的交易时进行验证。

③ 如凭买方来样成交，应考虑买家来样在政治、社会、宗教方面是否存在敏感的色彩、

造型、图案等问题，是否会造成不良影响；还应注意卖方在原材料、生产技术条件和工艺水平上能否落实，以免在交货时陷入被动。为慎重起见，外贸企业在签订合同时常在"一般交易条件"中写入相应说明，如凡根据买方提供的式样、商标、牌号及（或）印记等生产的任何棉布织物，如因涉及侵犯第三者的工业产权而引起纠纷，概由买方负责。

④ 买方来样时，最好将其制作成样品，以对等样品方式成交。

⑤ 无论是凭买方还是凭卖方样品销售，如果货物很难严格保证与样品完全一致，卖方往往可在合同中说明一些弹性品质条款。例如：

* 交货与样品近似；

* 品质与样品大致相同；

* 品质接近样品。

⑥ 无论是凭买方还是凭卖方样品买卖，必要时可使用"封样"的做法。

Section Four　General Catalog of E-Commerce Platform（电子商务平台的产品目录及分类）

C001 Electronics　数码电子产品

C001001 Computer & Networking C001　计算机&网络设备

C001001001 Tablets C001001　平板电脑

C001001002 Laptops C001001　笔记本电脑

C001001003 Desktops C001001　台式电脑

C001001004 Storage C001001　内存条

C001001005 Networking C001001　网络设备

C001001006 Tablet Accessories C001001　平板电脑配件

C001001007 Laptop Accessories C001001　笔记本电脑配件

C001001008 Computer Peripherals C001001　计算机外设

C001001009 Computer Components C001001　计算机部件

C001002 Consumer Electronics C001　消费电子产品

C001002001 Camera & Photography C001002　相机&摄影器材

C001002002 Home Audio & Video C001002　家庭影音设备

C001002003 TV Stick C001002　电视网络播放器

C001002004 Accessories & Parts C001002　相关配件&部件

C001002005 Video Games C001002　游戏机&配件

C001002006 Portable Audio & Video C001002　便携式影音设备

C001002007 Earphones & Headphones C001002　耳机&头戴式耳机

C001002008 Mini Camcorders C001002　微型摄像机

C001002009 Memory Cards C001002　内存卡

C001003 Phones & Accessories C001　手机&配件

C001003001 Mobile Phones C001003　手机

C001003002 Bags & Cases C001003　手机套&手机壳

C001003003 Batteries C001003　电池

C001003004 Chargers & Docks C001003　充电器

C001003005 Backup Powers C001003　充电宝

C001003006 Cables C001003　数据线

C001003007 Lenses C001003　手机镜头

C001003008 Parts C001003　手机部件

C001003009 LCDs C001003　手机屏

C001003010 Holders & Stands C001003　手机座

C001003011 Stickers C001003　手机贴

C002 Apparel & Accessories　服装&配饰

C002001 Women C002　女装

C002001001 Dresses C002001　连衣裙

C002001002 Coats & Jackets C002001　大衣&外套

C002001003 Blouses & Shirts C002001　上衣&衬衫

C002001004 Tops & Tees C002001　短袖&T恤

C002001005 Hoodies & Sweatshirts C002001　卫衣&运动衫

C002001006 Intimates C002001　内衣

C002001007 Swimwear C002001　泳衣

C002001008 Pants & Capris C002001　长裤&紧身裤

C002001009 Sweaters C002001　毛衣

C002001010 Skirts C002001　半身裙

C002001011 Leggings C002001　打底裤

C002001012 Accessories C002001　配饰

C002002 Men C002　男装

C002002001 Tops & Tees C002002　短袖&T恤

C002002002 Coats & Jackets C002002　大衣&外套

C002002003 Underwear C002002　内衣

C002002004 Shirts C002002　衬衫

C002002005 Hoodies & Sweatshirts C002002　卫衣&运动衫

C002002006 Jeans C002002　牛仔裤

C002002007 Pants C002002　长裤

C002002008 Suits & Blazer C002002　套装&西装

C002002009 Shorts C002002　短裤

C002002010 Sweaters C002002　毛衣

C002002011 Accessories C002002　配饰

C002003 Wedding & Events C002　婚礼&特殊场合礼服

C002003001 Wedding Dresses C002003　婚纱

C002003002 Evening Dresses C002003 晚礼服

C002003003 Homecoming Dresses C002003 校友返校日礼服

C002003004 Ball Gown C002003 舞会礼服

C002003005 Cocktail Dresses C002003 鸡尾酒会礼服

C002003006 Casual Party Dresses C002003 聚会礼服

C002003007 Celebrity-Inspired Dresses C002003 明星款礼服

C002003008 Quinceanera Dresses C002003 成人礼礼服

C002003009 Communion Dresses C002003 圣餐礼服

C002003010 Graduation Dresses C002003 毕业礼服

C002003011 Wedding Accessories C002003 婚纱配饰

C002003012 Wedding Party Dress C002003 婚礼礼服

C003 Bags & Shoes 箱包&鞋子

C003001 Luggage & Bags C003 行李箱&包

C003001001 Women's Shoulder Bags C003001 女式单肩包

C003001002 Women's Wallets C003001 女式钱包

C003001003 Women's Crossbody Bags C003001 女式长带包

C003001004 Women's Totes C003001 女式手提包

C003001005 Women's Clutches C003001 女士手包

C003001006 Women's Backpacks C003001 女式双肩包

C003001007 Men's Wallets C003001 男式钱包

C003001008 Men's Backpacks C003001 男式双肩包

C003001009 Men's Briefcases C003001 男式公文包

C003001010 Men's Crossbody Bags C003001 男式长带包

C003001011 School Bags C003001 书包

C003001012 Travel Duffle C003001 旅行包

C003002 Shoes C003 鞋子

C003002001 Women's Fashion Sneakers C003002 女式帆布鞋

C003002002 Women's Sandals C003002 女式凉鞋

C003002003 Women's Flats C003002 女式平底鞋

C003002004 Women's Pumps C003002 高跟鞋

C003002005 Women's Boots C003002 女靴

C003002006 Women's Slippers C003002 女式拖鞋

C003002007 Men's Fashion Sneakers C003002 男式帆布鞋

C003002008 Men's Flats C003002 男式平底鞋

C003002009 Men's Sandals C003002 男式凉鞋

C003002010 Men's Boots C003002 男靴

C003002011 Men's Loafers C003002 男式便鞋

C003002012 Men's Slippers C003002 男式拖鞋

C003003 Children's Shoes C003　童鞋

C003003001 Girls' Sneakers C003003　平底女童鞋

C003003002 Boys' Sneakers C003003　平底男童鞋

C003003003 Girls' Sandals C003003　女童凉鞋

C003003004 Boys' Sandals C003003　男童凉鞋

C003003005 Children's Boots C003003　童靴

C003003006 Girls' Leather Shoes C003003　女童皮鞋

C003003007 Boys' Leather Shoes C003003　男童皮鞋

C003003008 Baby First Walkers C003003　学步鞋

C003003009 Baby Leather Shoes C003003　婴儿皮鞋

C003003010 Baby Sneakers C003003　婴儿平底鞋

C003003011 Baby Boots C003003　婴儿靴子

C003003012 Baby Sandals C003003　婴儿凉鞋

C004 Home & Garden　家居&园艺

C004001 Home & Garden C004　家居用品

C004001001 Home Decor C004001　家居饰品

C004001002 Home Textile C004001　家纺

C004001003 Kitchen,Dining & bar C004001　厨具、餐具&酒具

C004001004 Bathroom Products C004001　卫浴用品

C004001005 Festive & Party Supplies C004001　节日&聚会用品

C004001006 Home Storage & Organization C004001　收纳用品

C004001007 Household Cleaning Tools & Accessories C004001　清洁用品

C004001008 Pet Products C004001　宠物用品

C004001009 Bedding Set C004001　床上用品

C004001010 Curtains C004001　窗帘

C004001011 Painting & Calligraphy C004001　装饰书画

C004001012 Furniture C004001　家具&配件

C004002 Outdoors & Garden C004　户外&花园用品

C004002001 Garden Pots & Planters C004002　花盆

C004002002 Garden Landscaping & Decking C004002　花园造景&美化

C004002003 Garden Tools C004002　园艺工具

C004002004 Watering & Irrigation C004002　浇水灌溉用具

C004002005 Temperature Gauges C004002　温度计&测温仪

C004002006 Fertilizer C004002　化肥

C004002007 BBQ C004002　烧烤用具

C004002008 Shade C004002　遮阳用具

C004002009 Mailboxes C004002　信箱

C004002010 Garden-Buildings C004002　篱笆&温室

C004002011 Outdoor Furniture C004002 户外家具

C004002012 Bonsai C004002 盆景

C004003 Home Improvement C004 灯具&杂货

C004003001 Lighting C004003 灯具

C004003002 Home Security C004003 家用安全装置

C004003003 Home Appliances C004003 小家电

C004003004 Hardware C004003 小五金件

C004003005 Hand Tools C004003 家用小工具

C004003006 Kitchen & Bath Fixtures C004003 厨房&卫浴设施

C004003007 Faucets,Mixers & Taps C004003 水龙头&花洒

C004003008 CCTV Product C004003 闭路电视设备

C004003009 Indoor Lighting C004003 室内灯具

C004003010 Outdoor Lighting C004003 室外灯具

C004003011 Lighting Bulbs & Tubes C004003 灯泡&灯管

C004003012 LED Lighting C004003 LED 灯具

C005 Toys, Kids & Baby 玩具&婴幼用品

C005001 Clothing & Accessories C005 童装&配饰

C005001001 Girls C005001 女童装

C005001002 Boys C005001 男童装

C005001003 Baby Girls C005001 女婴装

C005001004 Baby Boys C005001 男婴装

C005001005 Clothing Sets C005001 童装套装

C005001006 Girls' Dress C005001 女童连衣裙

C005001007 Boys' T-shirts C005001 男童 T 恤

C005001008 Baby Rompers C005001 婴儿背带裤

C005001009 Children's School Bags C005001 儿童书包

C005001010 Baby First Walkers C005001 学步鞋

C005001011 Children's Shoes C005001 儿童鞋

C005001012 Children's Accessories C005001 儿童配饰

C005002 Toys C005 玩具

C005002001 Stuffed Animals & Plush C005002 毛绒玩具

C005002002 RC Helicopters C005002 遥控玩具直升机

C005002003 Action Figures C005002 卡通人偶玩具

C005002004 Balloons C005002 气球

C005002005 Model Building C005002 拼装玩具

C005002006 Blocks C005002 积木玩具

C005002007 Dolls & Accessories C005002 洋娃娃&配饰

C005002008 Electronic Toys C005002 电子玩具

C005002009 Learning & Education C005002 益智玩具

C005002010 Baby Toys C005002 婴儿玩具

C005002011 Outdoor Fun & Sports C005002 户外玩具&体育用品

C005003 Baby & Maternity Products C005 母婴用品

C005003001 Nappy Changing C005003 妈咪包

C005003002 Activity & Gear C005003 出行用品

C005003003 Baby Care C005003 婴儿护理

C005003004 Safety Gear C005003 安全用品

C005003005 Feeding C005003 喂养用品

C005003006 Bedding C005003 婴儿床上用品

C005003007 Swimming Pool C005003 婴儿游泳池

C005003008 Baby Monitors C005003 婴儿监视器

C005003009 Maternity Dress C005003 孕妇裙

C005003010 Intimates C005003 孕妇内衣

C005003011 Maternity Tops C005003 孕妇上衣

C006 Automotive 汽车

C006001 Car Electronics C006 车用电子产品

C006001001 Motor Electronics C006001 车用小电子产品

C006001002 Car DVD C006001 车载 DVD

C006001003 Alarm Systems & Security C006001 报警系统&安全装置

C006001004 DVR/Camera C006001 行车记录仪

C006001005 Radar Detectors C006001 测速仪

C006001006 GPS C006001 GPS 导航仪

C006001007 Car Video Players C006001 车载播放器

C006001008 Motorcycle C006001 摩托车用品

C006001009 Motorbike Brakes C006001 摩托刹车片

C006001010 Protective Gears C006001 摩托车手保护装备

C006001011 Electrical System C006001 摩托车电气装置

C006002 Replacement Parts C006 汽车配件

C006002001 Car Parts C006002 汽车部件

C006002002 Car Lights C006002 车灯

C006002003 External Lights C006002 外灯

C006002004 Car Light Source C006002 车用 LED 灯

C006002005 Interior Lights C006002 内灯

C006002006 Engine C006002 引擎

C006002007 Fuel Injector C006002 喷油嘴

C006002008 Car Accessories C006002 汽车配件

C006002009 Car Stickers C006002 车饰

C006002010 Chromium Styling C006002　车身保护条

C006002011 Bumpers C006002　保险杠保护条

C006002012 Car Covers C006002　车罩

C006003 Tools Maintenance & Care C006　汽车保养工具

C006003001 Tools & Equipment C006003　车用工具&装置

C006003002 Diagnostic Tools C006003　汽车诊断仪

C006003003 Code Readers & Scan Tools C006003　汽车扫描仪

C006003004 Car Washer C006003　洗车用具

C006003005 Car Chargers C006003　车载充电器

C006003006 Steering Covers C006003　方向盘套

C006003007 Seat Covers C006003　汽车座套

C006003008 Floor Mats C006003　汽车置物防滑垫

C007 Sports & Outdoor　运动&户外

C007001 Sports Clothing C007　运动服装

C007001001 Hiking Jackets C007001　登山服

C007001002 Hiking T-shirts C007001　登山 T 恤

C007001003 Hiking Pants C007001　登山长裤

C007001004 Rucksacks C007001　登山包

C007001005 Running T-Shirts C007001　跑步 T 恤

C007001006 Running Bags C007001　跑步包

C007001007 Cycling Jersey C007001　自行车骑行服

C007001008 Cycling Jackets C007001　自行车骑行外套

C007001009 Cycling Shorts C007001　自行车骑行短裤

C007001010 Cycling Eyewear C007001　自行车骑行眼镜

C007001011 Skiing Jackets C007001　滑雪服

C007001012 Soccer Jersey C007001　足球球衣

C007002 Sport Shoes C007　运动鞋

C007002001 Running Shoes C007002　跑步鞋

C007002002 Basketball Shoes C007002　篮球鞋

C007002003 Soccer Shoes C007002　足球鞋

C007002004 Hiking Shoes C007002　登山鞋

C007002005 Skateboarding Shoes C007002　滑板鞋

C007002006 Tennis Shoes C007002　网球鞋

C007002007 Walking Shoes C007002　健走鞋

C007002008 Dance Shoes C007002　舞鞋

C007002009 Skate Shoes C007002　轮滑鞋

C007002010 Fitness Shoes C007002　健身鞋

C007003 Sport Equipment C007　运动装备

C007003001 Bicycle C007003 自行车

C007003002 Bicycle Parts C007003 自行车部件

C007003003 Bicycle Helmet C007003 自行车头盔

C007003004 Bicycle Light C007003 自行车灯

C007003005 Bicycle Bags & Panniers C007003 自行车骑行包&车筐

C007003006 Fishing Reels C007003 鱼线轮

C007003007 Fishing Rods C007003 钓竿

C007003008 Fishing Lines C007003 鱼线

C007003009 Ffishing Lures C007003 鱼饵

C007003010 Tent C007003 帐篷

C007003011 Yoga C007003 瑜伽用品

C007003012 Guitar C007003 吉他

C008 Jewelry & Watches 首饰&手表

C008001 Fashion Jewelry C008 时尚饰品

C008001001 Necklaces & Pendants C008001 项链&吊坠

C008001002 Bracelets & Bangles C008001 手镯&手链

C008001003 Earrings C008001 耳饰

C008001004 Rings C008001 戒指

C008001005 Jewelry Sets C008001 首饰套装

C008001006 Hair Jewelry C008001 发饰

C008001007 Tie Clips & Cufflinks C008001 领带夹&袖扣

C008001008 Brooches C008001 胸针

C008001009 Charms C008001 小饰品

C008001010 Body Jewelry C008001 鼻饰&肚脐饰品

C008001011 Anklets C008001 脚链

C008001012 Jewelry Findings & Components C008001 饰品小配件

C008002 Watches C008 手表

C008002001 Sports Watches C008002 运动手表

C008002002 Wristwatches C008002 腕表

C008002003 Fashion & Casual Watches C008002 时尚休闲手表

C008002004 Pocket & Fob Watches C008002 怀表

C008002005 Women's Fashion Watches C008002 女式时尚手表

C008002006 Men's Casual Watches C008002 男士休闲手表

C008002007 Lover's Wristwatches C008002 情侣手表

C008002008 Watch Accessories C008002 手表配件

C008003 Fine Jewerly C008 高档首饰

C008003001 Diamond Series C008003 钻石首饰

C008003002 Pearl Collection C008003 珍珠首饰

C008003003 Ruby Jewelry C008003 红宝石首饰

C008003004 Sapphire Jewelry C008003 蓝宝石首饰

C008003005 Silver C008003 银饰

C008003006 Necklaces & Pendants C008003 项链&吊坠

C008003007 Rings C008003 戒指

C008003008 Earrings C008003 耳饰

C008003009 Jewelry Sets C008003 首饰套装

C008003010 Charms C008003 小饰品

C008003011 Bracelets & Bangles C008003 手镯&手链

C009 Beauty & Health 美容美发&保健

C009001 Beauty C009 美发

C009001001 Hair Styling C009001 美发用品

C009001002 Hair Rollers C009001 卷发器

C009001003 Straightening Irons C009001 直发器

C009001004 Hair Trimmers C009001 电动理发器

C009001005 Hair Dryers C009001 吹风机

C009001006 Hair Scissors C009001 理发剪刀

C009001007 Hair Color C009001 一次性染发粉

C009001008 Hair Loss Products C009001 头发生长精华素

C009001009 Shaving & Hair Removal C009001 剃须&脱毛用品

C009001010 Combs C009001 梳子

C009001011 Mirrors C009001 镜子

C009002 Hair C009 假发

C009002001 Human Hair C009002 真发制假发

C009002002 Hair Weaves C009002 织发补发片

C009002003 Hair Extension C009002 驳发

C009002004 Wigs C009002 假发片

C009002005 Closure C009002 一片式假发

C009002006 Synthetic Hair C009002 合成纤维假发

C009002007 Blended Hair C009002 真发与合成纤维混合制假发

C009002008 Feather Hair C009002 羽毛假发

C009002009 Accessories & Tools C009002 假发配件&工具

C009003 Additional Categories C009 美容用品及其他

C009003001 Makeup C009003 美妆用品

C009003002 Nail & Tools C009003 美甲用品

C009003003 Skin Care C009003 护肤用品

C009003004 Health Care C009003 保健用品

C009003005 Oral Hygiene C009003 口腔保健

C009003006 Tattoo & Body Art C009003 文身用品

C009003007 Sex Products C009003 成人用品

C009003008 Fragrances & Deodorants C009003 香水&香体露

C009003009 Bath & Shower C009003 沐浴用品

C009003010 Sanitary Paper C009003 尿片

Part B　Terminology Practice

1. **Spread**: the price difference between two related markets or commodities. For example, the April-August live cattle spread.

2. **Speculator**: a market participant who tries to profit from buying and selling futures and option contracts by anticipating future price movements. Speculators assume market price risk and add liquidity and capital to the futures markets. They do not hold equal and opposite cash market risks.

3. **Option**: a contract that conveys the right, but not the obligation, to buy or sell a futures contract at a certain price for a specified time period. Only the seller (writer) of the option is obligated to perform.

4. **Maintenance margin**: a set minimum margin (per outstanding futures contract) that a customer must maintain in a margin account.

5. **Cash (spot) market**: a place where people buy and sell the actual (cash) commodities, that is, a grain elevator, livestock market, or the like.

6. **Adding value**: adding something that the customer wants that was not there before.

7. **Benchmarking**: comparing your product to the best competitors'.

8. **Bring to the table**: refers to what each individual in a meeting can contribute to a meeting, for example, a design or brainstorming meetings.

9. **Concurrent (or simultaneous) engineering**: integrating the design, manufacturing, and test processes.

10. **Continuous improvement**: the PDSA (Plan-Do-Study-Act) process of iteration which results in improving a product.

11. **Customer satisfaction**: meeting or exceeding a customer's expectations for a product or service.

12. **Design**: the creation of a specification from concepts.

13. **Flow charting**: creating a "map" of the steps in a process.

14. **Manufacturing**: creating a product from specifications.

15. **Metrics**: ways to measure: e.g., time, cost, customer satisfaction, quality.

16. **Process**: what is actually done to create a product.

17. **Six-sigma quality**: meaning 99.999 997% perfect; only 3.4 defects in a million.

18. **Statistical Process Control (SPC)**: used for measuring the conformance of a product to specifications.

19. **Test**: a procedure for critical evaluation; a means of determining the presence, quality, or truth of something, e.g.. Testing the product for defects.

20. **Total Quality Management (TQM)**: controlling everything about a process.

Part C　Useful Expressions

1. sales conditions　销售条件

2. special orders　特殊订货

3. conduct confirmation　作出确认

4. in duplicate　一式两份

5. in triplicate　一式三份

6. above the average quality　中等以上质量

7. below the average quality　中等以下质量

8. to execute the order　执行订单

9. plain sailing　一帆风顺

10. Fair Average Quality(F.A.Q.)　良好平均品质

11. mutual consent　双方同意

12. Sales Confirmation　销售确认书

13. conclude a deal　达成交易

14. offer is subject to…　报盘以……为准

15. make a ××% reduction　减价××%

16. market condition　市场状况

17. market fluctuation　市场波动

18. market information　市场情报

19. market price　市场价格

20. market report　市场报告

21. market risk　市场风险

22. market survey　市场调查

23. domestic market　国内市场

24. foreign market　国外市场

25. money market　货币市场

26. product market　产品市场

27. spot market　即期市场

28. stock market　股票市场

29. market glut　市场饱和

30. market structure　市场结构

31. market shortfall 市场供应不足

32. market value 市场价

33. full range of samples 全套样品

34. representative sample 有代表性样品

35. sample book 样品册

36. sample pad 样品

37. counter sample 对等样，回样

38. sample of no value 无价值的样品

39. free sample of no charge 免费样品

40. sample free of charge 免费样品

41. free sample 免费样品

42. as per sample 按照样品

43. equal to sample 和样品相同

44. sample post 样品邮寄

45. sample for reference 参考样品

46. sample invoice 样品发票

47. up to sample 与样品相符

48. inferior quality 低劣质量

49. superior quality 优等质量

50. prime quality tip-top quality 一流质量

51. quality shipped 装船品质

52. quality landed 卸岸品质

53. pattern sample 型式样品

54. duplicate sample 复样

Part D   Exercise

I. Give the Chinese equivalents for the following English terms.

1. intrinsic attribute

2. luster, modeling, structure

3. endurability

4. marketability

5. social attributes

6. disinfected

7. serviceability

8. hygiene

9. specifications

10. aquatic products

11. transnational corporation

12. life of quality assurance

II. Two columns are given for you to decide which method is best suited for a certain commodity, please match them.

(   )1. mineral ore   A. sample

(   )2. ordinary garments   B. manual

(　　)3. fish　　　　　　　　　　C. F.A.Q.

(　　)4. Haier washing machines　D. G.M.Q.

(　　)5. medical apparatus　　　E. famous brand

(　　)6. wheat　　　　　　　　F. specification

(　　)7. calligraphic works　　　G. origin

(　　)8. power plant generator　　H. drawing or diagram

III. Monomial Choice.

1. Quality latitude is used for (　　).

A. 初级产品　　　B. 工业制成品　　　C. 机械产品　　　　D. 机电产品

2. 凡货、样不能做到完全一致的商品，一般都不适宜凭（　　）买卖。

A. specification　B. size　　　　　C. standard　　　　D. sample

3. 我国出口大豆一批，合同规定大豆的水分为最高 14%、含油量为最低 18%、杂质为最高 1%，这种规定品质的方法是（　　）。

A. sale by specification　　　　　B. sale by grade

C. sale by standard　　　　　　　D. sale by instruction

4. Plain Satin Silk：

Width (inch)	Length (YDS)	Weight (m/m)	Composition
55	38/42	16.5	100% Silk

Which of the following refers to the quality of plain silk is sale? (　　).

A. Sample　　　　B. Grade　　　　C. Standard　　　　D. Specification

5. F.A.Q. is used for (　　).

A. agricultural and by-product products　　B. industrial products

C. mechanical products　　　　　　　　　D. wood and aquatic products

6. G.M.Q. is used for (　　).

A. agricultural and by-product products　　B. wood and aquatic products

C. industrial products　　　　　　　　　　D. man-made products

7. 在我国花生出口合同中规定：水分每增减 1%，则（　　）。

A. 合同价格增减 0.5%　　　　　　B. 合同价格减增 0.5%

C. 合同价格增减 1%　　　　　　　D. 合同价格减增 1%

8. "四川榨菜"中用来表明商品品质的方法是（　　）。

A. sale by brand or trade mark　　B. sale by standard

C. sale by specification　　　　　D. sale by origin

9. Description of Goods 条款就是合同的（　　）。

A. 品质条款　　B. 数量条款　　　C. 品名条款　　　D. 说明条款

10. Grey Duck Feather Soft Nap 18% allowing 1% more or less，此段文字表明了品质指标（　　）。

A. 差异的范围　　B. 变动的上下限　　C. 上下变动幅度　　　D. 误差

11. 凡货、样难以达到完全一致的，不宜采用（　　　）。

A. 凭说明买卖　　　B. 凭样品买卖　　　　C. 凭等级买卖　　　　D. 凭规格买卖

12. 在交货数量前加上"约"或"大约"字样，按惯例，UCP600 的规定这种约定可解释为交货数量不超过（　　　）的增加幅度。

A. 10%　　　　　　B. 5%　　　　　　　C. 2.5%　　　　　　　D. 1.5%

13. 在品质条款的规定上，对某些比较难掌握其品质的工业制成品或农副产品，我们多在合同中规定（　　　）。

A. 溢短装条款　　　　　　　　　　B. 增减价条款

C. 品质公差或品质机动幅度　　　　D. 商品的净重

14. 凭卖方样品成交时，应留存（　　　）以备交货时核查之用。

A. 回样　　　　　　B. 复样　　　　　　C. 参考样　　　　　　D. 对等样品

15. 对于价值较低的商品，往往采取（　　　）计算其重量。

A. 以毛作净　　　　B. 法定重量　　　　C.净重　　　　　　　D.理论重量

16. 对于大批量交易的散装货，因较难掌握商品的数量，通常在合同中规定（　　　）。

A. 品质公差条款　　　　　　　　　B. 溢短装条款

C. 立即装运条款　　　　　　　　　D. 仓至仓条款

17. 合同中未注明商品重量是按毛重还是净重计算时，则习惯上应按（　　　）计算。

A. 毛重　　　　　　B. 净重　　　　　　C. 以毛作净　　　　　D. 公量

18. 某公司与外商签订了一份出口某商品的合同，合同中规定的出口数量为 500 吨。在溢短装条款中规定，允许卖方交货的数量可增减 5%，但未对多交部分货物如何作价给予规定。卖方依合约规定多交了 20 吨，根据《公约》的规定，此 20 吨应按（　　　）作价。

A. 到岸价　　　　　B. 合同价　　　　　C. 离岸价　　　　　　D. 议定价

19. 我某进出口公司拟向马来西亚出口服装一批，在洽谈合同条款时，就服装的款式可要求买方提供（　　　）。

A. 样品　　　　　　B. 规格　　　　　　C. 商标　　　　　　　D. 产地

20. 我国现行的法定计量单位制是（　　　）。

A. 公制　　　　　　B. 国际单位制　　　C. 英制　　　　　　　D. 美制

IV. Fill in the blanks with the most appropriate terms in the box.

samples	vivid	outdated	marked	rejected material
qualify	outturn samples	official seal	regular orders	as per

1. If the quality of your products is satisfactory, we may place＿＿＿＿＿＿.

2. There is no ＿＿＿＿＿＿qualitative difference between the two.

3. The new varieties have very ＿＿＿＿＿＿designs and beautiful colors.

4. The quality is all right, but the style is a bit ＿＿＿＿＿＿.

5. No doubt you've received the ＿＿＿＿＿＿of the inferior quality goods.

6. You know we sell our tea according to our ＿＿＿＿＿＿.

7. We sell goods _____ the sales sample, not the quality of any previous supplies.

8. If you find the quality of our products unsatisfactory, we're prepared to accept return of the _____ within a week.

9. The quality of this article cannot _____ for first-class.

10. Our Certificate of Quality is made valid by means of the _____ .

Chapter Eight   International Payments for Cross-Border E-Commerce

第八章   跨境电子商务国际支付

Part A   Text

A Brief Introduction to Cross-Border E-Commerce Payments

Cross-border e-commerce payment methods can be divided into two broad categories: online payment (including electronic account payment and international credit card payment, suitable for small cross-border retail sales) and bank remittance models (suitable for large amounts of cross-border transactions). Cross-border online payment methods mainly include: credit card payment, PayPal, Cashpay, Moneybookers, Payoneer, ClickandBuy, Paysafecard, WebMoney, CashU, and etc.; offline cross-border payment methods include: Wire transfer, Western Union, MoneyGram, Hong Kong offshore company bank accounts, and etc.

跨境电子商务支付方式可以分为两大类：网上支付（包括电子账户支付和国际信用卡支付，适合小额的跨境零售）和银行汇款模式（适合大金额的跨境交易）。线上的跨境支付方式主要包括信用卡收款，PayPal，Cashpay，Moneybookers，Payoneer，ClickandBuy，Paysafecard，WebMoney，CashU 等；线下的跨境支付方式主要包括电汇（T/T）、西联汇款、速汇金汇款，香港离岸公司银行账户等。

In international trade, how and when an exporter receives payment for the goods he sends abroad are problems that concern him the most. Payment in domestic trade is a fairly simple matter. It can be made either in advance or within a reasonably short period after delivery. However, these problems are magnified many times in international trade. Much time is unavoidable lost in correspondence, dispatch and delivery.

在国际贸易中，出口商最关心的事就是怎样以及什么时候才能得到他销往国外商品的货款。国内贸易的支付比较简单，它可以是先付款后交货，也可以是在交货后的一小段合情合理的时间内付款。然而，国际贸易的支付要比国内贸易的支付复杂得多。在通信、发货、交货的过程中不可避免地要浪费很多时间。

Because of these problems, different methods of payment have been adopted in international trade. Generally, in every contract for the sale of goods abroad, the clause dealing with the payment of the purchase price consists of four elements: time, mode, place, and currency of payment. The various methods of financing exports represent the order and variations of these four elements.

由于这些原因，国际贸易采用不同的支付方式。一般来说，在每一笔出口合同中，涉及货款支付的条款包括下列 4 个方面：支付时间、支付方式、支付地点和支付货币。各种不同的出口资金融通的方法是这 4 个方面不同排列的变体。

Section One　Cross-Border E-Commerce On-line Payment Methods（跨境电子商务线上跨境支付方式）

1. Credit Card

Cross-border e-commerce website can open a port to receive overseas bank credit card payment through cooperation with international credit card organizations such as Visa and MasterCard, or directly with overseas banks.

Advantages: the most popular payment methods in both Europe and the United States, where the credit card user population is very large.

Disadvantages: inconvenient to access to, deposit needed, high fees, small amount of payment. risk of protest.

Scope: for cross-border e-commerce retail platforms and independent B2C. Currently the world's top five credit card brands are Visa, MasterCard, America Express, Jcb, Diners club, among which Visa, MasterCard, America Express are the most widely used ones.

1. 信用卡收款

跨境电子商务网站可通过与 Visa，MasterCard 等国际信用卡组织合作，或直接与海外银行合作，开通接收海外银行信用卡支付的端口。

优点：是欧美最流行的一种支付方式，信用卡的用户有着非常庞大的人群基础。

缺点：接入方式麻烦，需预存保证金，收费高昂，付款额度偏小，存在拒付风险。

适用范围：从事跨境电子商务零售的平台和独立 B2C。目前国际上五大信用卡品牌包括 Visa，MasterCard，America Express，Jcb，Diners club，其中 Visa，MasterCard，America Express 使用最为广泛。

2. PayPal

PayPal is quite similar to the domestic Alipay, and PayPal has a high international reputation and is a common payment method for customers in many countries. PayPal allows funds to be transferred between users who use e-mail to identify themselves.

Advantages: the transaction is completely conducted online. With a wide range of applications, PayPal is especially applied by North American users. In order to form a "closed-loop transaction", both parties involved must be PayPal users, so as to achieve risk control and reduce transaction risk.

Disadvantages: PayPal users consumers (buyers) benefit more than PayPal users sellers (merchants), transaction costs are mainly provided by the merchants; wire transfer fees, in addition to charge fee, each transaction also needs to pay transaction processing fees; accounts are easily to be frozen with the losses of business interests.

Scope: cross-border e-commerce retail industry, more cost-effective for small transactions.

2. PayPal

PayPal 类似于国内的支付宝，PayPal 在国际上知名度较高，是很多国家客户的常用付款方式。PayPal 允许使用电子邮件来标识身份的用户之间进行资金转移。

优点：交易完全在线上完成。适用范围广，尤其受北美用户信赖。收付双方必须都是 PayPal 用户，以此形成"闭环交易"，实现风控，降低交易风险。

缺点：PayPal 用户消费者（买家）利益较大于 PayPal 用户卖家（商户）的利益，交易费用主要由商户提供；电汇费用，每笔交易除手续费外还需要支付的交易处理费；由于商业利益的损失账户很容易被冻结。

适用范围：跨境电子商务零售行业，对于小额交易更划算。

3. Cashpay

Advantages: fast pay, usually 2 to 3 days, fast settlement; support mall shopping channel integration; no account fees nor user fees; no withdrawal of fees nor surcharges, provide more choice of payment gateway, support currency preferred by the businesses for cash withdrawal.

Disadvantages: less-known in the domestic market.

Security: a special risk control fraud system Cashshield, more secure data preservation.

Features: safe, fast, reasonable rate, PCIDSS specification, a multi-channel integrated payment gateway.

3. Cashpay

优点：偿付速度快，一般为 2~3 天，结算快；支持商城购物车通道集成；无开户费及使用费；无提现手续费及附加费，提供更多支付网关的选择，支持商家喜欢的币种提现。

缺点：在中国国内的市场知名度不高。

安全性：有专门的风险控制防欺诈系统 Cashshield，资料数据较安全。

特点：安全，快速，费率合理，PCIDSS 规范，是一种多渠道集成的支付网关。

4. Moneybookers

Advantages: safer, because Moneybookers is based on E-Mail as a payment identifier, its payer does not expose personal information such as credit cards; transfer can be done just via e-mail address; customers must activate the certification before they trade; fees can be received and paid through the network in real time.

Disadvantages: do not allow customers to have multiple accounts, that is, a customer can only register an account; Moneybookers currently does not support minors' registration, the threshold of age is 18 years old for registration; withdrawals will be charged a small fee.

4. Moneybookers

优点：比较安全，由于 Moneybookers 是以 E-Mail 为支付标识的，所以其付款人不会暴露

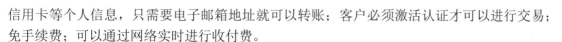

信用卡等个人信息，只需要电子邮箱地址就可以转账；客户必须激活认证才可以进行交易；免手续费；可以通过网络实时进行收付费。

缺点：不允许客户拥有多个账户，即一个客户只能注册一个账户；目前不支持未成年人注册，需年满 18 岁才可以注册；提现会收取少量费用。

5. Payoneer

Payoneer is a New York-based online payment company in the United States. Its main business is to help its partners to distribute funds worldwide. It also provides Bank of America / European Bank to receive accounts to customers worldwide, so as to receive trade payments from European and American e-commerce platforms and businesses.

Advantages: convenient, Payoneer account online registration can be done with Chinese ID card, and automatically bind the Bank of the United States and the European bank account; official, being the same as the European and American enterprises to accept the remittance of European companies, and the online foreign exchange declaration and settlement are completed through the cooperation of Payoneer and China Payment Corporation.

Scope of application: cross-border e-commerce website or seller with a single small amount of funds but a large client base.

5. Payoneer

Payoneer 是一家总部位于纽约的美国在线支付公司，主要业务是帮助其合作伙伴将资金下发到全球，同时也为全球客户提供美国银行/欧洲银行收款账户，用于接收欧美电商平台和企业的贸易款项。

优点：便捷，凭中国身份证即可完成 Payoneer 账户在线注册，并自动实现绑定美国银行账户和欧洲银行账户；正式，像欧美企业一样合规接收欧美公司的汇款，并通过 Payoneer 和中国支付公司的合作完成线上的外汇申报和结汇。

适用范围：单笔资金额度小但客户群分布广的跨境电子商务网站或卖家。

6. ClickandBuy

ClickandBuy is an independent third-party payment company that receives payments from ClickandBuy and receives payment within 3-4 business days. The minimum amount per transaction is $ 100 and the maximum daily transaction amount is $ 10,000. If the customer chooses to send money through ClickandBuy, they can withdraw money through ClickandBuy. The business reserves the right to choose a refund via ClickandBuy.

6. ClickandBuy

ClickandBuy 是独立的第三方支付公司，收到 ClickandBuy 的汇款确认后，货款可以在 3～4 个工作日内收到。每次交易金额最低$ 100，每天最高交易金额$ 10,000。如果客户选择通过 ClickandBuy 汇款，则可以通过 ClickandBuy 提款。商家保留选择通过 ClickandBuy 退款的权利。

7. Paysafecard

Paysafecard is a means of payment mainly for European online game players. Being a bank draft, its purchase process is simple and safe. In most countries, most Paysafecards can be used in news-stands, gas stations and other places. The user finishes the payment with a 16-digit account number. To open Paysafecard payment, a business license is required.

7. Paysafecard

Paysafecard 主要是欧洲游戏玩家的网游支付手段，是一种银行汇票，购买手续简单而安全。在大多数国家，Paysafecards 大多可以用在报摊、加油站等场所。用户用 16 位账户数字完成付款。要开通 Paysafecard 支付，需要有企业营业执照。

8. WebMoney

WebMoney is Russia's most mainstream electronic payment method; major banks in Russia are free to conduct recharge and withdrawals.

8. WebMoney

WebMoney 是俄罗斯最主流的电子支付方式，在俄罗斯各大银行均可自主充值取款。

9. CashU

CashU is currently used by a vast majority of Internet users in the Middle East and North Africa and is one of the most widely used electronic payment methods in the Middle East and North Africa. CashU is mainly used to pay for online games, VoIP technology, telecommunications and IT services, and foreign exchange transactions. CashU allows the customer to pay in any currency, but the trading funds in the account will always be shown in US Dollars.

9. CashU

CashU 目前主要是中东和北非的广大网民在使用，是中东和北非地区运用最广泛的电子支付方式之一。CashU 主要用于支付在线游戏、VoIP 技术、电信和 IT 服务，以及实现外汇交易。CashU 允许客户使用任何货币进行支付，但该账户将始终以美元显示交易资金。

Section Two　Cross-Border E-Commerce Off-line Payment Methods（跨境电子商务线下跨境支付方式）

1. Wire transfer

Telegraphic Transfer (T/T) is a process that the remitting bank, at the request of the remittance, sends a cable to its correspondent bank in the country concerned instruction, to make a certain amount of payment to the payee. The payee can receive payment promptly, but the charges for this type of transfer are relatively high.

Advantages: payment is received quickly; payment can be credited to the account within a few minutes; due to delivery against payment, the interests of businesses are guaranteed.

Disadvantages: delivery against payment, so the buyers are likely to have suspicion; due to the small number of users, the volume of business transactions is limited; buyers and sellers have to pay fees, two-way charges, a large amount will be changed a high fee; bank information is highly required.

Scope of application: T/T is the traditional B2B payment model, suitable for large transaction payment.

Cost: The buyer and seller bear the bank's charge locally and individually. Specific costs are calculated based on the bank's actual rates.

1．电汇（T/T）

电汇（T/T）是汇出行应汇款人的申请，电报通知另一国家的代理行指示解付一定金额给收款人的一种汇款方式。电汇方式下收款人可以迅速收到汇款，但费用较高。

优点：收款迅速，几分钟就能实现到账；先付款后发货，可以保证商家利益不受损失。

缺点：先付款后发货，买方容易产生不信任；由于用户量少，所以限制了商家的交易量；买卖双方都要支付手续费，双向收费，数额较大的手续费高；对银行信息要求非常高。

适用范围：电汇是传统的 B2B 付款模式，适合大额的交易付款。

费用：买卖双方各自承担所在地的银行费用。具体费用根据银行的实际费率进行计算。

2．Western Union

Western Union is currently the world's leading express mail remittance method, which can be remitted and withdrawn from Western Union agent locations in most countries in the world. Western Union fee is borne by the buyer.

Advantages: credited fast; fees are borne by the buyer; it is the most cost-effective for the seller, who can get the payment before the goods are shipped, leading to good security.

Disadvantages: high risk to the buyer, the buyer is hard to accept; buyers and sellers need to go to the counter under the Western Union operation, with higher charges.

Scope of application: Medium amount of payment.

2．西联汇款

西联汇款是目前世界上比较领先的特快汇款方式，可以在全球大多数国家的西联代理所在地汇出和提款。西联手续费由买家承担。

优点：到账速度快；手续费由买家承担；对于卖家来说最划算，可先提钱再发货，安全性好。

缺点：对买家来说风险极高，不易接受；买卖双方需要去西联线下柜台操作，手续费较高。

适用范围：中等额度支付。

3．MoneyGram

MoneyGram is a fast and reliable way to send money internationally. The payee can collect the money with the number provided by the sender.

Advantages: remittance faster, ten minutes to account; remittance amount is not high, the cost is relatively low, no intermediate fee, no telegraph fee; simple procedures.

Disadvantages: remitter and payee must be based on personal identity; remittances abroad are needed; if the customer holds cash remittance accounts, a fee for the change of cash is charged.

3. 速汇金汇款

速汇金汇款是一种比较快捷、可靠的国际汇款方式，收款人凭汇款人提供的编号就可以收款。

优点：汇款速度较快，十几分钟即可到账；汇款金额不高时，费用相对较低，无中间费，无电报费；手续简单。

缺点：汇款人及收款人都必须是个人的身份；必须是境外汇款；如果客户持现钞账户汇款，还需缴纳一定的现钞变汇的手续费。

4. Hong Kong, China Offshore Company Bank Accounts

Sellers receive offshore remittances from overseas buyers by opening offshore bank accounts in Hong Kong, China, and remitting their mainland accounts from their H.K. counterpart.

Advantages: no limit to receive wire transfers; different currencies are freely convertible.

Disadvantages: China Hong Kong bank account money also needs to go to mainland China account, which is not so convenient; with a certain financial risk.

Scope of application: both traditional foreign trade and cross-border e-commerce are suitable for sellers who already have a certain transaction size.

4. 中国香港离岸公司银行账户

卖家在中国香港开设离岸银行账户，以接收海外买家的汇款，再从中国香港账户汇往中国内地账户。

优点：接收电汇无额度限制；不同货币可自由兑换。

缺点：中国香港银行账户的钱还需要转到中国内地账户，较为烦琐；有一定的资金风险。

适用范围：传统外贸及跨境电子商务都适用，适合已有一定交易规模的卖家。

Section Three　Instruments of Payment in International Trade（国际贸易中的支付工具）

In international sales of commodities, the main issues concerning the settlement of payment are means of payment, time and place of payment, and mode of payment, etc. Issues in this regard should be clearly specified in the contract by the parties concerned.

在国际贸易中，货款的结算主要涉及支付工具、付款时间和地点，以及支付方式等问题，交易双方应在合同中对此做出明确的规定。

In international trade, the most frequently used means of payment include currencies and bills.

The former is used for account, settlement and payment; the latter for settlement and payment. In practice, sellers of goods, in general, almost never insist on their rights to demand cash for payment, but readily take certain bills, such as bill of exchange(draft), promissory note and cheque (check) for substitutes, among which draft is widely used.

在国际贸易中，最常使用的支付工具包括货币和票据。前者用于计价、结算和支付；后者用于结算和支付。实际上，销售货物的人，总的来说，他们几乎从不坚持要求用现金支付的权利，而是乐意用一些票据，如汇票、本票和支票来代替现金支付，其中以使用汇票为主。

Draft is an unconditionally written order drawn by the drawer for the money to be paid by the drawee (payer). Drafts are negotiable instruments and may be sold.

汇票是出票人要求受票人（付款人）无条件付款的书面命令。汇票可以议付，可以转卖。

Promissory Note is a written and signed promise to pay a stated amount of money to a particular person.

本票是向某人支付一定金额款项的书面承诺。

Cheque is a written order to a bank to pay a certain sum of money from one's bank account to another person. The payer of a check is the drawer of the check. A cheque drawn on a bank overseas cannot be readily negotiated by the exporter. If the exporter's bank was prepared to negotiate it for him then he would receive payment right away but at the cost of the discount. Failing this the exporter would have to ask his bank to collect the cheque for him and this would be both time-consuming and relatively expensive.

支票是向银行开出的，要求银行从出票人自己的银行账户上向另一人支付一定金额款项的书面命令。支票的出票人就是付款人。出口商不能凭在海外银行开立的支票立即议付货款。如果出口商的银行愿意议付，那么出口商就可以立即得到付款，但他需要支付贴现的费用。如果出口商的银行不愿议付，那么出口商只有委托其银行收款，这既费时又费钱。

Section Four　Cross-Border Payments and Process（跨境支付业务与流程）

1. Cross-Border Payments

Cross-border payment refers to the process that when Chinese consumers buy overseas products on the net with foreign merchants or foreign consumers buy Chinese products with China's dealers, due to the different currency, the adoption of certain settlement tools and payment system are both required to realize conversion of funds between two countries or regions, so as to finally complete the transaction.

1．跨境支付业务

通俗来讲，跨境支付就是中国消费者在网上购买国外商家产品或国外消费者购买中国商家产品时，由于币种不同，需要通过一定的结算工具和支付系统实现两个国家或地区之间的资金转换，最终完成交易。

2．The Classification of Cross-Border Payments

Cross-border transfer remittance way: the third remittance payment platform, commercial banks and professional company.

Overseas offline consumption way: credit card, debit card, foreign currency cash and RMB cash.

Cross-border network consumption way: third-party payment platform, e-bank online payment, credit card online payment, electronic remittance, mobile phone and fixed phone payment.

2．跨境支付的分类

跨境转账汇款途径：第三方支付平台、商业银行和专业汇款公司。

境外线下消费途径：信用卡刷卡、借记卡刷卡、外币现金和人民币现金。

跨境网络消费途径：第三方支付平台、网银线上支付、信用卡在线支付、电子汇款、移动手机支付和固定电话支付。

3．Third-Party Cross-Border Payment Process

Cross-border settlement way has two kinds: a cross-border payment remittance way and a cross-border settlement way, as shown by the payment process diagram.

As shown in Figure 8-1, the foreign exchange cross-border payment business carried out by the third-party payment license company is mainly the bank card acquiring business, which includes two modes: offshore acquiring and foreign card acquiring. Among them, the overseas acquiring business of the third-party payment license company collects the foreign exchange payment paid by the domestic individual to the overseas website through the identity of the non-financial institution. The basic process of the business is that after the domestic individual purchases the goods on the overseas website according to the displayed foreign currency quotation, the third-party pays the license company to pay the corresponding RMB amount, and then the third-party payment license company's domestic cooperative bank purchases the foreign exchange and enters the foreign exchange. After receiving the payment success information issued by the non-financial institution, the overseas merchants will send the goods to the domestic residents by post. After receiving the goods, the domestic residents will send the clearing instructions to the third-party payment license company. The third-party payment license company remits the foreign currency payment to the overseas merchant bank settlement account through the domestic cooperative bank in accordance with the settlement agreement with the overseas merchant, and completes the cross-border settlement. The foreign card acquiring business of the third-party payment license company is to collect the foreign exchange payment from the overseas individuals to the domestic non-financial institution on behalf of the domestic website through its status as a non-financial institution. The business process is that after the overseas individual purchases the goods on the domestic website, the overseas payment company that cooperates with the domestic third-party payment license company pays the license to the domestic third-party payment company to open the foreign bank account to pay the foreign exchange payment (the payment method can be Credit cards issued overseas such as Visa/MasterCard can also be T/T wire transfers). After the domestic third-party payment license company confirms receipt of foreign exchange payment, it notifies the domestic website to deliver the goods to overseas individuals. After receiving the goods, the overseas individual confirms and instructs the domestic third-party to pay the license company to transfer the payment to the domestic website. The cooperative bank of the domestic third-party payment license company handles the cross-border settlement of foreign exchange funds according to the instructions, and after the settlement of foreign exchange, transfers the RMB funds to the domestic website.

(1) Outflow of funds:

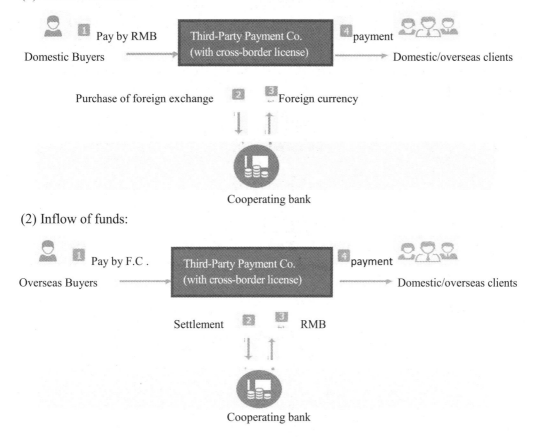

Figure 8-1   Payment Process of Domestic Consumers Shopping Overseas

3．第三方跨境支付流程

跨境电子商务的结算方式有跨境支付购汇方式和跨境收入结汇方式两种，支付流程如图 8-1 所示。

第三方支付许可公司开展的外汇跨境支付业务主要是银行卡收单业务，包括境外收购和外国卡收购两种模式。其中，第三方支付许可公司的海外收购业务通过非金融机构的身份将国内个人支付的外汇支付收入海外网站。业务的基本过程是，国内个人根据显示的外币报价在海外网站上购买商品后，第三方支付许可公司支付相应的人民币金额，然后，第三方支付许可公司的国内合作银行购买外汇并进入外汇流程。海外商家收到非金融机构发出的支付成功信息后，将货物邮寄给国内居民。收到货物后，国内居民将清算指示发送给第三方支付许可公司。第三方支付许可公司根据与境外商户的清算协议，通过境内合作银行向外国商业银行结算账户支付外币，完成跨境结算。第三方支付许可公司的外卡收购业务旨在通过其作为非金融机构的身份，代表国内网站向海外个人收取外汇，并支付给国内非金融机构。其具体业务流程是海外个人在国内网站上购买商品后，与国内第三方支付许可公司合作的境外支付公司会向国内第三方支付公司开出支付许可，通过已开立的国外银行账户进行外汇支付（支付方式可以是 Visa/MasterCard 等海外发行的信用卡，也可以是 T/T 电汇）。国内第三方支付许可证公司确认收到外汇付款后，通知国内网站将货物交付给海外个人。海外人员收到货物后，确认并指示国内第三方支付许可证公司将款项转入国内网站。国内第三方支付许可公司合作银行按照指示办理外汇资金跨境结算，结汇后，将人民币资金转入国内网站。

（1）资金出境：

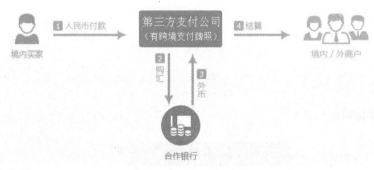

（2）资金入境：

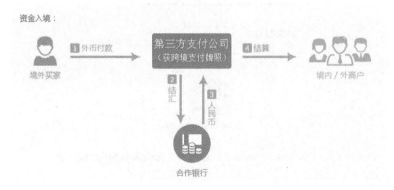

图 8-1　境内消费者在境外购物支付流程图

As shown in Figure 8-2, in the process of cross-border e-commerce, domestic consumers are accompanied by information flow in addition to commodity flow and cash flow. The details are as shown in the following eight steps.

① Log in to the overseas online shopping platform and purchase goods (the domestic consumers log in to the overseas website to determine the goods or services to be purchased, and place an order).

② Commodity information (external e-commerce sends the consumer's order, ie the merchandise message, to the third-party for payment).

③ Obtain a certification letter (a third-party payment is obtained in the domestic consumer certification information).

④ Enter the authentication information, select the RMB payment method, and confirm the payment (the domestic consumer input information and choose the payment method).

⑤ Payment information (third-party payment will send payment information to the custodian bank).

⑥ Purchase payment information (receive the purchase remittance information of the custodian bank).

⑦ Purchase payment information (foreign e-commerce receives the purchase remittance information paid by the third-party).

⑧ Sending goods (sending products and related services to domestic consumers).

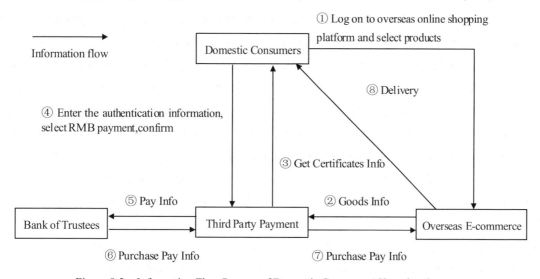

Figure 8-2　Information Flow Process of Domestic Consumers Shopping Overseas

如图 8-2 所示，在跨境电子商务中，境内消费者在境外购物过程除了商品流和现金流外，还伴随着信息流。具体如以下 8 个步骤所示。

① 登陆境外网购平台、选购商品（境内消费者登陆境外网站确定要购买的商品或服务，并下订单）。

② 商品信息（境外电商将消费者的订单，即商品消息发送给第三方支付）。

③ 获取认证信息（第三方支付获取境内消费者认证信息）。

④ 输入认证信息,选择人民币支付方式,确认支付(境内消费者输入信息并选择支付方式)。

⑤ 支付信息（第三方支付将支付信息发给托管银行）。

⑥ 购汇付款信息（接收托管银行的购汇付款信息）。

⑦ 购汇付款信息（境外电商收到第三方支付的购汇付款信息）。

⑧ 发送货物（向境内消费者发送产品和有关服务）。

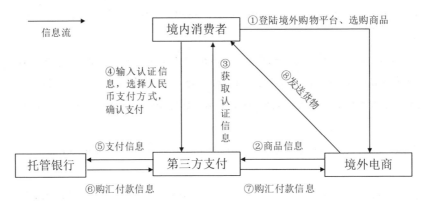

图 8-2 境内消费者在境外购物信息流流程图

As shown in Figure 8-3, cross-border e-commerce items become orders after they are placed on the overseas consumer online. Foreign consumers also choose logistics and online payment online. Domestic consumers directly purchase overseas e-commerce products, according to "Notice on Launching the Pilot Program for Cross-border E-Commerce Payment Services of Payment Agencies", the payment enterprise shall handle the payment business. Then, cross-border e-commerce items are packaged into small parcels overseas and imported through postal and express mail channels. Among them, the implementation area of logistics is mainly the postal express mail supervision center, the postal international mail processing center, and the airport express mail supervision center. Domestic customers in the overseas shopping logistics process also involves completing their own filing management process in the customs clearance management platform, that is, the filing entity pre-recording, commodity filing, and e-commerce account book filing. The logistics enterprise declares the information such as the recipient's personal identification number to complete the receipt information. E-commerce companies or agency declarations are the core documents for judging the authenticity of e-commerce transactions. The payment voucher is signed by the payment institution and attached to the electronic payment in the electronic order, which becomes one of the bases for the customs to determine the duty-paid price, but it is not used as a document for customs clearance. The Customs handles customs clearance procedures in the centralized supervision area, and conducts inspection and release. After the customs list is released, the import of e-commerce items is included in the customs statistics. The import tax is levied on the basis of the postal tax standard, and the commodity tax rate is determined when the goods are filed.

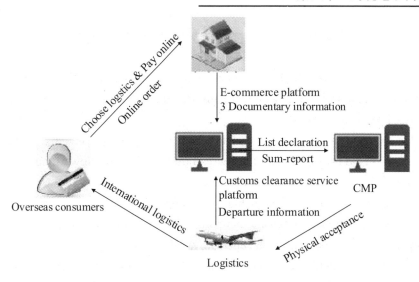

Figure 8-3　Logistics Flow Process of Domestic Consumers Shopping Overseas

如图 8-3 所示，跨境电子商务物品在境外消费者网上下单后成为订单物品，境外消费者同时在网上选择物流与在线支付，境内消费者直接网购境外电子商务产品的，按照《关于开展支付机构跨境外汇支付业务试点的通知》的要求，由支付企业代办支付业务。然后，跨境电子商务物品在境外打包成小包裹，通过邮政、快件渠道进口。其中，物流的实施区域主要是邮政快件监管中心、邮政国际邮件处理中心、机场快件监管中心。境内消费者在境外购物物流流程还涉及在通关管理平台完成其自身的备案管理流程，即申报主体预先备案、商品备案和电子商务账册备案。物流企业申报包含收件人个人身份证号等信息以完成签收信息。电子商务企业或代理申报是判断电子商务交易真实性的核心单证。支付凭证由支付机构申报并附在电子订单中的支付电子单里签章，成为海关判定完税价格的根据之一，但是不作为通关的单证。海关在集中监管区办理清关的手续，操作查验和放行。物品清单海关放行后，电子商务物品进口纳入海关统计。进口缴税统一按行邮税标准征收进口税，商品备案时确定商品税率。

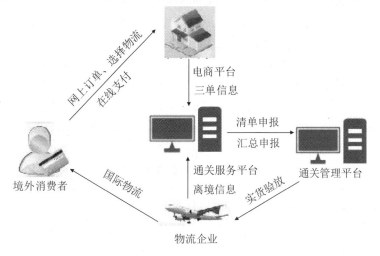

图 8-3　境内消费者在境外购物物流流程图

Part B   Terminology Practice

1. **Telegraphic Transfer (T/T)**: a process that the remitting bank, at the request of the remittance, sends a cable to its correspondent bank in the country concerned instruction, to make a certain amount of payment to the payee.

2. **PayPal**: PayPal is a payment instrument which has a high international reputation and is a common payment method for customers in many countries. PayPal allows funds to be transferred between users who use e-mail to identify themselves.

3. **Negotiable**: transferable or assignable, when applied to a draft or a check, means that the value it represents can be transferred to another party, if it is endorsed by the drawer.

4. **Accepted**: a draft is said to be accepted when the drawee signs name on it, with the word "accepted", thus undertaking to pay the value of the draft to the drawer at a specified future date.

5. **On demand**: payable as soon as a request for payment is made; a sight draft is payable on demand, and is also called a demand draft.

6. **Honored**: a bill of exchange is said to be honored when it is paid at maturity, that is, when it is due to be paid.

7. **Maturity**: the date when a draft is due to be paid.

8. **Notary Public**: a legal officer whose office is of great antiquity; his chief function is the certifying of documents.

9. **Noted**: a bill of exchange is said to be noted when a Notary Public inscribed on it a note to the effect that it has been dishonored at maturity, that is, that the drawee has failed to make payment against the draft when it fell due.

10. **Protest**: a declaration by a Notary Public that payment or acceptance of a draft has been demanded, but refused by the drawee.

11. **Endorsed**: a draft like a check, may be endorsed by the drawee; this amounts to a declaration that the amount payable against the draft be received by another party, to whom the draft is given. The endorsement is usually a signature on the back of the documents.

12. **Discount**: a percentage deduction made for cash payment, e.g. against a draft before its maturity.

13. **Cash in advance**: payment for goods in which the price is paid in full before shipment is made. This method usually is used only for small purchase or when the goods are built.

14. **Cash on delivery**: the buyer must pay for the goods when there is delivery to him.

15. **Guaranteed payment**: a room set aside by the hotel, at the request of the customer, in advance of the guest's arrival. Payment for room is guaranteed and will be paid unless an appropriate cancellation is made. The company or organization should receive a cancellation code or the name of the person accepting the cancellation from the hotel.

16. **Financing**: loan from banking services contractor for money to purchase equipment or other high priced items.

17. **Exchange rate**: the price at which US Currency can be bought with another currency or gold.

18. **Offshore bank**: a bank located in a jurisdiction different from that where its depositors reside. Countries that have a history and reputation as a haven for offshore banks can be referred to as offshore financial centres.

Part C   Useful Expressions

1. in advance 提前
2. consists of 包括
3. through cooperation with 通过与······的合作
4. access to 获得······
5. be quite similar to 与······相似
6. have a high international reputation 国际上知名度高
7. a wide range of 各式各样
8. risk control 风控
9. cost-effective 划算
10. independent third-party 独立的第三方

Part D   Exercise

I. Answer the following questions according to the information you have got.

1. What categories can cross-border e-commerce payment methods be divided into ?
2. What payment instrument does cross-border online payment method mainly include?
3. What payment instrument does cross-border offline payment method mainly include?
4. What is PayPal and how does it function?
5. What is Payoneer and how does it function?
6. What is Paysafecard?
7. What is T/T and how does it run?
8. What is Western Union?
9. What is MoneyGram?
10. What is an "offshore company"?

II. Write a word that fits naturally in each blank space.

The most generally used _____ of payment in the _____ trade is the _____ of credit. It is _____ for individual transactions or _____ a series, makes _____ with unknown buyers easy and _____ protection to both seller and buyer. The process of establishing an L/C _____ with the buyer. He instructs his bank to _____ an L/C for the _____ of the purchase _____ in favor of the seller. The _____ contain full details of the _____ as agreed upon between the buyer and the seller. The buyer's bank _____ the L/C to its _____ in the seller's country. _____ receiving the L/C, the _____ advises the seller of the arrival the _____. In foreign trade it is _____ for the correspondent to _____ the credit. This means that the correspondent _____ to pay the seller the money _____ to him, provided the conditions set _____ in the

L/C have been complied ____. The seller can now execute the buyer's order, ____ that when he has done so, the ____ will be paid at once by the correspondent. The buyer is equally ____, because the correspondent will pay on his ____ only if the conditions of the transaction are fully ____ by the seller.

III. Translate the following terms and phrases into Chinese.

1. Credit card

2. retail industry

3. small transactions

4. more cost-effective

5. fast settlement

6. maximum daily transaction amount

7. Wire transfer

8. two-way charges

9. actual rates

10. Western Union

IV. Case study for cross-border e-commerce.

Case Description:

55 Overseas Online Shopping Network is aimed at the consumer to fulfill its rebates on offshore online shopping website, and their major rebate merchants are B2C, C2C websites in the United States, Britain, Germany, such as Amazon, eBay, etc.; the profit ratio is in the range of 2% to 10% or so, the product scope is with goods of mother & child, beauty makeup, clothing, food and other comprehensive category.

Questions:

What model does 55 Overseas Online Shopping Network belong to? What are its characteristics?

案情介绍：

55 海淘网是针对消费者进行海外网购的返利网站，其返利商家主要是美国、英国、德国等 B2C、C2C 网站，如亚马逊、eBay 等，返利比例在 2%～10%不等，商品覆盖母婴、美妆、服饰、食品等综合品类。

问题：

55 海淘网属于哪种模式？有何特色？

V. Describe one or two cases about the latest feature of cross-border e-commerce payment, in terms of means, procedures or styles.

VI. Please determine whether the following statements are TRUE or FALSE. Then put T for TRUE or F for FALSE in the bracket at the end of each statement.

1. In international trade, it is always necessary for the seller to urge the buyer to open the covering L/C in good time. (   )

2. When the buyer fails to issue the covering L/C within the specified time of the contract, the

seller holds the right of declaring the contract avoid. (　　)

3. When the contract requires payments to be effected in US dollar, the relevant L/C may choose to effect payment in RMB. (　　)

4. If the L/C prohibits partial shipments and the goods are shipped in full quantity with the price not reduced, a short drawing of 5 percent in the amount is permissible.(　　)

5. Quantity, the seller may still have the right of delivering 5 percent more or less.(　　)

6. According to the UCP500, a freely negotiable credit must stipulate a place for presentation of documents for negotiation. (　　)

7. According to Article 20 of the UPC600, when the shipment date and the expiry date of L/C are August 30 and September 15 respectively, the beneficiary may present the documents between September 16 and 20 because these dates have not exceeded a period of 21 days.(　　)

8. When the goods are posted, the latest date of shipment refers to the date of Post Receipt. (　　)

9. If the Issuing Bank appoints the Bank of China as its Advising Bank of L/C, then the Issuing Bank may ask the Bank of Asia to advise amendments to the L/C.(　　)

10. The Beneficiary of a L/C may indicate his acceptance or rejection of the amendments till when he presents the relevant documents. (　　)

11. In our country goods for export must go through customs clearance. (　　)

12. When exporting goods on CFR, CPT or FOB terms, the seller must pay the insurance premium. (　　)

13. According to UCP600, if documents are in correspondence with L/C's stipulations, discrepancies between the documents themselves are allowed. (　　)

14. Banks will refuse to pay if the documents which are not required by the L/C are presented to them. (　　)

15. When documents are presented to the Opening Bank, they shall be examined carefully within one month. (　　)

16. As a L/C beneficiary, the buyer must act on any suggestions written in the L/C even if they are not documents. (　　)

17. If a L/C stipulates some conditions but does not require the related documents, the banks may disregard them as not stated. (　　)

18. According to the UCP500, Commercial Invoice must be issued by the beneficiary named in the L/C. (　　)

19. The beneficiary of a L/C may choose to present one copy of the Insurance Policy if it has more than one original copy. (　　)

20. A Certificate of Origin can be used only to prove the time when the export commodities were produced. (　　)

VII. Translate the following sentences into English.

1. 跨境电子商务网站可通过与 Visa，MasterCard 等国际信用卡组织合作，或直接与海外银行合作，开通接收海外银行信用卡支付的端口。

2. PayPal 类似于国内的支付宝，PayPal 在国际上知名度较高，是很多国家客户的常用付款方式。PayPal 允许使用电子邮件来标识身份的用户之间进行资金转移。

3. Payoneer 是一家总部位于纽约的美国在线支付公司，主要业务是帮助其合作伙伴将资金下发到全球，其同时也为全球客户提供美国银行/欧洲银行收款账户，用于接收欧美电商平台和企业的贸易款项。

4. ClickandBuy 是独立的第三方支付公司，收到 ClickandBuy 的汇款确认后，货款可以在 3～4 个工作日内收到。每次交易金额最低 $ 100，每天最高交易金额 $ 10 000。

5. 西联汇款是目前世界上比较领先的特快汇款方式，可以在全球大多数国家的西联代理所在地汇款和提款。西联手续费由买家承担。

6. 速汇金汇款是一种比较快捷可靠的国际汇款方式，收款人凭汇款人提供的编号就可以收款。

7. 在国际贸易中，货款的结算主要涉及支付工具、付款时间和地点，以及支付方式等问题，交易双方应在合同中对此做出明确的规定。

8. 汇票是出票人要求受票人（付款人）无条件付款的书面命令。汇票可以议付，可以转卖。

VIII. Multiple Choices.

1. If an account is set up in AliExpress with a U.S. dollar account, which of the following payment methods is used by the buyer to pay for the payment to the U.S. dollar account? (   ).

A. Moneybookers   B. PayPal

C. T/T   D. Credit Card

2. Which of the following types can be selected for AliExpress product shipping settings? (   ).

A. Standard Shipping   B. Free Shipping

C. Custom shipping   D. No delivery

3. In Taobao, Taobao members can enjoy the following rights after passing Alipay certification (   ).

A. selling goods for free   B. selling shop for free

C. owns a personal website URL   D. free window recommendation

4. Which of the followings belongs to the transaction states of Alipay deals In Taobao? (   ).

A. Waiting for buyer payment   B. Buyer paid

C. Waiting for the seller to ship   D. The seller has shipped

E. The transaction was successful

5. In Taobao Mall, the packaging elements of baby selling points are (   ).

A. planning   B. design   C. material   D. process

6. In the Taobao Mall baby description, we can choose to associate sales items with (   ).

A. shop unsold items

B. store hot items

C. the unit price of goods is close to a single product

D. package matching single product

7. What is the maximum number of company images can the company website put on the international station? (　　).

A. One　　　　　B. Two　　　　　C. Three　　　　　D. Four

8. In AliExpress, the percentage rate of commissions charged for registered regular member transactions is (　　).

A. 3%　　　　　B. 4%　　　　　C. 5%　　　　　D. 6%

9. If the account in AliExpress only has a renminbi account, which of the following payment methods can be used by the buyer when paying the purchase price?(　　).

A. Moneybookers　　　B.TT　　　C. Debit cards　　　D. Credit cards

10. Under normal circumstances, which of the following documents is correct for the documents requested by the L/C? (　　)

A. The seller sent directly to the buyer.

B. The seller sends it to the issuing bank and the issuing bank gives it to the buyer.

C. The seller handed over to the negotiating bank and the negotiating bank to the buyer.

D. The seller handed over to the negotiating bank, the negotiating bank sent it to the issuing bank, and then the issuing bank to the buyer.

11. When using Western Union to receive remittances from foreign customers, the required information is (　　).

A. company name　　　　　　　B. contact name

C. company telephone　　　　　D. company Tax ID

12.A complete quotation should include (　　).

A. unit price, currency, amount, unit of quantity, trade terms

B. payment method, delivery date

C. arbitration, litigation clause

D. quote validity period

13. U.S. customer Joymeal Inc. signed a contract with our company. The product sold was plastic tableware with a quantity of 2 000 units. The transaction price was USD 1.50/set, CIF New York, and the payment method was 100% L/C at sight. In the entire process, the department that will surely deal with (　　).

A.bureau of foreign trade and economic cooperation

B. bank

C. freight forwarding

D. entry and exit inspection and quarantine bureau

Chapter Nine　Cross-Border E-Commerce International Logistics

第九章　跨境电子商务国际物流

Part A　Text

A Brief Introduction to International Logistics

Nowadays, more and more cross-border e-commerce foreign trade sellers are mushrooming. Whenever the cross-border businesses begin to have orders, how to choose express logistics to send the goods abroad becomes one of the important considerations. Cross-border e-commerce International logistics is a key link in cross-border e-commerce.

现在跨境电子商务外贸卖家越来越多，每当有跨境订单时，其中一个重要考虑因素就是怎么选择快递物流把货发到国外去。跨境电子商务国际物流是跨境电子商务的一个关键环节。

In general, international packages and other channels can be used for cross-border e-commerce sellers to ship the goods through the platform. However, cross-border e-commerce big sellers or cross-border e-commerce independent platform sellers now need to optimize their logistics costs and need to consider the customer experience. They need to integrate cross-border e-commerce logistics resources and explore new cross-border e-commerce logistics formats.

一般来讲，跨境电子商务可以通过国际包裹和其他渠道将货物通过平台发货。但是现在跨境电子商务大卖家或者跨境电子商务独立平台的卖家需要优化物流成本，需要考虑客户体验，需要整合跨境电子商务物流资源并探索新的跨境电子商务物流形式。

Therefore, this chapter introduces the main modes and processes of cross-border e-commerce international logistics.

因此，本章介绍跨境电子商务国际物流的主要模式和流程。

Section One　The Main Modes and Features of Cross-Border International Logistics（跨境国际物流的主要模式及其特征）

1. International Express Mode

There are currently four major commercial express delivery giants conducting international express delivery business, namely DHL, TNT, FEDEX and UPS. These international cross-border express merchants bring excellent cross-border logistics experience to overseas users of online shopping products through their own global cross-border network, utilizing powerful IT systems and cross-border localization services all over the world. Some packages sent to the United States arrive as quickly as in 48 hours. Of course, good service comes with high prices. In general, domestic merchants will only use cross-border international commercial couriers to deliver their products only if the client's timeliness requirements are very high. Table 9-1 is the comparison of the four giants.

Table 9-1　Comparison of the Four Major Commercial Courier Companies

Commercial express giant	FEDEX (U.S.)	UPS(U.S.)	DHL(Germany)	TNT(Holland)
Characteristics	More than 21kg items are sent to Asian countries faster and more cost-effective. But the overall price is high	6-21kg items have a price advantage in the United States and the United Kingdom, especially in the United States	The items below 5.5kg have a price advantage of being sent to North America and the United Kingdom, and the price of 21kg or more has an independent large price	It generally takes within 3 working days to send to Europe, and customs clearance is faster in Western European countries

1. 国际快递模式

目前有四大商业快递巨头做国际快递，即 FEDEX、UPS、DHL 和 TNT。这些国际跨境快递商通过自建的全球跨境网络，利用强大的 IT 系统和遍布世界各地的跨境本地化服务，为网购各国产品的海外用户带来极好的跨境物流体验。有些寄送到美国的包裹，最快可在 48 小时内到达。当然，优质的服务往往伴随着昂贵的价格。一般国内的商户只有在客户时效性要求很强的情况下，才会使用跨境国际商业快递来派送商品。表 9-1 是四大商业快递巨头的比较。

表 9-1　四大商业快递巨头对比

商业快递巨头	FEDEX (U.S.)	UPS(U.S.)	DHL(Germany)	TNT(Holland)
特　　点	21kg 以上物件发送到亚洲国家速度较快，性价比较高，但总体而言价格偏高	6～21kg 物件发到美国和英国具有价格优势，特别是寄往美国本土速度快	5.5kg 以下物件发往北美和英国的价格有优势，21kg 以上物件有独立的大货价格	发送欧洲一般3个工作日内可到，在西欧国家通关速度较快

2. Domestic Express Mode

Domestic express delivery mainly includes EMS, SF and Sengtong, Yuantong, Zhongtong, Huitong and Yunda. In terms of cross-border logistics, Sengtong & Yuantong have been deployed earlier, but they have also only recently made efforts to expand. For example, Sengtong was only available online in March 2014 and Yuantong opened only with the CJ Korea Express in April 2014 Cooperation, while Zhongtong, Huitong and Yunda are just to start cross-border logistics business. SF's international business is going to be more mature. At present, express delivery services to the United States, Australia, South Korea, Japan, Singapore, Malaysia, Thailand, Vietnam and other countries have been established. Express shipments to Asian countries are usually delivered within 2-3 days. In the domestic express delivery, EMS's international business is the most perfect. Relying

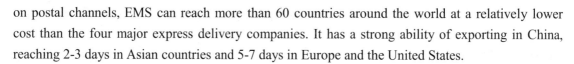

on postal channels, EMS can reach more than 60 countries around the world at a relatively lower cost than the four major express delivery companies. It has a strong ability of exporting in China, reaching 2-3 days in Asian countries and 5-7 days in Europe and the United States.

2. 国内快递模式

国内快递主要包括 EMS、顺丰和"四通一达"（申通、圆通、中通、汇通、韵达）。在跨境物流方面，"四通一达"中的申通、圆通布局较早，但也是近期才发力拓展，比如申通2014 年 3 月才上线，圆通也是 2014 年 4 月才与 CJ 大韩通运展开合作，而中通、汇通、韵达则是刚刚启动跨境物流业务。顺丰的国际化业务则要成熟些，目前已经开通到美国、澳大利亚、韩国、日本、新加坡、马来西亚、泰国、越南等国家的快递服务，发往亚洲国家的快件一般 2～3 天可以送达。在国内快递中，EMS 的国际化业务是最完善的。依托邮政渠道，EMS可以直达全球 60 多个国家，费用相对四大快递巨头要低，中国境内的出关能力很强，到达亚洲国家 2～3 天，到欧美国家则需 5～7 天。

3. Postal Parcel Mode

The postal network basically covers the whole world, so it is more extensive than any other logistics channels. This mainly benefits from both the Universal Postal Union and the Ka-Ha postal organization (KPG). The Universal Postal Union is a specialized agency on international postal affairs set up by the United Nations. Its function is to improve international postal services through a number of conventions and laws so as to achieve the purpose of international cooperation in the development of postal services. Due to the large membership and the uneven development of the postal system between Member States, the Universal Postal Union makes it difficult to promote deep cooperation among member countries. So in 2002, the Kahala Post Office was established, and later Spain and the United Kingdom joined the office. The Kahala Organization requires delivery deadlines of 98% to all member countries. If the goods can not be delivered to the recipient on the specified date, the operator responsible for the delivery will pay the customer 100% of the price of the goods. These stringent requirements all promote deepening cooperation among member countries and strive to improve service levels. For example, postal parcels sent from China to the United States can arrive within 15 days. According to incomplete statistics, 70% of Chinese cross-border e-commerce exporters' parcels are delivered through the postal system, of which China Post occupies about 50%. Other postal services used by Chinese sellers include Hongkong Post, Singapore Post and others.

3. 邮政包裹模式

邮政网络基本覆盖全球，所以它比其他的任何物流渠道都要广。这主要同时也得益于万国邮政联盟和卡哈拉邮政组织（KPG）。万国邮政联盟是联合国下设的一个关于国际邮政事务的专门机构，其功能是通过一些公约法规来改善国际邮政业务，从而达到发展邮政方面的国际合作的目的。万国邮政联盟由于会员众多，而且会员国之间的邮政系统发展很不平衡，因此很难促成会员国之间的深度邮政合作。于是在 2002 年，成立了卡哈拉邮政组织，后来西班牙和英国也加入了该组织。卡哈拉邮政组织要求所有成员国的投递时限要达到 98%的质量标准。如果货物没能在指定日期投递给收件人，那么负责投递的运营商要按货物价格的 100%赔付客户。这些严格的要求都促使成员国之间深化合作，努力提升服务水平。例如，从中国发往美国的邮政包裹，一般 15 天以内可以到达。据不完全统计，中国出口跨境电子商务 70%的包裹都是通过邮政系统投递，其中中国邮政占据 50%左右。中国卖家使用的其他邮政服务包括香港邮政、新加坡邮政等。

4．Overseas Warehouse Service Mode

Overseas Warehouse Service Model refers to the one-stop control and management service for the seller in the storage, sorting, packing and delivery of goods at the sales destination. General concept of overseas warehousing mainly includes three parts, namely the first journey of transport, storage management and local distribution. As shown in Table 9-2.

Table 9-2　Comparison of Three Parts of Overseas Storage Modes

Head transport	Warehouse management	Local delivery
Domestic merchants transport cross-border goods to overseas warehouses by sea, air, land or intermodal	Domestic merchants use the cross-border logistics information system to remotely operate cross-border overseas warehousing goods and manage inventory in real time across borders	Overseas warehousing centers distribute cross-border goods to cross-border customers via local postal or express delivery based on cross-border order information

4．海外仓储模式

海外仓储服务模式指为卖家在销售目的地进行货物仓储、分拣、包装和派送的一站式控制与管理服务。广义概念上的海外仓储主要包括头程运输、仓储管理和本地配送三个部分，如表 9-2 所示。

表 9-2　海外仓储模式三部分比较

头 程 运 输	仓 储 管 理	本 地 配 送
国内商家通过海运、空运、陆运或者联运将跨境商品运送至海外仓库	国内商家通过跨境物流信息系统，远程操作跨境海外仓储货物，实时跨境管理库存	海外仓储中心根据跨境订单信息，通过当地邮政或快递将跨境商品配送给跨境客户

5．Dedicated-line logistics mode

Cross-border dedicated-line logistics is generally carried out by means of air parcel delivery to foreign countries, together with the cooperation of the destination country's delivery. The advantage of dedicated-line logistics lies in its ability to focus on large quantities of goods to a particular country or region, reducing costs through economies of scale. Therefore, its price is generally lower than that of commercial courier. In terms of timeliness, it is much faster than the postal parcel logistics, but slightly slower than commercial delivery. The most common dedicated-line logistics products in the market include US-line, Australia-line, Russia-line and Europe-line. Many logistics companies have also launched special routes in South America, South Africa and the Middle East.

5. 专线物流模式

跨境专线物流一般是通过航空包舱方式运输到国外，再通过合作公司进行目的国的派送。专线物流的优势在于其能够集中大批量到某一特定国家或地区的货物，通过规模效应降低成本。因此，其价格一般比商业快递低。在时效上，比邮政包裹快得多，但比商业配送要慢得多。市面上最普遍的专线物流产品包括美国专线、澳洲专线、俄罗斯专线和欧洲专线等，也有不少物流公司推出了南美专线、南非专线和中东专线等。

Section Two Methods to Choose Bross-Border International Logistics（跨境国际物流的选择方法）

For cross-border e-commerce sellers, how to choose cross-border international logistics is a key issue that concerns both of the cost and efficiency of the company. First of all, cross-border e-commerce sellers should choose suitable cross-border logistics models based on the characteristics of their cross-border products sold (size, safety, customs clearance, etc.), for example, large cross-border products , such as furniture, are not suitable for postal parcel channels, but rather, more suitable for overseas warehouse mode.

对于跨境电子商务的卖家来说，如何选择跨境国际物流是一个涉及公司成本和效率的关键问题。首先，跨境电子商务的卖家应该根据所售跨境产品的特点（尺寸、安全性、通关便利性等）来选择合适的跨境物流模式，比如，大件跨境产品（如家具）就不适合走邮政包裹渠道，而更适合海外仓模式。

Second, as for the time, peak season and off season should be considered. Flexible use of different logistics methods shall vary according to the peak season and off season, such as in the off season, the use of postal parcels can reduce logistics costs, whilst during peak season or large-scale promotional activities, using Hongkong Post or Singapore Post and even Belgium Post can guarantee the timeliness.

其次，在时间方面要考虑淡旺季，要根据淡旺季灵活使用不同的物流方式，例如在淡季时邮包的使用可以降低物流成本，在旺季或者大型促销活动时采用香港邮政或者新加坡邮政甚至比利时邮政可以保证时效。

Finally, the pre-sale cross-border e-commerce sellers must clearly state the characteristics of different cross-border logistics modes to cross-border buyers and provide cross-border buyers with diversified cross-border logistics options so that they can choose their suitable logistics mode.

最后，售前跨境电子商务卖家要明确向跨境买家列明不同跨境物流方式的特点，为跨境买家提供多样化的跨境物流选择，让跨境买家根据实际需求来选择跨境物流方式。

As shown in Figure 9-1, cross-border e-commerce mainly involves four main entities: producer/manufacturer (domestic seller), cross-border e-commerce platform (direct mail export), third-party service providers, rendering services in logistics, payment and customs clearance, consumers/enterprises (foreign buyers). The biggest difference between cross-border e-commerce and general e-commerce lies in the big feature of "cross-border". The goods that are sold need to enter and leave the country through customs, and the way in which goods enter and leave determines the way of cross-border logistics.

如图 9-1 所示，跨境电子商务主要涉及四个主体：生产商/制造商（国内卖家），跨境电子商务平台（直邮出口），包括物流、支付、通关服务在内的第三方服务提供商，消费者/企业（国外买家）。跨境电子商务与一般电子商务的最大区别就在于"跨境"这一大特征，成交商品需要通过海关进出境，货品进出境的方式决定了跨境物流的运作方式。

Commodities traded by cross-border e-commerce mainly enter and exit through three modes: customs clearance of goods, customs clearance of express mail and post mail. Cross-border retail (B2C and C2C) are mostly cleared by post mail and express mail, especially for small platforms and individual consumers who are not large-scale. As shown in Figure 9-1, the free trade zone or bonded zone logistics model is also a new type of logistics distribution model under cross-border e-commerce. It transports goods to the free trade zone or bonded warehouse, and then cross-border e-commercial enterprise is responsible for the sales of goods. At the same time, the free trade zone or the bonded warehouse is responsible for the sorting, quarantine and packaging of goods, and finally realizes the centralized logistics distribution mode of goods through the free trade zone or the bonded zone. The biggest advantage of this model is that it can make full use of the advantages of the free trade zone and the bonded zone to provide guarantee for the fast operation of cross-border e-commerce international logistics.

跨境电子商务成交的商品主要通过三种方式进出境：货物方式通关、快件方式通关和邮件方式。跨境零售（B2C 和 C2C）多数通过邮件方式和快件方式通关，特别是未成规模的小型平台和个人消费者基本都采用这种方式。如图 9-1 所示，自贸区或保税区物流模式也是跨境电子商务之下的一种新型物流配送的模式，它是通过将货物运输至自贸区或保税区仓库，再由跨境电子商务企业负责商品销售，同时由自贸区或保税区仓库负责货物分拣、检疫和包装等环节，最后通过自贸区或保税区实现商品集中物流配送的模式。这种模式的最大优势就是可以在最大程度上利用自贸区及保税区自身优势，为跨境电子商务国际物流的快速运行提供保障。

Customs is an important cross-border gateway in the shipping process. Foreign trade e-commerce (B2B) goes mainly through customs clearance of goods, that is, import and export enterprises and foreign wholesalers and retailers conduct product display and trading online, while import and export goods offline as to general trade. In fact, currently , domestic large-scale e-commerce platform goods transfer, to a certain extent, is still carried out by means of customs clearance, so as the overseas warehouses .

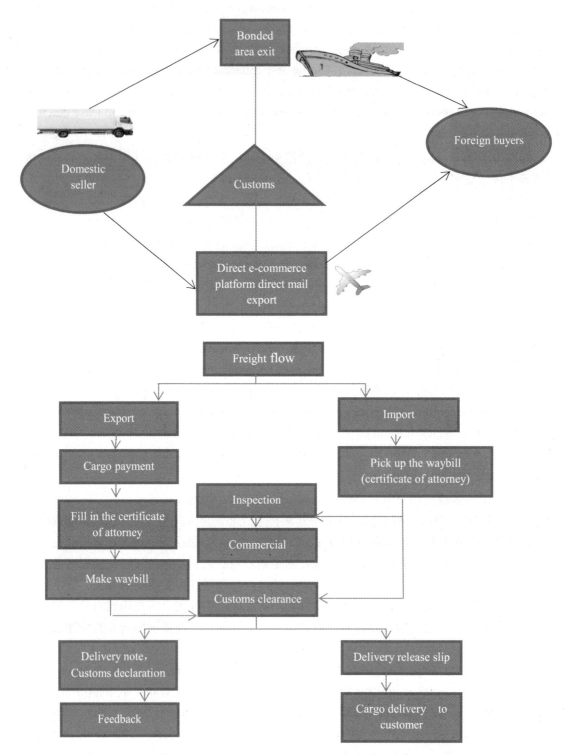

Figure 9-1   Cross-Border E-Commerce International Logistics Process Diagram

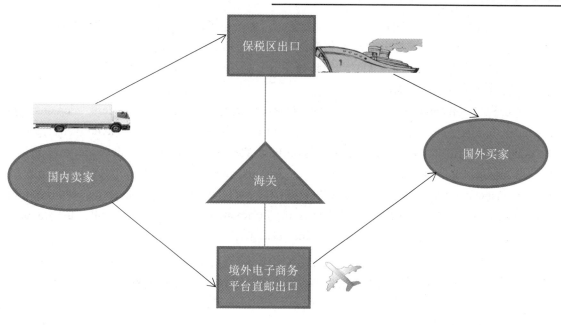

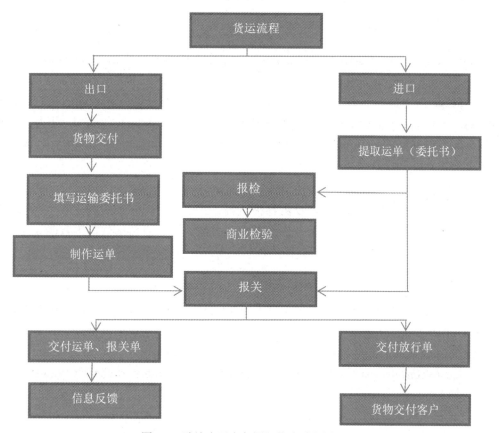

图 9-1 跨境电子商务国际物流过程图

在货运流程中，海关是跨境的一道重要关口。外贸电子商务（B2B）主要通过货物方式通关，即进出口企业与外国批发商和零售商通过互联网在线上进行产品展示和交易，线下按一般贸易完成货物进出口。国内大型电子商务平台目前在一定程度上仍旧通过货物方式通关，海外仓也通常采用货物方式通关。

Figure 9-1 referring to cross-border e-commerce international logistics process demonstrates how cross-border e-commerce goods are transported from the export side into the delivery phase of the goods. First, fill in the transport commission book for inspection, and at the same time make a waybill, conduct commercial inspection at the customs; importers fill in the pick-up waybill for customs inspection. After the customs declaration, the exporter delivers the shipping order with the customs declaration and simultaneously gives the information feedback. Eventually, the importer delivers the release and delivers the goods to the customer.

图 9-1 所示的跨境电子商务国际物流过程图中，跨境电子商务货物从出口方进入货物交付阶段，先填写运输委托书进行报检，同时制作运单，在海关进行商业检验；进口方则填写提取运单进行海关报检。报关后，出口方交付运单和报关单并同时进行信息反馈，进口方交付放行，把货物交付客户。

Section Three　Methods of the International Logistics Delivery（国际物流装运方式）

As to the methods of delivery in international practice, there are many methods to deliver the goods purchased, such as ocean transport, railway transport, air transport, river and lake transport, postal transport, road transport, pipelines transport, land bridge transport and international multimodal transport and so on. The buyer and seller can decide which method will be the best for goods to be transported according for goods characteristics, quantity, transit journey, value, time, the natural conditions and so on.

国际货物运输有多种方式：海洋运输、铁路运输、航空运输、江河运输、邮包运输、公路运输、管道运输、大陆桥运输以及由各种运输方式组合的国际多式联运等。买卖双方应根据商品特点、数量多少、路程远近、价值大小、时间长短、自然条件等因素商定应采用的运输方式。

1. Ocean Transport

Ocean transport is the most widely used form of transportations in international trade as well as the most efficient form in terms of energy. It still has the attraction of being a cheap mode of transport for delivering large quantities of goods over long distance. Before a shipment is made, the exporter has to consider many different factors influencing his transport considerations such as cost, safety, speed and convenience.

So far as foreign trade is concerned, goods transport is mostly (over 80% of world trade in volume terms) done by ocean vessel. There are several features for ocean transportation.

- Large transport volume.
- Great capability of transport.
- Low freight.
- Sound adaptability to various goods.
- Low speed.
- High risky.

Because of the prominent advantages over large capability of transport and low freight, the ocean transport still plays a very important role in international transportation even with its low speed and high risks. Nowadays more than 2/3 of transports are done by ocean transportation. There are two kinds of ocean vessels: chartering and liner.

1. 海洋运输

海洋运输是国际贸易运输中采用最广泛的一种形式，从能源角度来讲也是最有效的形式。对于长途运送大批量货物，它还具有作为一种廉价运输方式的吸引力。在安排货物运输之前，出口商必须考虑各种不同的影响运输条件的因素，例如，费用、安全性、速度和便利条件。

就货物运输来说，大多数的国际贸易运输（80%以上）都是由远洋运输船舶来完成的，海洋运输有以下特点。

- 运量大。
- 通过能力大。
- 运费低。
- 对货物的适应性强。
- 航速低。
- 风险较大。

由于海运运量大和费用低的突出优点，尽管它存在航速低、风险大的不足，但仍在国际贸易货运中占有十分重要的地位，在国际贸易总运量中有 2/3 以上利用海运。运输船可分为租船运输和班轮运输。

(1) Shipping by Chartering.Shipping by chartering is also called tramp. Shipping by chartering is a freight-carrying vessel which has no regular route or fixed schedule of sailing, or definite freight, or specific port. It is first in one trade and then in another, always seeking those ports where there is a demand at the moment for shipping space. So it is usually used to transport bulk cargo with low value, such as rice, minerals, oil and timber, etc. The shipper charters the ship from the ship-owner and uses it to carry the goods. The owner of the cargoes should sign a charter party with the shipper owner. The freight is paid according to the agreement between the two parties.

Shipping by chartering falls into three kinds: voyage charter, time charter and demise charter.

（1）租船运输。租船运输又称不定期货船。租船运输没有固定的船期表，没有固定的航线，不定运价和不定港口。哪里有货就向哪里开航，哪里装船最好就去哪里接货。因此，通常用来运输货值较低的大宗货物，如粮食、矿石、石油、木材等。发货人从船东处租货船装运货物，货主与船主签订租船合同，按双方商定的运价收取运费。

国际上使用的租船方式主要有 3 种：定程租船、定期租船和光船租船。

① Voyage Charter. The voyage charter is one for the carriage of goods from one specified port to another, or for a round trip. It includes single voyage charter, return voyage charter, successive voyage charter and contract of affreightment, COA or quantity contract/volume contract. According to the route stipulated in the charter party, the ship-owner is responsible for delivering the goods to the port of destination and for managing the ship as well as bearing all expenses.

Under a voyage charter, payment by the charterer is usually based on an agreed rate per ton for a "full and complete cargo". Should he fail to provide sufficient cargo to fill the ship he is liable for what is termed dead freight, a prorata payment for the space not used. A voyage charter also stipulates the number of days known as lay days, for loading and unloading. Should these be accessed, the charter is liable for a demurrage charge for each day in excess, and conversely is entitled to dispatch money for each day not taken up. The liability of the shipowner is to provide a ship that is seaworthy and to avoid unjustifiable deviation en route.

① 定程租船。定程租船又称程租船或航次租船，是租船人按照航程租赁全部舱位，并由船舶所有人负责将货物运至指定目的港的运输方式。定程租船就其租赁方式的不同可分为单程租船（又称单航次租船）、来回航次租船、连续航次租船、包运合同/运量合同。根据租船合同规定的路线，船东负责将货物交到目的港，并负责船只管理，以及支付所有费用。

在定程租船情况下，租船人常常按议定的装满货物的吨计费率支付费用。如果不能使船只载满，空舱费用由租船人按载重吨支付。定程租船还规定了装卸货的受载日期。如果受载日期超过规定，租船人需支付每天的滞期费。反之，船方支付在受载日期内提前完成装卸的速遣费（按天计）。船方的责任是保证船舶的适航性，并避免航途中不必要的绕航。

② Time Charter. The time charter, also called transport vessel or vehicle charter is a kind of transport based on a fixed period instead of on a certain number of voyages or trips. The charterer charters the ship for a period of time during which the ship is deployed and managed by the charterer. What concerns the charterer most is the period, not the voyage. The chartering may be for a period of one year or of several years.

During the period of chartering, the ship is managed, deployed and used by the charterer. A series of work, such as loading, unloading, stowing and trimming and the so-caused fuel expenses, port expenses, loading and unloading expenses, etc., should be borne by the charterer. The ship-owner should bear the wages and board expenses of the crew, and be responsible for seaworthiness during the period of chartering and the so-caused expenses and the vessel insurance premium.

② 定期租船。定期租船又称期限租船，是以期限为基础的租船方式，而不是以某一航线或航程为基础。即由船舶所有人将船舶出租给租船人使用一定期限，在此期限内由租船人自行调度和经营管理。租用时间可以是一年或数年。

在租船期间，货船的经营、管理和使用权都归承租人。同时，由于装卸货物、平仓理仓等引起的燃油费、港口费、装卸费等也都由承租人负担。船东要负责支付船员的工资，并保证在租用期间货船适合海洋运输及相关费用和货船的保险费。

③ Demise Charter. Demise charter, is also called bare-boat charter, the charterer takes a lease of the entire ship for an agreed time. So demise charter belongs to time charter, but there are some differences: as to time charter, during the period of chartering, the ship-owner provides the charterer with a crew, while as to bare-boat charter, the ship-owner only provides the charterer with a bare-boat, the charterer shall employ the crew and pay the crew's wages and provisions, ship's maintenance and stores, etc. by himself, apart from those expenses he is responsible for under the time charter.

③ 光船租船。光船租船也是定期船租的一种，所不同的是：在定期租船方式下，船主不仅提供货船，还有船员，而在光船租船方式下，船主不提供船员，只有一条船交给租方使用，由租方自行配备船员，负责船舶的经营管理和航行各项事宜（如船舶的维护、修理及机器的正常运转等）。

(2) Charter Party. The charter party is a contract concluded between the ship-owner and the charterer when the latter charters the ship or booking shipping space from the former. It stipulates the rights and obligations of the two parties. The main terms on the charter party include the interested parties, name and flag of the ship, description and quantity of the shipments, time of chartering, freight, loading and unloading expenses, time limit of loading and unloading, demurrage and dispatch money.

（2）租船合同。租船合同是租船人和船舶所有人之间所订立的载明双方权利、义务的契约。主要条款包括有关当事人、船名和货船标识、装运货物的名称和数量、租期、运费、装卸费、装卸时限、滞期费、速遣费。

The freight may be stipulated in the charter party as follows.

a. Freight can be paid in advance.

b. Freight can be paid after the goods have arrived at the port of destination.

c. Part of freight is paid in advance, the rest of which is paid after the goods have arrived at the port of destination.

Before the charterer pays off freight and other charges, the ship-owner is entitled to refuse to deliver the goods, this kind of right is called lien.

租船合同中有关运费的规定如下。

a. 运费预付。

b. 货到目的港时再付运费。

c. 已付部分运费，余下的货到目的港之后再付。

在租船人付清运费之前，船主有权拒绝装运货物，这叫留置权。

When discussing the problem of whom will be responsible for the charges of loading and unloading, both the ship-owner and the charterer should make it very clear in the charter party. There are four methods to be used to stipulate the expenses of loading and unloading.

a. The ship-owner bears gross terms.

b. The ship-owner is free in (FI).

c. The ship-owner is free out (FO).

d. The ship-owner is free in and out (FIO). When adopting this method, the interested parties shall indicate who will bear the expenses of stowing and trimming. If they agree that the charterer shall be responsible for them, then the interested parties shall stipulate "ship-owner is free in and out, stowed, trimmed (FIOST)".

在签订租船合同时，必须明确装卸费用是由租船人还是船方负担。对这个问题有 4 种规定方法。

a. 船方负担装货费和卸货费（Gross Terms）。

b. 船方管卸不管装 （Free In，FI）。

c. 船方管装不管卸（Free Out，FO）。

d. 船方不管装卸（Free In and Out，FIO）。如果采用这种方法，应该在租船合同中写明由谁负责平仓理仓费。如果租船合同中规定由租船人负担这些费用，那么就必须在租船合同中订立："船主不负责货物的装卸及平仓理仓费（FIOST）"。

The time of loading and unloading will affect the turn-over rate of the ship, and thus, will affect the interest of the ship-owner. Therefore, it is the main clause specified in the charter party. The time limit of loading and unloading may be indicated by.

a. Fixed days.

b. Efficiency of loading and unloading.

c. Customary quick dispatch.

装卸时间影响装卸费用，进而影响船方的利益。所以，装卸时间是租船合同的主要条款，装卸时限的规定方法有：

a. 在一定天数内装卸完毕。

b. 规定装卸速度。

c. 按惯常的速度装卸。

During the time limit of loading and unloading, in case the charterer does not finish the work of loading and unloading, in order to compensate the ship-owner for his losses, the charterer should pay certain amount of fine for the exceeding time, this is the so-called demurrage.

在规定的装卸时限内，如果租船人没有完成货物的装卸工作，租船人就必须因此而向船主支付一定数目的罚款，这就是滞期费。

During the time limit of loading and unloading, in case the charterer finishes the work of loading and unloading ahead of schedule, then the ship-owner shall pay certain amount of bonus to the charterer, this is the so-called dispatch money.

在规定的装卸时限内，如果租船人提前完成了货物的装卸工作，船主就必须因此而向租船人支付一定数目的奖励费，这就是速遣费。

(3) Shipping by Liner. A liner is a vessel with regular sailing and arrival on a stated schedule between a group of specific ports. The main features of liners usually include.

a. The liner has a regular line, port, timetable and comparatively fixed freight, which is the basic features of liners.

b. The ship-owner usually leases part of shipping space instead of the whole ship.

c. The carrier is responsible for loading and unloading operations, i.e., Gross Terms.

d. The B/L drawn by the shipping company is the shipping contract between the carrier and the consignor. The rights and obligations of the carrier and the consignor are based on the B/L drawn by the shipping company.

（3）班轮运输。班轮运输是指船舶在固定的航线上和港口间按事先公布的船期表航行。班轮运输主要有下列优点。

a. 有固定航线、固定港口、固定船期和相对固定的费率。这是班轮运输的基本特点。

b. 船东通常出租部分舱位，而不是全部舱位。

c. 管装管卸，有关装卸费均包括在运费内，如船方负责装卸费。

d. 承托双方的权利、义务和责任豁免以签发的提单条款为依据。

2. Railway Transport

Railway transport is capable of attaining relatively high speeds with large quantities and is safe, at low cost, punctual, rather economical and less influence by weather.

2. 铁路运输

铁路运输具有货运量大、速度快、安全可靠、运输成本低、运输准确和受气候影响较小等特点。

Railway transport falls into three kinds.

(1) Railway transport at home.

(2) International railway transport between two countries.

(3) International railway through transport.

铁路运输有 3 种。

（1）内地铁路运输。

（2）国与国之间的铁路运输。

（3）国际铁路货物联运。

According to the stipulations of the International Union of Railways, the International Railway Cargo Through Transport Agreement and the International Convention Concerning the Carriage of Goods by Rail, the goods belonging to the export country may be transported directly to the place of destination as long as the carrier issues a railway bill of lading at the place of dispatch.

The main transport documents are the railway bill and its duplicate. The railway bill is the transportation contract and binding upon the consignee, the consignor and the railway department. The railway bill together with the goods is transported from the place of dispatch to the place of destination and then is delivered to the consignee after he has paid off the freight and other charges. The consignor may make exchange settlement with the bank against the duplicate of railway bill.

根据"国际铁路联盟"《国际铁路货物联运协定》和《国际铁路货物运送公约》的规定，

只要承运人在起运地签发铁路运输提单，出口货物就可以直接运往目的地。

铁路运输单据主要有铁路货运提单及其复印件。铁路货运提单实质上是约束收货人、托运人和承运人三者之间的一种运输合同。它随货物一起从出发地运至目的地，然后由收货人付款索单。托运人也可通过银行交换铁路货运提单的复印件。

3．Air Transport

The advantages of air transport are high speed and quick transit, low risk of damage and pilferage with very competitive insurance, saving in packing cost, reducing amount of capital tied up in transit and so on; while the chief disadvantage is the limited capacity of air freight and overall dimensions of acceptable cargo together with weight restrictions. It is also subject to the influence of weather. However, it is suitable those goods that are of time pressing, small quantity of cargoes but urgent need, light but precious. The air transport can be divided into the following kinds.

(1) Scheduled airliner.

(2) Charted carrier.

(3) Consolidation.

(4) Air express.

3．航空运输

航空运输的优点是航行速度快、交货迅速、货损率低以及节省包装、储存等费用，货物可以运往世界各地而不受地面条件的限制；缺点是运量小、运价高，易受恶劣气候的影响。因此，它适用于一些时间性强、体轻而贵重、量少而急需的货物运输。航空运输可分为以下4种。

（1）班机运输。

（2）包机运输。

（3）集中托运。

（4）急件运送。

The airway bill, also called air consignment note, is a document or consignment note used for the carriage of goods by air supplied by the carrier to the consignor.

空运提单，也称为航空托运单，是用来证明货物已由承运人通过航空方式交给收货人。

Airway bill has the following features.

a. It is a transport contract signed between the consignor/shipper and the carrier/ airline.

b. It is a receipt from the airline acknowledging the receipt of the consignment from the shipper.

c. The airway bill is an internationally standardized document mostly printed in English and in the official language of the country of departure, which facilitates the on-carriage of goods going through 2 to 3 airlines in different countries to the final destination. Generally, there are usually 12 copies of each airway bill for distribution to the various parties, such as the shipper, consignee, issuing carrier, second carrier (if applicable), third carrier (if applicable), airport of destination, airport of departure, and extra copies for other purposes (if required). Copies 1, 2 and 3 are the originals.

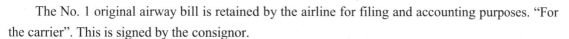

The No. 1 original airway bill is retained by the airline for filing and accounting purposes. "For the carrier". This is signed by the consignor.

The No. 2 original airway bill is to be carried with the consignment and delivered to the consignee at the destination. "For the consignee". This is signed by the carrier, as well as the consignor, and is sent with the goods to the consignee.

The No. 3 original airway bill is for the shipper, who may present it to the negotiating bank as a shipping document evidencing shipment having been made. "For the consignor". This is signed by the carrier and sent back to the consignor.

空运提单有以下特点。

a. 空运提单是托运人/发货人与承运人/航空公司之间签订的货物运输协定。

b. 空运提单是航空公司开给托运人的托运货物的收据。

c. 空运提单通常都是按国际标准用英语和起运地的语言印制，这样方便途中经由 2～3 个不同国家转到目的地。一般来说，空运提单可以有 12 份以便交给不同的有关当事人，如托运人、收货人、承运人、第二承运人（如果有的话）、第三承运人（如果有的话）、目的地机场、起飞机场以及其他用途（如果有的话）。每份空运提单有 3 份正本。

第 1 份由托运人签署，交给承运人或其代理人保存，作为运输契约凭证。

第 2 份由承运人与托运人共同签署，连同货物交收货人，作为核收货物的依据。

第 3 份由承运人签署，于收到货物后，交付托运人，作为收到货物的运输契约的证明。

4. International Combined Transport/International Multimodal Transport

International combined transport means the conveyance of cargo includes at least two modes of transport by which the goods are carried from the place of dispatch to destination on the basis of combined transport or a multimodal transport contract. Under this method, the container is used an intermedium and make up of an international multimodal and join transport mode by sea, air and land.

4. 国际多式联运

国际多式联运是在集装箱运输的基础上产生和发展起来的一种综合性的连贯运输方式。它一般是以集装箱为媒介，把海、陆、空多种传统的单一运输方式有机地结合起来，组成一种国际的连贯运输。

It usually includes:

(1) Train-Air (or Truck-Air, or Ship-Air). The export goods are carried to Hong Kong by train or truck or ship and then loaded into airplanes at Hong Kong.

(2) Train-Ship. The export goods from Chinese interior provinces may also be transported to Hong Kong by railway for transshipment to foreign ports by vessels.

(3) Container Transport/Containerized Traffic.

国际多式联运通常包括：

（1）火车、飞机的联合运输方式。出口货物先由火车、卡车或船运往香港，然后在香港将货物装上飞机。

（2）火车、船的联合运输方式。中国内地的出口货物先由火车运往香港，然后在香港转船运往国外港口。

（3）集装箱运输方式。

Part B　Terminology Practice

1. **Logistics**: in a general business sense, logistics is the management of the flow of things between the point of origin and the point of consumption in order to meet requirements of customers or corporations.

2. **Inbound logistics**: one of the primary processes of logistics concentrating on purchasing and arranging the inbound movement of materials, parts, or unfinished inventory from suppliers to manufacturing or assembly plants, warehouses, or retail stores.

3. **Outbound logistics**: is the process related to the storage and movement of the final product and the related information flows from the end of the production line to the end user.

4. **Parcel delivery**: also known as package delivery, which refers to the delivery of shipping containers, parcels, or high value mail as single shipments. The service is provided by most postal systems, express mail, private courier companies, and less than truckload shipping carriers.

5. **Post**: mail or post is a system for physically transporting postcards, letters, and parcels.

6. **Postal service**: a postal service can be private or public, though many governments place restrictions on private systems.

7. **Shipping documents**: documents such as commercial invoices, bills of lading, policies of insurance, etc. , involved in the shipping of goods.

8. **Commercial invoice**: a document prepared by a seller giving details of goods supplied, their price, contract terms and the total amount due to be paid by the buyer.

9. **Bill of Lading(B/L)**: a document signed by a ship's Master, acknowledging receipt of cargo. It also serves as a contract of freight, and as title to the cargo.

10. **Consignment**: a parcel of goods sent by one party to another.

11. **Consignee**: the person, firm, or representative to whom a seller of shipper sends merchandise and who, upon presentation of the necessary documents, is recognized as the owner of the merchandise.

12. **transshipment**: transferring a cargo from one carrying vessel to another at an immediate port, before arrival at the ultimate port of destination.

13. **On board B/L**: an on board Bill of Lading certifies that a consignment has actually been loaded on the carrying vessel; opposed to an alongside Bill of Lading.

14. **Customs clearance**: completion of customs formalities when exporting or importing goods.

15. **Shipper**: the person whose household goods are being moved.

16. **Irregular route carrier**: a carrier operating within a specified and defined territory, as set

forth in the carrier's Certificate, but not over specified route or routes between fixed termini. Our industry members are irregular route carriers.

17. **Individual shipper**: the owner of household goods being shipped.

18. **Interline**: the transfer of a shipment from one carrier to another for further transportation.

19. **Carrier**: a company that transports passengers, freight or household goods.

20. **Cartons**: containers used for packing smaller odds and ends. Breakables and non-breakables may be packed in cartons.

21. **S.I.T. (Storage-In-Transit)**: temporary storage of household goods in the warehouse of the carrier or his agent, pending further transportation.

22. **Inventory**: the detailed descriptive list of household goods showing number and condition of each item.

23. **Connecting flight**: a segment of ongoing journey that requires passengers to change aircraft, but not necessarily carriers. Under International Air Transportation Association (IATA) regulations, a flight connection becomes a stopover if the passenger is required to wait more than 24 hours for the next flight.

24. **Container**: a container is any receptacle or enclosure for holding a product used in storage, packaging, and shipping.

Part C　Useful Expressions

1. …be mushrooming… 不断涌现
2. one of the important considerations 一个重要考虑因素是……
3. make efforts to 努力……
4. set up by 由……创建
5. achieve the purpose of 达到……目标
6. should be considered… 必须考虑
7. clearly state 明确注明……
8. the most widely used 最广泛使用……

Part D　Exercise

I. Answer the following questions according to the information you have got.

1. What are currently four major commercial express delivery giants ?

2. What are currently domestic express delivery firms?

3. What is the definition of "Overseas Warehouse Service Mode"?

4. What are the advantages of dedicated-line logistics?

5. What is the most widely used form of transportations in international trade?

6. Why does ocean transport still play a very important role in international transportation nowadays?

7. What is a time charter?

8. What is a demise charter?

9. What is the edge of railway transport?

10. What are the advantages and drawbacks of air transport?

II. Match each one on the left with its correct meaning on the right.

1. Consignee   A. a system for physically transporting postcards, letters, and parcels

2. Post   B. the owner of the merchandise

3. Parcel delivery   C. most widely used form of transportations

4. Logistics   D. special routes

5. Customs clearance E. management of the flow of things

6. Carrier   F. completion of customs formalities exporting or importing goods

7. Inventory   G. a company that transports passengers, freight or household goods

8. Container   H. enclosure for holding a product

9. Ocean transport   I. package delivery

10. Dedicated-line   J. detailed descriptive list of household goods showing number and condition of each item

1. (   )   2. (   )   3. (   )   4. (   )   5. (   )

6. (   )   7. (   )   8. (   )   9. (   )   10. (   )

III. Translate the following terms and phrases into Chinese.

1. international logistics

2. a key link

3. independent platform

4. customer experience

5. international express mode

6. domestic express mode

7. postal parcel

8. overseas warehouse service

9. air transport

10. international multimodal transport

IV. Case study for cross-border e-commerce.

Case Description:

Bud-honey Baby has dominated the "maternal and infant brands limited-time sale", in that Bud-honey Baby recommends hot sale maternal and infant brands at its website. Bud-honey Baby pushes the limited sales within 72 hours every day for the price lower than the market price, aiming to open the cross-border e-business. Bud-honey Baby supply chain is divided into four patterns: ① from the brand of domestic generation procurement system; ② order direct purchase from abroad, through each port away general trade; ③ and orders from abroad, Ningbo and Guangzhou cross-border e-pilot pattern; ④ honey bud orders from abroad, overseas companies with the pattern

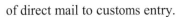

of direct mail to customs entry.

Question:

Please comment on the pattern.

案情介绍:

蜜芽宝贝主导"母婴品牌限时特卖",每天在网站推荐热门的进口母婴品牌,以低于市场价的折扣力度,在 72 小时内限量出售,致力于打开跨境电子商务业务。蜜芽宝贝的供应链分为 4 种模式:① 从品牌方的国内总代采购体系采购;② 从国外订货直接采购,经过各口岸走一般贸易形式;③ 从国外订货,走宁波和广州的跨境电子商务试点模式;④ 蜜芽的海外公司从国外订货,以直邮的模式报关入境。

问题:

请评论这种模式。

V. Describe one or two cases about the latest development of cross-border e-commerce logistics.

VI. Please determine whether the following statements are TRUE or FALSE. Then put T for TRUE or F for FALSE in the bracket at the end of each statement.

1. Sometimes when the buyer cannot determine a specific port of discharge, he may require two or three ports to be written on the contract for option. (　　)

2. When there are optional ports in the contract, the goods may be unloaded at any one of the ports at the shipping company's disposal. (　　)

3. When importing on FOB terms, we can generally stipulate the port of discharge. (　　)

4. An order B/L may be negotiable after being endorsed. (　　)

5. A B/L is a transport contract in which the shipping company promises to transport the goods received to the destination. (　　)

6. A letter of indemnity is issued by the seller to the buyer to certify that the goods delivered are in goods condition. (　　)

7. According to the UCP500, a B/L which is issued subject to a Charter Party must be accepted unless the Credit stipulates otherwise. (　　)

8. When you transport your goods by a Time Charter, you have to pay for loading and unloading. (　　)

9. When the shipowner speeds up his ship and arrives at the destination at an earlier date than is stipulated, he can obtain dispatch money from the shipper. (　　)

10. When the charterer fails to load or unload the goods within the stipulated period of time, he has to pay demurrage to the shipowner. (　　)

VII. Translate the following sentences into English.

1. 一般来讲,只要是跨境电子商务小卖家就可以通过平台发货,可以选择国际小包等渠道。现在跨境电子商务大卖家或者跨境电子商务独立平台的卖家需要优化物流成本,需要考虑客户体验,需要整合跨境电子商务物流资源并探索新的跨境电子商务物流形式。

2. 当然,优质的服务往往伴随着昂贵的价格。一般国内的商户只有在客户时效性要求很强的情况下，才会使用跨境国际商业快递来派送商品。

3. 在国内快递中，EMS 的国际化业务是最完善的。依托邮政渠道，EMS 可以直达全球 60 多个国家，费用相对四大快递巨头要低，中国境内的出关能力很强，到达亚洲国家 2～3 天，到欧美国家 5～7 天。

4. 万国邮政联盟是联合国下设的一个关于国际邮政事务的专门机构，其功能是通过一些公约法规来改善国际邮政业务，从而达到发展邮政方面的国际合作的目的。

5. 万国邮政联盟由于会员众多，而且会员国之间的邮政系统发展很不平衡，因此很难促成会员国之间的深度邮政合作。于是在 2002 年，成立了卡哈拉邮政组织，后来西班牙和英国也加入了该组织。卡哈拉组织要求所有成员国的投递时限要达到 98%的质量标准。

VIII. Multiple Choices.

1. Before shipment, the buyers generally send their (　　) to the sellers, informing them of the packing and marking, mode of transportation,etc.

　　A. shipping documents 　　　　　　B. shipping requirements

　　C. shipping advice 　　　　　　　　D. shipping marks

2. We are very anxious to know when you can definitely (　　) shipment.

　　A. affect 　　　　B. effect 　　　　　C. carry 　　　　　　D. load

3. Our advice of despatch was mailed to you three days ago and you no doubt (　　) it by now.

　　A. will receive 　　B. have received 　　　C. received 　　　　　D. have had received

4 .We look forward to (　　) the goods in the fourth quarter.

　　A. delivery 　　　　B. your delivery 　　　C. deliver 　　　　　　D. delivery of

5 . (　　) any change in the date of delivery, please let us know in advance.

　　A. There should be 　　　　　　　B. Should there be

　　C. There would be 　　　　　　　D. Would there be

6. We regret to say that your price is not (　　) the current world market.

　　A. on a level with 　　　　　　　B. at a level with

　　C. in a level with 　　　　　　　D. in level with

7. The goods are urgently needed, we (　　) hope you will deliver them immediately.

　　A. in the case 　　B. therefore 　　　　C. so 　　　　　　D. for

8.For all the remaining items the stated dates of delivery are approximate, but (　　)caused us certain expenses.

　　A. under any circumstances 　　　　B. in no case

　　C. by all means 　　　　　　　　D. in any case

9. Because of the heavy demand (　　) the limited supply in the market it sells fast.

　　A. for 　　　　　B. to 　　　　　　C. from 　　　　　　D. on

10. If direct steamer is not available for the transportation, (　　).

　　A. the goods will not be shipped 　　　B. partial shipment should be allowed

　　C. the goods have to be separated 　　　D. the goods have to be transshipped

Chapter Ten   Order Procedure of Cross-Border E-Commerce

第十章　跨境电子商务订单流程

Part A   Text

A Brief Introduction to E-Order

Order system, as a cross-border e-commerce system key "link", runs through the whole cross-border e-commerce system process. Other modules of cross-border e-commerce systems are built around an order system. Order is actually the core of the entire e-commerce. The evolution of the order system is also evolving with the business changes of e-commerce platforms. This chapter introduces the "link of life" of cross-border e-commerce platforms—orders.

订单系统作为跨境电子商务系统的纽带，贯穿了整个跨境电子商务系统的关键流程。跨境电子商务系统的其他模块都是围绕订单系统进行构建的。订单实际上就是整个电子商务的核心。订单系统的演变也是随着电子商务平台的业务变化而逐渐演变进化着的，本章介绍跨境电子商务平台的"生命纽带"——订单。

Section One   Role of Cross-Border E-Commerce Order System（跨境电子商务订单系统的作用）

The role of the order system is to manage order types, order status, collect a series of real-time orders of goods, discounts, customers, goods receiving information, payment information and so on. The role of the order system is also to carry out a series of actions such as inventory update and order issuance. The basic model of the order system business involves users, goods (inventory), orders, payments; the basic flow of the order is to place an order→minus inventory, these two steps must be completed at the same time, that is, the order can not be placed without the reduction of inventory (otherwise oversold), or reducing the inventory without generating orders (otherwise undersold). Oversold merchants tend to confront the dilemma of out -of -stock, where consumers fail to buy the article, leading to a lousy experience; undersold sellers tend to have an overstock inventory or need to repeatedly modify the product information, which is troublesome, also leading to a lousy experience.

订单系统的作用是：管理订单类型、订单状态，收集关于商品、优惠、用户、收货信息、支付信息等一系列的订单实时数据，进行库存更新、订单下发等一系列动作。订单系统业务的基本模型涉及用户、商品（库存）、订单、付款；订单基本流程是下订单→减库存，这两

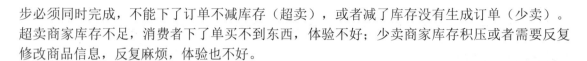

步必须同时完成，不能下了订单不减库存（超卖），或者减了库存没有生成订单（少卖）。超卖商家库存不足，消费者下了单买不到东西，体验不好；少卖商家库存积压或者需要反复修改商品信息，反复麻烦，体验也不好。

Section Two　Procedure of Cross-Border E-Commerce Buyer Order（跨境电子商务买家订单流程）

1．Cross-Border Buyers' Orders

After cross-border buyers select cross-border products, they can successfully enter the order creation page by clicking "Buy Now" on the cross-border product details page. After the cross-border buyers successfully fill in the order information, they can submit it and submit the order to generate the corresponding order.

1．跨境买家下单

跨境买家选择跨境产品后，在跨境产品详细信息页面单击 Buy Now，就可以成功进入创建订单页面。跨境买家成功填写订单信息后，就可以提交，提交后就可以生成相应的订单。

2．Modify the Price

① Cross-border sellers can check the information of the corresponding order in "Transaction"-"Manage Order"-"Order in Progress" page.

② Cross-border sellers can adjust the price of their products before cross-border buyers pay. In the "Order in progress" page, select the order which is to be modified with the discount, click "adjust the price" to enter the order details page, modify the discount information. If cross-border buyers have already paid, cross-border sellers can no longer adjust the transaction price.

2．修改价格

① 跨境卖家可以在"交易"—"管理订单"—"进行中的订单"页面中查询相应订单的信息。

② 在跨境买家未付款之前，跨境卖家可以调整产品的价格。可以在"进行中的订单"页面中，选择需要修改折扣的订单，单击"调整价格"，进入订单详情页面，对折扣信息进行修改。如果跨境买家已经付款，跨境卖家就无法再调整交易价格。

3．Cross-Border Buyers' Payment

① After cross-order buyers choose any cross-border payment method, click "Pay My Order" to enter the cross-border payment page for payment. If a cross-border buyer fails to make any payment within 20 days after the order is placed, the cross-border order will be automatically closed.

② If a cross-border seller only sets up a RMB collection account without setting up a USD collection account, the seller can only pay for cross-border goods by credit card. Cross-border buyers can use Moneybookers, PayPal, debit cards and bank transfer payments if cross-border sellers set up a U.S. dollar collection account.

3. 跨境买家付款

① 跨境买家选择任意一种跨境支付方式后，单击 Pay My Order 即可进入跨境支付页面进行支付。若跨境买家在订单生成后 20 天内逾期不付款，跨境订单就会自动关闭。

② 如果跨境卖家只设置了人民币收款账户，而没有设置美元收款账户，那么该卖家只能通过信用卡方式支付跨境商品的货款。如果跨境卖家设置了美元收款账户，那么跨境买家就能使用 Moneybookers、PayPal、借记卡和银行汇款付款方式。

4. Waiting for Delivery

① Cross-border sellers can view the information of cross-border orders in the "Trading" - "Manage Orders"-"Order in Progress" page. If the cross-border buyers' payment is successful, the order status automatically reads "Waiting for you to ship".

② If the cross-border buyer has not paid yet, the seller can check the remaining payment time of cross-border buyer through the order details. If cross-border buyers overdue payment (20 days), cross-border orders will automatically shut down. Cross-border sellers must pay attention to the remaining time of cross-border buyers' payment so as to remind cross-border buyers to pay as soon as possible, and pay attention to the delivery after cross-border buyers' payment is effected successfully.

4. 等待发货

① 跨境卖家可以在"交易"—"管理订单"—"进行中的订单"页面中查看跨境订单的信息。如果跨境买家付款成功，订单状态就会自动显示"等待您发货"。

② 如果跨境买家还未付款，可以通过订单详情查看跨境买家剩余付款时间。如果跨境买家逾期未付款（20 天），跨境订单就会自动关闭。跨境卖家必须关注跨境买家付款的剩余时间，提醒跨境买家尽快付款，同时注意在跨境买家付款成功后进行发货。

Section Three　Procedure of Cross-Border E-Commerce Seller Order（跨境电子商务卖家订单流程）

1. Cross-Border Sellers' Delivery

Cross-border sellers can contact their cross-border freight forwarding company for shipping, besides, the UPS online delivery can also be applied. In the delivery page, the seller can view the remaining delivery time.

Cross-border sellers can communicate with cross-border buyers promptly within the delivery time. If they can not be confirmed before the deadline, cross-border sellers may request cross-border buyers to extend the delivery time before the deadline.

1. 跨境卖家发货

跨境卖家可以自己联系跨境货代公司发货，也可以使用 UPS 线上发货功能。在发货页面，卖家可以查看剩余的交货时间。

跨境卖家在交货时间内,可以及时与跨境买家沟通,如果在交货时间截止前确认无法发货,跨境卖家可以在截止时间前要求跨境买家延长发货时间。

2. Cross-Border Sellers to Extend Delivery Time

After the successful delivery by cross-border sellers, sellers can fill in the shipping and logistics information, after which the order display reads "waiting for the buyer's receipt". Sellers can select "Waiting for Buyer Goods Receipt" to inquire the order information in the "Trading"- "Manage Orders"-"Order in Progress" page.

2. 跨境卖家延长发货时间

跨境卖家发货成功后,可以填写发货及物流信息,完成后订单显示状态"等待买家收货"。卖家可以在"交易"—"管理订单"—"进行中的订单"页面中选择"等待买家收货"查询订单信息。

① If cross-border buyers can not receive the goods they want on time within the receiving time, cross-border sellers may extend the time.

② After the cross-border sellers have shipped, they can advise the cross-border buyers that they have already shipped and notify cross-border buyers to check.

③ After cross-border buyers receive cross-border goods, cross-border sellers should timely communicate with cross-border buyers for inspection, follow up in time, and confirm the goods receipt and settlement.

④ If the cross-border buyer fails to confirm the receipt (within 30 days), the order will be automatically terminated and the order amount will be automatically paid back to the cross-border sellers.

① 如果跨境买家在收货时间内不能按时收到自己所要的货物,跨境卖家可适当延长跨境买家确认收货的时间。

② 跨境卖家发货后可以告诉跨境买家已经发货,通知跨境买家注意查收。

③ 在跨境买家收到跨境货物之后,跨境卖家应及时与跨境买家沟通验货,及时跟进,与买家确认收货和放款。

④ 如果跨境买家逾期未确认收货(30天之内),则该订单将自动结束,该笔订单款项将会自动支付给跨境卖家。

Section Four　Goods Receipt and Settlement(收货与放款)

1. Cross-Border Buyers' Goods Receipt

After cross-border buyers receive the goods during the delivery period, they conduct cross-border inspection of goods, confirm the receipt if there is no objection, and confirm that the order payment can be paid to cross-border sellers.

1. 跨境买家收货

跨境买家在发货期内收到货物，对跨境货物进行验收，若无异议则确认收货，并确认订单支付款项可支付给跨境卖家。

2. Cross-Border Sellers Receive the Payment

Cross-border platforms will only effect payment to cross-border sellers only if both the transaction being closed and the conditions for cross-border goods properly delivered. Cross-border platform settlement conditions:

① cross-border buyers confirm the receipt and agree to settle.

② cross-border platform receives the information of goods properly delivered.

2. 跨境卖家收款

只有同时满足交易成功和跨境货物妥投两个条件，跨境平台才会放款给跨境卖家。跨境平台放款条件：

① 跨境买家确认收货并同意放款。

② 跨境平台查到货物妥投信息。

Section Five　Cross-Border Order's Numeric Fields（跨境订单字段）

The order numeric field contains the information that needs to be recorded in the order. Its main function is to communicate with other systems and provide information for the downstream system. Specific information can be broken down into the following categories.

订单字段包含订单中需要记录的信息，它的作用主要在于沟通其他系统，为跨境下游系统提供信息依据。具体信息可以细分为以下几类。

1. Order Information

The order number is generally generated according to a specific rule and used as an identifier for cross-border order recognition. The order number automatically increases according to the increase of order quantity. In order to prevent the cross-border competitors or third parties from estimating the order quantity when designing the order number, the non-ordering setting shall be taken into account. The order number follow-up can be used as an order-unique identifier for order recognition when WMS (warehouse management system) and TMS (shipping management system) are docked.

1. 订单信息

订单号一般是按照某种特定规则生成，并作为跨境订单识别的标识，根据订单的增加进行自增，同时，在设计订单号时，为了防止跨境竞争者或者第三方来估算订单量，必须考虑订单的无序设置。订单号后续可以被用作订单唯一标志，用来对接 WMS（仓存管理系统）和

TMS（运输管理系统）的订单识别。

2．Order Status

The current stage of order is shown in this column.

2．订单状态

显示当前订单所处的阶段。

3．User Information

Refers to cross-border buyers' relevant information, including name, address, phone number. Self-pick-up point is included when it comes to an O2O case, so that address will become a self-pick-up point address. Address information is subsequently used on WMS and TMS to distinguish between regions and delivery arrangements.

3．用户信息

指跨境买家的相关信息，包括名称、地址、手机号。O2O 还会多一种情况就是自提点，这样地址则会变为自提点的地址。地址信息在后续会作用在 WMS 和 TMS 上用于区分区域和配送安排。

4．Goods' Information

Refers to the basic information and inventory of cross-border goods. Cross-border products information mainly impacts two aspects: inventory update and warehouse management system.

4．商品信息

商品信息指跨境商品的基本信息和库存，跨境商品信息主要影响两个方面：库存更新和仓存管理系统产生。

5．Amount Information

Cross-border product information generated by orders, and cross-border amounts belong to special product information. It also belongs to cross-border product information category. In addition to the amount of money inside the information to record the final amount, the amount of the process also needs to be recorded, such as the cross-border commodity distribution discount amount, payment amount, payable amount. It can be further used in follow-up order settlement, returns, financial and other areas.

5．金额信息

订单产生跨境商品信息，跨境金额属于特殊的商品信息，它也属于跨境商品信息范畴。这里面金额信息除了要记录最终的金额外，过程金额也需要记录。比如跨境商品分摊的优惠金额、支付金额、应付金额等。可进一步用于后续的订单结算、退换货、财务等环节。

6．Time Information

This information records the trigger time for each status node throughout the order process.

6．时间信息

时间信息记录整个订单流程每个状态节点的触发时间。

Part B　Terminology Practice

1. **Order processing**: refers to the process or work-flow associated with the picking, packing and delivery of the packed items to a shipping carrier. Order processing is a key element of order fulfillment.

2. **Distribution centers**: order processing operations or facilities are commonly called "distribution centers".

3. **Order picking**: order picking or order preparation operation is one of a logistic warehouse's processes. It consists in taking and collecting articles in a specified quantity before shipment to satisfy customers' orders. It is a basic warehousing process and has an important influence on supply chain's productivity. This makes order picking one of the most controlled logistic processes.

4. **Warehouse**: a warehouse is a commercial building for storage of goods. Warehouses are used by manufacturers, importers, exporters, wholesalers, transport businesses, customs, etc. They are usually large plain buildings in industrial areas of cities, towns and villages.

5. **Loading dock**: it is an area of a building where goods vehicles (usually road or rail) are loaded and unloaded. They are commonly found on commercial and industrial buildings, and warehouses in particular.

6. **Quantity**: it is a property that can exist as a multitude or magnitude. Quantities can be compared in terms of "more", "less", or "equal", or by assigning a numerical value in terms of a unit of measurement.

7. **Quality**: in business, engineering and manufacturing, quality has a pragmatic interpretation as the non-inferiority or superiority of something; it's also defined as fitness for purpose. Quality is a perceptual, conditional, and somewhat subjective attribute and may be understood differently by different people. Consumers may focus on the specification quality of a product/service.

8. **WMS**: a warehouse management system (WMS) is a software application, designed to support and optimize warehouse or distribution center management. They facilitate management in their daily planning, organizing, staffing, directing, and controlling the utilization of available resources, to move and store materials into, within, and out of a warehouse, while supporting staff in the performance of material movement and storage in and around a warehouse.

9. **ASRS**: an automated storage and retrieval system (ASRS or AS/RS) consists of a variety of computer-controlled systems for automatically placing and retrieving loads from defined storage locations.

10. **Payment**: is the trade of value from one party (such as a person or company) to another for goods, or services, or to fulfill a legal obligation.

Part C   Useful Expressions

1. run through 贯穿

2. the core of... ……的核心

3. evolving with 与……共同演变

4. a series of 一系列

5. carry out 执行

6. place an order 下订单

7. confront the dilemma of 面临……困境

8. lead to 导致……

9. fill in 填……

10. be applied 应用，得到应用

11. communicate with 与……沟通

12. be broken down into 被分解成

13. be further used 被进一步使用

14. generated by 由……产生

15. be taken into account 考虑

Part D   Exercise

I. Answer the following questions according to the information you have got.

1. What is the role of the order system?

2. What does the basic mode of the order system business involve?

3. How to modify the price? Please demonstrate the process.

4. What are the two prerequisites for cross-border platform settlement?

5. What does order numeric field contain?

6. What is order numeric field's usage?

7. What is the definition of goods' information?

8. What is time information's usage?

II. Match each one on the left with its correct meaning on the right.

1. order system   A. an identifier for cross-border order recognition

2. order number   B. stock

3. WMS   C. rewards

4. TMS   D. settlement

5. order status   E. online to offline

6. inventory   F. trigger time for each status node

7. time information   G. current stage of order

8. returns   H. shipping management system

9. payment   I. warehouse management system

10. O2O   J. e-commerce system key "link"

1. (　　)　2. (　　)　3. (　　)　4. (　　)　5. (　　)

6. (　　)　7. (　　)　8. (　　)　9. (　　)　10. (　　)

III. Translate the following terms and phrases into Chinese.

1. manage order types   2. order status

3. real-time   4. discounts

5. customers   6. goods receiving information

7. payment information   8. oversold

9. undersold   10. credit card

11. waiting for you to ship 12. manage orders

13. order in progress   14. freight forwarding company

15. online delivery   16. remaining delivery time

17. deadline

IV. Case study for cross-border e-commerce.

Case Description:

"The United States Shopping Net" is focused on the purchase of the local brand goods, clothing, bags, shoes, health care products, cosmetics, watches, jewelry, outdoor equipment, household maternal and infant supplies, home theater, etc. The site is of wholesale and retail, mainly with direct-mail as purchasing agency. Goods are delivered by unified logistics distribution by the United States—New York express, one-step shipment sent directly to the customers, with no domestic transshipment.

Question:

Please comment on the pattern.

"美国购物网"专注代购美国本土品牌商品，涵盖服饰、箱包、运动鞋、保健品、化妆品、名表首饰、户外装备、家居母婴用品、家庭影院等。该网站兼顾批发与零售，主打直邮代购。代购的商品均由美国分公司采用统一的物流配送——纽约全一快递，由美国发货直接寄至客户手中，无须经过国内转运。

问题：

请评论这种模式。

V. Describe one or two cases about the ordering system in doing cross-border e-commerce.

VI. Please determine whether the following statements are TRUE or FALSE. Then put T for TRUE or F for FALSE in the bracket at the end of each statement.

1. Price terms are mainly applied to determine the prices of commodities in international trade. (　　)

2. Warsaw-Oxford Rules clearly explain the thirteen kinds of trade terms incurrent use. (　　)

3. As an exporter, you concluded a deal with an American on basis of EXW; then your

transaction risk is reduced the minimum degree. (   )

4. According to the interpretation of the Revised American Foreign Trade Definition, FAS is suitable for all kinds of transportation. (   )

5. On CIP terms, the seller must pay the freight rate and insurance premium as well as bear all the risks until the goods have arrived at the destination. (   )

6. The common feature of an FOB contract and an FAS contract is that the seller must load the goods on a named ship. (   )

7. With "Delivered Duty Paid" , the buyer bears all the costs and risks involved in bringing the goods to the place of destination. (   )

8. With "Delivered Duty Paid" , the buyer has an obligation to clear the goods not only for export but also for import, to pay any duty for both export and import and to carry out all customs formalities. (   )

9. "Free Alongside Ship" means that the seller delivers when the goods are placed alongside the vessel nominated by the buyer at the named port of shipment. (   )

10. With "Free Alongside Ship", the risk of loss of or damage to the goods passes when the goods are alongside the ship, and the buyer bears all costs from that moment onwards. (   )

VII. Translate the following sentences into English.

1. 订单实际上就是整个电子商务的核心。订单系统的演变也是随着电子商务平台的业务变化而逐渐演变进化着的。

2. 订单系统的作用是：管理订单类型、订单状态，收集关于商品、优惠、用户、收货信息、支付信息等一系列的订单实时数据。

3. 订单系统的另一个作用是进行库存更新、订单下发等一系列动作。

4. 在跨境买家未付款之前，跨境卖家可以调整产品的价格。

5. 跨境买家选择任意一种跨境支付方式后，单击 Pay My Order 即可进入跨境支付页面进行支付。若跨境买家在订单生成后 20 天内逾期不付款，跨境订单就会自动关闭。

6. 跨境卖家可以自己联系跨境货代公司发货，也可以使用 UPS 线上发货功能。在发货页面，卖家可以查看剩余的交货时间。

7. 如果跨境买家逾期未确认收货（30 天之内），则该订单将自动结束，该笔订单款项将会自动支付给跨境卖家。

8. 订单字段包含订单中需要记录的信息，它的作用主要在于沟通其他系统，为跨境下游系统提供信息依据。

Chapter Eleven　Cross-Border E-Commerce Market Selection

第十一章　跨境电子商务市场选品

Part A　Text

A Brief Introduction to Market Selection

Cross-border e-commerce market is based on the selection of cross-border e-commerce platform, combined with certain data analysis and its own situation to select cross-border business and the breakdown of cross-border products under specific categories. Before choosing products, cross-border e-commerce businesses shall understand the essence of the selection is that the selection is to select those commodities of which quality, price, features and others are most suitable for cross-border market demand, and also to highlight their competitive advantage.

跨境电子商务市场选品就是要根据跨境电子商务平台的情况，结合一定的数据分析和自身的情况来选择要跨境经营的行业，并细分具体类目下的跨境产品。在选品之前，跨境电子商务商家必须了解选品的本质就在于，选品就是要精选那些质量、价格、特性等最符合跨境目标市场需求的跨境商品，并且突出自己的竞争优势。

The selection of cross-border e-commerce market actually embodies the thoroughness of e-commerce businesses in their own foreign trade industry. Many enterprises involved in cross-border e-commerce have the basis of traditional foreign trade. Therefore, cross-border e-commerce enterprises that have done traditional foreign trade often have some advantages or resources for foreign trade. Cross-border e-commerce is only an upgrade and transformation of traditional foreign trade. The process of market selection is actually a process in which e-commerce enterprises sort out their core strengths in the foreign trade sector and think about how to apply core strengths to new cross-border e-commerce businesses mode.

跨境电子商务市场选品实际上也是体现电子商务商家对自身所处的外贸行业的了解透彻程度，不少涉足跨境电子商务的企业都有做传统外贸的基础。因此，做过传统外贸的跨境电子商务企业往往都会有一些外贸优势或资源。跨境电子商务只是传统外贸的一次升级和转型，市场选品过程实际上也是电子商务企业梳理自身所处外贸行业的核心优势，并思考如何把核心优势应用到跨境电子商务的新模式上面的过程。

Section One　The Definition and Classification of the Product Selection（选品的定义和分类）

In the field of cross-border e-commerce, the selection of products or market selection refers to the selection of industries and cross-border products under specific categories according to the circumstances of the e-commerce platform in combination with certain data analysis and their own circumstances. According to the specific size, selection of products can be categorized into:

选品，或市场选品，在跨境电子商务领域，是指根据电子商务平台的情况，结合一定的数据分析和自身的情况来选择要经营的行业及具体类目下的跨境产品。选品按从大到小可以细分为：

(1) Selection in terms of industry categories. According to the current situation of cross-border e-commerce platform, the e-businesses have to determine the foreign trade business in which they operate, such as sports and entertainment, healthcare, beauty, baby products, clothing, toys, etc.

（1）行业大类选品。根据跨境电子商务平台目前的情况确定要经营的外贸行业，如运动及娱乐、健康养生、美容、婴儿用品、服装、玩具等。

(2) Selection in terms of general products. In a sub-industry, e-businesses have to determine what kind of products to sell, such as under the clothing industry are the adult clothing, baby clothes, children's clothing, etc.

（2）类目中类选品。在某个细分行业下，确定要卖哪些类目的产品，如服装行业下有成人服装、婴儿服装、童装等类目。

(3) Selection in terms of particular product. In a middle class category, e-businesses have to determine what products to sell, such as under adult clothing are the casual wear, high-end clothing, jeans, etc.

（3）产品小类选品。在某个中类类目下确定卖哪些产品，如成人服装目下有休闲服装、高档服装、牛仔服等产品。

Cross-border e-commerce product selection is a process of understanding the cross-border e-commerce market. The selection is all about the market. Therefore, businesses have to find the Blue Ocean product line in the e-commerce platform where market competition is relatively small, that is, to occupy the Niche Market. Businesses have to optimize the information display of cross-border e-commerce products, and improve the quality and establish word-of-mouth, that is, to achieve excellence amongst the participants. Finally, to make distinctions, make products special, that is, select specialty products, in accordance with the "long-tail theory", there is a big market for small needs.

跨境电子商务选品是一个认识跨境电子商务市场的过程，选品就是了解市场。因此，要找到在电子商务平台市场竞争比较小的蓝海产品线，即做到人无我有。优化跨境电子商务产品的信息展示，提高质量，做口碑，即做到人有我优。最后，要做出特色，人优我特，即选择特种产品，按照"长尾理论"，小需求也有大市场。

Section Two　Cross-Border E-Commerce Positioning（跨境电子商务定位）

Cross-border e-commerce products also involve the positioning of cross-border e-commerce websites, namely the target market of the e-store, the target customers and the unique core competencies of the website operators.

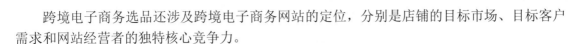

跨境电子商务选品还涉及跨境电子商务网站的定位，分别是店铺的目标市场、目标客户需求和网站经营者的独特核心竞争力。

1. Cross-Border E-Commerce Target Market

Through cross-border e-commerce industry platform, e-commerce businesses can subsequently implement the industry research and market segmentation, so as to determine the potential of each market segment and match up with the store.

1. 跨境电子商务目标市场

企业通过跨境电子商务平台的行业调研进行市场细分，判断各细分市场的潜力及与店铺的匹配度。

2. Cross-Border E-Commerce Target Customer Demands

For cross-border e-commerce businesses, the data is the core. Data analysis tools can be applied to determine the supply and demand of selected products in cross-border markets. Through the search of product keywords, the market opportunities of the chosen category can be generally understood.

2. 跨境电子商务目标客户需求

对于跨境电子商务企业而言，数据是核心。利用数据分析工具判断相关已选品类在跨境市场上的供求情况。通过搜索产品关键词大致了解该品类在市场的商机情况。

3. Unique Core Competencies Of Cross-Border E-Shop

After understanding the relevant market conditions based on data surveys, and then cross-border e-commerce businesses will shape their core competitiveness. The market positioning can be further clarified through high product cost-effective strategy or fill the market blank strategy.

3. 跨境电子商务店铺经营者的独特核心竞争力

基于数据调研了解相关市场的情况后，跨境电子商务企业接着就要塑造自己的核心竞争力。可以通过高的产品性价比战略或产品填补市场空白战略来进一步明确市场定位。

Section Three Cross-Border E-Commodity Selection Method Procedures（跨境电子商务选品方法程序）

1. Determining the Hot Product by the Approach of Searching Cross-Border E-Commerce Platform

This is the most common practice, e-businesses can first enter the AliExpress website, and then enter a keyword, the search box will appear keyword reads HOT SEARCHES, and then these words can be combined with third-party data tools to search those "hot"products.

1. 以跨境电子商务平台作为搜索平台确定热销产品方法

这是最常见的做法，电子商务企业可以首先进入速卖通网站，然后输入某个关键词，搜索框就会出现 HOT SEARCHES 的关键词字样，再将这类热词结合第三方数据工具进行搜索就可以得出热销产品。

2. Browsing Foreign Websites To Choose "Hot" Products

E-commerce businesses can often visit some of the industry's foreign web sites, such as "Google"by entering keywords to search some target overseas market sites, clicking into the hot sales of these overseas websites, especially those of the latest models of products. This procedure leads to the result of hot-sale products.

2. 浏览国外网站选择热销产品方法

电子商务企业可以通过经常浏览一些行业的国外网站，如通过 Google 输入关键词去搜索一些目标海外市场的网站，进入这些海外网站的热销排行，关注那些最新款式的产品，从而得出热销产品。

3. Social Media Hot Words Method

To seize the end-users is the core of cross-border e-commerce platform website. At present, social media is the largest gathering of market demand information, such as Facebook, Twitter and so on, E-commerce businesses can focus on social media hot words via understanding these foreign social media habits and interest. Seizing social media is to capture the real market tone.

3. 社交媒体的热词方法

跨境电子商务平台网站的核心就是抓住终端客户，目前，社交媒体就是最大的市场需求信息聚集地，如 Facebook、Twitter 等，电子商务企业可以通过了解这些国外社交媒体的习惯和兴趣，关注社交媒体的热词。抓住了社交媒体就等于抓住了真正的市场风口。

4. Entering AliExpress and Other Cross-Border Platforms to Learn From Example Sellers

New cross-border e-commerce businesses can figure out an AliExpress model store by searching keyword of a category of products, through the analysis of AliExpress buyers page, a lot of cross-border selections of business opportunities are to be found. With the study of other cross-platform example sellers on the seller page, the new cross-border e-commerce enterprises can understand the title of prevailing products, keywords, market positioning, market activity and so on. Transaction records, which are similar to Taobao's buyer records , can be visited to understand the product source of the customer, the buyers' satisfaction rate as well as the buyer's customer rating.

4. 进入速卖通等跨境平台学习榜样卖家

新入门的跨境电子商务企业还可以把想做某个产品的品类通过关键词搜索到一个速卖通榜样店铺，进入速卖通店铺的买家页面，通过研究分析速卖通买家页面，可以找到很多跨境选品的商机。通过研究速卖通等跨境平台榜样卖家的买家页面，新入门的跨境电子商务企业可以了解到爆款产品的标题、关键词、市场定位、市场活跃度等。也可以通过查询类似于淘宝的交易记录这样的买家记录了解这个产品的客户来源、买家满意度、买家的客户评价。

Section Four　Pricing of Cross-Border E-Goods（跨境电子商品的定价）

In international trade practice the terms of price is one of the most important terms of a contract. So the price of goods is certainly among the chief terms. Pricing is a complex and generally unscientific activity in most firms discussed in business negotiations. Actual practice is much more difficult than following the theories and simple suggestions of the economists. So pricing become trial and error and hard calculations in decision making. Setting the price level is not just a question of determining the lowest possible price at which will achieve the optimum balance between the performance desired by customers and the costs incurred by the exporter. Pricing means a serious of techniques relating to a single product or a group of products. Price is the amount of money (plus possible some goods) that is needed to acquire some combination of a product and its accompanying services. Practice indicates that price is simply an offer or an experiment to test the pulse of the market. If they reject it, the price usually will be changed quickly, or the product may even be withdrawn from the market. In managing the price portion of a firm's marketing mix, the exporter must, first of all, decide on its pricing objectives or targets, and then set the base price for a product or service.

在国际货物买卖中，对大多数公司来说定价工作是很复杂的，而且一般来说也不科学，真正实践起来要比经济学家的理论和简单的建议困难得多。在定价决策过程中，既需要反复试验纠正其错误，又要不厌其烦地进行计算。确定价格水准，不仅是确定可能的最低供货价格，还要确定什么样的价格既能使客户满意又能补偿出口商的费用。定价意味着有关一种或一组产品的一系列技巧。所谓价格指的是为获得某种产品及有关服务所需支付的金额（可能还要加上某些商品）。实践表明，价格只是一种报盘，或者说，是一种对市场"脉搏"的测试。如果客户接受，则说明所定的价格可行；如果客户都不接受，则往往需要马上对价格做出变动，甚至将商品撤出市场。在处理公司营销组合中的价格部分时，出口商必须首先明确其定价目标或目的，并确定其产品或劳务的基价。然后，根据结构的各种因素，采取适当的策略、方法和政策。

1．Pricing Strategy

Pricing strategy is part of the process of developing an overall marketing strategy. According to objections of a company, the pricing strategy may be demand-oriented or competition-oriented. Demand-oriented pricing examines the intensity of demand as expressed by consumers. Price varies with the intensity of demand for a product, with a high price charged where there is a high degree of interest in the product and a low price when demand is weak. Competition-oriented pricing examines the pricing behavior of competitors. Firms which rely entirely on the competitive element to determine a price will set it at a level which is just above or below the prices obtaining in the market.

Three well-known pricing strategies are penetration pricing, skimming pricing and early cash recover pricing, which are often used by firms introducing new products to a market. The first two are direct opposite, while the third can incorporate features of the other two. These may be used as a promotional device, or as a contributory element in developing a company image.

1. 定价策略

定价策略是制定整个营销策略过程中的一部分。根据公司的目标，定价策略可以分为需求型和竞争型两种。需求型定价策略考虑的是消费者表现出的对商品的强烈需求愿望。由于消费者对商品需求愿望的不同，价格也随之不同。如果对某种商品的需求特别强烈，其价格就会高很多；如果需求量小，该商品的价格就会很低。竞争型价格策略考虑的是竞争对手的问题，如果公司完全依靠竞争来决定价格，该价格将高于或低于市场预期。

三个广为人知的定价策略是渗透定价法、撇脂定价法和资金速期回收定价法，公司向市场推销新产品时常使用这些定价法。前两种策略针锋相对，而第三种是前两种策略的结合。这些定价策略可以作为经销方式，或可以有助于塑造公司形象。

(1) Penetration pricing. A very important way to achieve a large share of the market for a new product is to set a relatively low price initially to stimulate demand and attract more buyers. If the market appears to be highly price sensitive, setting a low price will bring additional buyers into the market. It is helpful to unlock markets that may not have even been anticipated. A low initial price strategy also has the benefit of discouraging actual and potential competition and is consequently an important protective element in the firm's armory. When a product is being produced under conditions which give rise to scale economies and unit production and distribution costs fall with increased output, this strategy will be workable.

（1）渗透定价法。使某一新产品占据较大市场份额的一种方法就是在最初阶段以相对低价来刺激需求。如果该市场显示出很大的价格弹性，定低价就能吸引更多的买主进入市场。渗透定价策略可以用来开拓预料之外的市场。初期低价策略也有益于降低实际和潜在的竞争，进而也是保护公司的重要因素。当出现大量订单积压时，公司不能调整价格。只有对能促成规模经济、单位生产和经销成本随产量的增加而降低的情况下生产的产品，此策略方可奏效。

(2) Skimming pricing. This strategy is designed to gain a premium from those buyers who want to take advantage of the readiness of a market. After a time, when the premium segment is saturated, the firm gradually reduces prices to draw in the more price sensitive segments of the market. Typically a price skimming strategy works well where there are significant entry barriers such as patents, high development costs, raw material advantages sometimes accrue to the firm setting a high initial price; this strategy leaves room for a price reduction if a miscalculation has been made; it is always easier to reduce price than to raise it once a product has been established on the market. A high price may also create an impression of a superior product in the minds of consumers.

（2）撇脂定价法。这种策略目的在于从买主身上赚取高额利润。经过一段时间，当高价市场部分趋于饱和时，公司逐渐减价以吸引价格弹性较大的市场部分。特别是在有重要市场壁垒，如专利权、高开发成本、原材料控制或促销成本长期偏高的情况下，撇脂定价策略才能充分发挥效应。初定高价的公司有时还有另外两方面的优势：如有定价失误，这种策略还有减价的余地；一旦某产品打开了市场，减价总比涨价容易。高价也可在消费者和用户心中留下优质产品的印象。

(3) Early cash recovery pricing. Companies sometimes do not believe that the market for their products will exist for a long period, or they experience a shortage of cash, or survival may be the overriding objective facing them. In such circumstances they tend to set a price which will bring in cash at an earlier stage rather than in the longer term. Market conditions dictate whether the price should be high or low. The firm can maximize immediate cash flow through a high price strategy because of the presence of a low demand elasticity and constant unit cost of production and distribution, and through a low price strategy because of the presence of a high demand elasticity and declining unit cost. The choice of strategy depends on the firm's objectives and its view of market condition.

（3）资金速期回收定价法。有时公司相信它们的产品市场不会持久，或者会经受缺少现金的困难，或者正面临着公司能否生存的困境。在这种情况下，公司倾向于制定一个在短期内而不是较长期限内收回现金的价格。市场条件决定价格应高还是应低。在需求弹性较低且单位生产和经销成本不变时，公司可采取高价策略；需求弹性较高且单位生产成本下降时，公司可采用低价策略。这样做公司可以最大限度地迅速收回现金。策略的选择取决于公司的目标及其对市场情况的了解。

2．Pricing Objectives

Every market task, including pricing especially, must be directed toward the achievement of a goal, in other words, management should decide on its pricing objectives before determining the price itself. The objectives can be divided into two kinds: long-term objectives and short-term objectives.

Long-term objectives are usually concerned with profitability and market share. Firms which consider price as a strategic marketing weapon will devote more attention to long-term price objectives than those which view price as a tactical instrument to gain short-term advantage in the market. Short-term objectives are usually specified in annual budgets developed by the firm for a number of items including profits, sales volume and market share. The main objectives whether long-term or short-term, established by the company are oriented either toward profits, toward sales, or toward maintaining the status quo.

2．定价目标

市场上每一项工作，尤其是定价，必定是为了达到某种目标。换言之，经营者在决定价格本身之前，必须首先明确定价目标。定价目标可分为两类：长期目标和短期目标。

长期目标通常关于盈利情况和市场份额。有些公司把价格作为一种战术手段以求在市场上取得短期优势，与此相比，那些将价格作为战略性营销武器的公司，则更重视定价的远期目标。短期目标一般体现在公司的年度预算中，包括利润、销售额和市场份额等几个方面。公司所确定的主要目标，无论长期的还是短期的，都是为了取得利润、扩大销量或维持现状。

3．Pricing Principles

It is very complicated to make a good price for a product in the import and export business. In order to do it well, we should carry out correctly pricing principles and be sure to master the changing trend of the international market. All the factors that may influence pricing should be taken into account. The calculation of cost, profit and loss must be reinforced.

In order to pricing properly, the following three principles should be adhered to.

(1) To price according to the international market. The international market price is made on the basis of international merits and formed in the international market competition, which can be accepted both by the buyer and the seller.

(2) To price based on the situations of different policies of various countries and regions. In order to let the foreign trade work in with the diplomatic policies, we should consider the policies of different countries and regions in the reference with the international market.

(3) To price based on the purpose of purchasing. The price of goods to be imported and exported can be made according to the international market, and be made based on the purpose of purchasing. That's to say, the price can be a little higher or lower than the international market.

3．定价原则

在进出口业务中，确定一个合理的价格是一项十分复杂的工作。为了做好这项工作，必须正确贯彻我国进出口商品的作价原则，切实掌握国际市场价格的变动趋势，充分考虑影响价格的各种因素，加强成本和盈亏的核算。

在确定进出口商品价格时，必须遵循下列 3 项原则。

（1）按照国际市场价格水平定价。国际市场价格是以商品的国际价值为基础并在国际市场竞争中形成的，它是交易双方都能接受的价格。

（2）要结合国别、地区政策定价。为了使外贸配合外交，在参照国际市场价格水平的同时，也可适当考虑国别、地区政策。

（3）要结合购销意图定价。进出口商品价格在国际市场价格水平的基础上，可根据购销意图来确定，即可略高于或略低于国际市场价格。

4．Pay Close Attention to the Ups and Downs of the International Market

The international market price is subject to the supply and demand, so it is not so stable. Therefore, in making the price of the goods, we should pay great attention to the ups and downs of the international market, make good prediction so as to avoid blindness of the making correct use of pricing.

4．注意国际市场价格动态

国际市场价格因受供求关系的影响而经常波动，不断变化。因此，在确定进出口价格时，必须注意市场供求关系的变化，要对国际市场价格走势做出正确判断，以避免定价上的盲目性。

Part B　Terminology Practice

1. **Marketing strategy**: refers to a long-term, forward-looking approach to planning with the fundamental goal achieving a sustainable competitive advantage. Strategic planning involves an analysis of the company's strategic initial situation prior to the formulation, evaluation and selection of market-oriented competitive position that contributes to the company's goals and marketing objectives.

2. **Commodity**: in economics, a commodity is an economic good or service that has full or substantial fungibility. The price of a commodity good is typically determined as a function of its market as a whole: well-established physical commodities have actively traded spot and derivative markets.

3. **Category of goods**: a retailing and purchasing concept in which the range of products purchased by a business organization or sold by a retailer is broken down into discrete groups of similar or related products.

4. **Duties**: are taxes levied by governments on the importation, exportation, or use of goods.

5. **Express**: a system for the prompt and safe transportation of goods at rates higher than standard freight charges.

6. **Bid**: a statement of what a vendor will take for a good or service. Vendor may bid either verbally or in writing and the bid is generally good for a defined period of time.

7. **Selection of products**: also known as market selection , refers to the selection of industries and cross-border products under specific categories according to the circumstances of the e-commerce platform in combination with certain data analysis and their own circumstances.

8. **Blue Ocean Strategy**: it is a marketing theory from a book published in 2005 which was written by W. Chan Kim and Renée Mauborgne, professors at INSEAD and co-directors of the INSEAD Blue Ocean Strategy Institute. Based on a study of 150 strategic moves spanning more than a hundred years and thirty industries, Kim & Mauborgne argue that companies can succeed by creating "blue oceans" of uncontested market space, as opposed to "red oceans" where competitors fight for dominance, the analogy being that an ocean full of vicious competition turns red with blood.

9. **Core competency**: a concept in management theory introduced by C. K. Prahalad and Gary Hamel. It can be defined as "a harmonized combination of multiple resources and skills that distinguish a firm in the marketplace" and therefore are the foundation of companies' competitiveness.

10. **Positioning**: refers to the place that a brand occupies in the mind of the customer and how it is distinguished from products from competitors. In order to position products or brands, companies

may emphasize the distinguishing features of their brand (what it is, what it does and how, etc.) or they may try to create a suitable image (inexpensive or premium, utilitarian or luxurious, entry-level or high-end, etc.) through the marketing mix.

Part C   Useful Expressions

1. rock-bottom price 最低价

2. type 型号

3. specification 规格

4. price 价格

5. quality 品质

6. weight 重量

7. quantity 数量

8. domestic subsidy 国内补贴

9. domestic support （农产品）国内支持

10. electronic commerce 电子商务

11. ex ante 采取措施前

12. ex post 采取措施后

13. export performance 出口实绩

14. export subsidy 出口补贴

15. free-rider 免费搭车者（享受其他国家最惠国待遇而不进行相应减让的国家）

16. *Lisbon Agreem*ent 《里斯本条约》（有关地理标识及其国际注册）

17. direct payment valuation request 直接支付估价申请

18. direct payment valuation 直接支付估价单

19. provisional payment valuation 临时支付估价单

20. payment valuation 支付估价单

21. quantity valuation 数量估价单

22. quantity valuation request 数量估价申请

23. contract bill of quantities-BOQ 合同数量单

24. No pricing tender BOQ 不计价投标数量单

25. priced tender BOQ 标价投标数量单

26. stores requisition 领料单

27. discount 折扣

28. reduction 降价

29. allowance 折扣

30. rebate 回扣

31. cash discount 即期付款折扣

32. quantity discount　数量折扣

33. special discount　特别折扣

34. average price　平均价

35. base price　底价

36. market price　市场价

37. maximum price　最高价

38. buying price　买价

39. bedrock price　最低价

40. ceiling price　最高价

41. closing price　收盘价

42. cost price　成本价

43. current price　先行价格

44. exceptional price　特别价

45. extra price　附加价

46. floor price　最低价

47. gross price　毛价

48. nominal price　有行无市价

49. opening price　开盘价

50. original price　原价

51. popular price　大众化的价格

52. present price　现价

53. prevailing price　通行价格

54. reserve price　保留价格

55. retail price　零售价

Part D　Exercise

I. Answer the following questions according to the information you have got.

1. What is the definition of selection of products?

2. What does positioning of cross-border e-commerce websites embody?

3. How to determine the hot products by the approach of searching cross-border e-commerce platform?

4. How to choose "hot" products via browsing foreign websites?

5. How to choose "hot" products via social media hot words method?

II. Match each one on the left with its correct meaning on the right.

1. rock-bottom price　　A. a harmonized combination of multiple resources and skills that distinguish a firm in the marketplace

2. positioning　　B. goods

3. core competency   C. uncontested market space

4. Blue Ocean   D. the place that a brand occupies in the mind of the customer

5. Commodity   E. fixing a price

6. pricing   F. goals

7. objectives   G. in vogue words

8. hot words   H. a system for the prompt and safe transportation of goods at rates higher than standard freight charges

9. Social media   I. the lowest price

10. Express   J. Facebook, Twitter, etc.

1. ( ) 2. ( ) 3. ( ) 4. ( ) 5. ( )

6. ( ) 7. ( ) 8. ( ) 9. ( ) 10. ( )

III. Translate the following terms and phrases into Chinese.

1. The selection of cross-border e-commerce market actually embodies the thoroughness of e-commerce businesses in their own foreign trade industry. Many enterprises involved in cross-border e-commerce have the basis of traditional foreign trade.

2. Cross-border e-commerce enterprises that have done traditional foreign trade often have some advantages or resources for foreign trade. Cross-border e-commerce is only an upgrade and transformation of traditional foreign trade. The process of market selection is actually a process in which e-commerce enterprises sort out their core strengths in the foreign trade sector and think about how to apply core strengths to new cross-border e-commerce businesses mode.

3. Selection in terms of industry categories. According to the current situation of cross-border e-commerce platform, the e-businesses have to determine the foreign trade business in which they operate, such as sports and entertainment, healthcare, beauty, baby products, clothing, toys, etc.

4. Selection in terms of general products. In a sub-industry, e-businesses have to determine what kind of products to sell, such as under the clothing industry are the adult clothing, baby clothes, children's clothing, etc.

5. Browsing foreign websites to choose "hot" products. E-commerce businesses can often visit some of the industry's foreign web sites, such as "Google"by entering keywords to search some target overseas market sites, clicking into the hot sales of these overseas websites, especially those of the latest models of products. This procedure leads to the result of hot-sale products.

6. In international trade practice the terms of price is one of the most important terms of a contract. So the price of goods is certainly among the chief terms.

IV. Case study for cross-border e-commerce.

Case Description:

JD.com has challenged China e-commerce rival Alibaba with the launch of a cross-border platform designed to bring foreign brands to the Chinese middle class. JD Worldwide enables international businesses to sell directly to China consumers without needing to establish a legal presence on the mainland, lowering the barriers to entry for brands. The cross-border platform

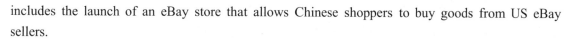

includes the launch of an eBay store that allows Chinese shoppers to buy goods from US eBay sellers.

Question:

Please comment on the pattern.

案情介绍：

中国电子商务集团京东（JD.com）向国内竞争对手阿里巴巴（Alibaba）发出挑战，推出了一个旨在为中国中产阶级带来国外品牌的跨境网购平台。京东全球购使国际企业能够直接面向中国消费者进行销售，不需要在中国内地设立法律实体，降低了品牌准入的壁垒。京东的这一跨境网购平台是"eBay 海外精选"频道，通过其中国消费者可以向美国 eBay 卖家购买商品。

问题：

请评论这种模式。

V. Describe one or two cases about the latest development of pricing system in doing cross-border e-commerce.

VI. Please determine whether the following statements are TRUE or FALSE. Then put T for TRUE or F for FALSE in the bracket at the end of each statement.

1. Auction is a public sale of items sold to the lowest bidder. (　　)

2. Bailee is a public warehouseman considered a "bailee for hire". One person who holds or stores goods for another. (　　)

3. Bailor is the owner of goods being stored, typically a shipper. (　　)

4. Barrels are iron used for packing odd dishes, glassware, lamp bases, and anything breakable. (　　)

5. Bid is a statement of what a vendor will take for a good or service. Vendor may bid either verbally or in writing and the bid is generally good for a defined period of time. (　　)

6. A confirmed reservation exists when a supplier acknowledges, either orally or in writing, that a booking has been refused. (　　)

7. Confirming order is a type of PO used when there is a rush for placing an order. (　　)

8. Declared valuation is a system for establishing the van line's minimum liability for loss or damage to shipment. (　　)

9. Direct Pay Request is a type of payment request. Used for employee reimbursement, petty cash, and other types of payments that do not require Purchasing approval. (　　)

10. Duties are taxes levied by governments on the importation, exportation, or use of goods. (　　)

VII. Translate the following sentences into English.

1. 跨境电子商务市场选品就是要根据跨境电子商务平台的情况，结合一定的数据分析和自身的情况来选择要跨境经营的行业，并细分具体类目下的跨境产品。在选品之前，跨境电子商务商家必须了解，选品的本质就在于要精选那些质量、价格、特性等最符合跨境目标市场需求的跨境商品，并且突出自己的竞争优势。

2. 跨境电子商务选品是一个认识跨境电子商务市场的过程，选品就是了解市场。因此，要找到在电子商务平台市场竞争比较小的蓝海产品线，即做到人无我有。优化跨境电子商务产品的信息展示，提高质量，做口碑，即做到人有我优。最后，要做出特色，人优我特，即选择特种产品，按照"长尾理论"，小需求也有大市场。

3. 跨境电子商务店铺经营者的独特核心竞争力：基于数据调研了解相关市场的情况后，跨境电子商务企业接着就要塑造自己的核心竞争力。可以通过高的产品性价比战略或产品填补市场空白战略来进一步明确市场定位。

4. 进入速卖通等跨境平台学习榜样卖家。新入门的跨境企业还可以把想做某个产品的品类通过关键词搜索到一个速卖通榜样店铺，进入速卖通店铺的买家页面，通过研究分析速卖通买家页面，可以找到很多跨境选品的商机。通过研究速卖通等跨境平台榜样卖家的买家页面，新入门的跨境企业可以了解到爆款产品的标题、关键词、市场定位、市场活跃度等。也可以通过查询类似于淘宝的交易记录这样的买家记录了解这个产品的客户来源、买家满意度、买家的客户评价。

5. 定价策略是制定整个营销策略过程中的一部分。根据公司的目标，定价策略可以分为需求型和竞争型两种。需求型定价策略考虑的是消费者表现出的对商品的强烈需求愿望。由于消费者对商品需求愿望的不同，价格也随之不同。如果对某种商品的需求特别强烈，其价格就会高很多；如果需求量小，其价格就会很低。竞争型价格策略考虑的是竞争对手的问题，如果公司完全依靠竞争来决定价格，该价格就会高于或低于市场预期。

VIII. Multiple Choices.

1. The core clause of the international sales of goods contract is (   ).

A. packing terms   B. transportation terms

C. price clause   D. quality terms

2. The determinants of export price usually is (   ).

A. international price movement   B. the international market price level

C. exporters operating intentions   D. importers business intentions

3. The important indicators of foreign trade enterprises and import and export trading profit and loss are (   ).

A. export foreign exchange income   B. export cost price

C. export profit and loss rate   D. export swap costs

4. The total cost of a goods for export is RMB 55 000, foreign exchange net income after export is $10 000, if the Bank of China's foreign exchange rate is $100 against 650 yuan, the export profit and loss rate is (   ).

A. 50.9%   B.33.7%   C. 45.9%   D. 36.7%

5. In general case, CIF shall take more (   ) into consideration than the FOB price.

A. foreign freight, domestic expenses   B. abroad freight, insurance premium

C. abroad costs, domestic expenses   D. abroad insurance premium and net profit

6. Our company's external price quoted is for CIF price $100, the foreign party demands to quote on FOB basis, assuming that the premium rate is 0.85%, freight $ 60, then we should offer ( ).

A. $ 930.65   B. $ 990.65   C. $ 903.65   D. $ 935

7. Some provisions of the contract are: "$1 000 per metric ton CIF Singapore", the price should be ( ).

A. price set after   B. provisional price   C. fixed price   D. to be determined

8. International trade pricing method which is often used in our country is ( ).

A. Pending price   B. Provisional price   C. Price set after   D. A fixed price

9. To solve the problem between the two sides in international trade with fixed price or a non fixed price differences, which of the following can be used? ( ).

A. Batch for   B. Provisional price   C. Pending price   D. Price set after

10. The hypothesis to adopt the fixed price is ( ).

A. choosing the pricing time   B. identifying the standard of pricing

C. provision for adjustment of price   D. analysis preparation for profit and loss

11. The price which is according to the date of bill of lading or the average price for the month of shipment is ( ).

A. price before shipment   B. price upon shipment

C. price after shipment   D. price upon the goods at the port of destination

12. A dealer or buyers abroad who earns "a double-charge commission" often uses ( ).

A. the price adjustment provisions   B. discount

C. commission   D. vague commission

13. An export contract stipulated in the "1, 000 us dollars per metric ton CIF Hong Kong, and 2% discount", then the seller net income should be ( ).

A. $ 960   B.$ 1 020   C. $ 980   D. $ 1 040

Chapter Twelve Cross-Border E-Commerce Regulation

第十二章 跨境电子商务监管

Part A Text

A Brief Introduction to Cross-Border E-Commerce Regulation Problems

With the emergence and rapid development of the new type of international trade cross-border e-commerce, its regulation faces many problems to be solved urgently. Cross-border e-commerce features its small quantities, lots of batches, complex sources and diverse sales patterns, all of which determine the need to upgrade and strengthen regulatory oversight in terms of quality and safety, prevention and control of disease outbreaks, guarantee of consumer rights and interests, traceability of product origin and so on.

随着跨境电子商务这种国际贸易新型业态的出现与迅速发展，其监管也面临着许多亟待解决的问题。跨境电子商务的特点是数量少、批量多、来源复杂、销售模式多样等，这些特点决定了质量安全、疫病疫情预防、违禁物品、消费者权益保证、产品来源追溯等各个方面的监管需要升级和加强力度。

Section One The Rights and Obligations of Cross-Border E-Commerce Market Participants（跨境电子商务市场主体的权利和义务）

Cross-border e-commerce industry chain involves many market players, including: manufacturers or producers, cross-border e-commerce companies, cross-border e-commerce platform, cross-border e-commerce supporting services businesses (including payment enterprises, logistics firms, warehousing firms, etc.), cross-border consumers. Therefore, it is necessary to clarify the rights and obligations of all the market participants. Due to the diversity of the main bodies of cross-border e-commerce, as well as the geography of the region and the complexity of the transactions, the boundaries of the rights and obligations of all the market players become vague or even missing.

跨境电子商务的产业链中涉及许多市场主体，主要包括制造商或生产商、跨境电子商务企业、跨境电子商务平台、跨境电子商务配套服务型企业（包括支付、物流、仓储等企业）、跨境消费者等。跨境电子商务主体的多样性、地域的广泛性、交易的复杂性，导致各个市场主体的权利义务界限出现模糊甚至缺失现象，所以有必要厘清各市场主体的权利义务。

1. Clear Responsibilities

Most of the import and export commodities sold through the cross-border e-commerce platform have integrated the import and export trade links and market sales links. Therefore, the inspection and quarantine, customs, industry and commerce, health, food and drug administration and other administrative law enforcement departments' duties and boundaries need urgent clarification. The legal system of inspection and quarantine supervision are needed to improve.

1. 明确职责

通过跨境电子商务平台销售的进出口商品，大多已经将进出口贸易环节和市场销售环节等多个环节合为一体，所以检验检疫、海关、工商、卫生、食药等各行政执法部门的监管职责权限和边界急需厘清。检验检疫监管法律制度需要完善。

2. Clear Legal Obligations

Consumers, who purchase cross-border goods through cross-border e-commerce methods or platforms, have the obligation to declare actively and receive quarantine inspection for those goods that should be subject to quarantine inspection. Cross-border e-commerce platforms are obliged to file records with relevant inspection and quarantine authorities; they are also obligated to conduct a reasonable review of the authenticity and legitimacy of cross-border e-commerce businesses and cross-border goods traded on their platforms. E-commerce companies have the obligation to submit the relevant information of the cross-border sales to cross-border inspection and quarantine departments for the record. It is forbidden to sell banned-entry items stipulated by the state to domestic and foreign consumers on the cross-border e-commerce trading platform. For those e-commerce products within the scope of quarantine, e-commerce companies should also take the initiative to declare and accept quarantine. When the sale of products is at risk of being dangerous or perilous, e-commerce companies have the obligation to recall. For the logistics enterprises, who offer customs clearance and other customs clearance services to cross-border businesses, have the obligation to offer the information to the inspection and quarantine departments for the record; they are also obligated to check whether the arrival parcel goods are consistent before the closure.

The main obligations of the cross-border e-commerce market described above are shown in Figure 12-1.

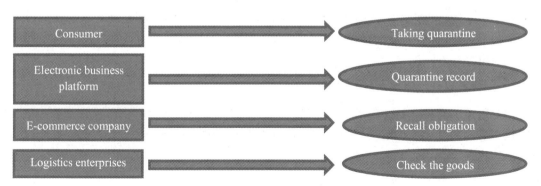

Figure 12-1　Cross-Border E-Commerce Market Obligations Corresponding Map

2．明确法定义务

消费者通过跨境电子商务方式或平台购买跨境商品，对于那些应当接受检疫的商品，消费者负有主动申报和接受检疫的义务。跨境电子商务平台有义务向相关检验检疫部门备案；并有义务对在其平台上交易的跨境电子商务企业和跨境商品的真实性、合法性进行合理审查。电子商务企业有义务将跨境销售的电子商务产品的有关信息向所在跨境平台地检验检疫部门备案。不得在跨境电子商务交易平台上向境内外消费者销售国家规定的禁止进出境物品。电子商务产品属于检疫范围的，电子商务企业还应当主动申报并接受检疫。当销售的产品出现风险时，电子商务企业负有召回的义务。为跨境电子商务从事报关报检等通关服务的物流企业有义务向检验检疫部门备案，对其运抵的邮包在封闭之前有义务查验货证是否相符。

以上介绍的跨境电子商务市场主体义务如图 12-1 所示。

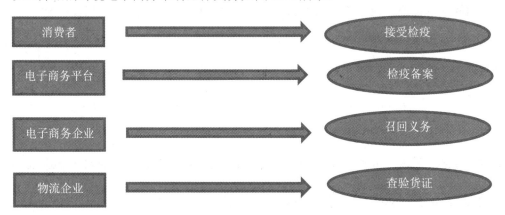

图 12-1　跨境电子商务市场主体义务对应图

Section Two　Regulation Problems Confront the Cross-Border E-Commerce（跨境电子商务监管面临的问题）

1．It is Difficult for the Rights and Interests of Consumers to Obtain a Good Guarantee

In the process of cross-border e-commerce transaction, since the sellers or manufacturers are located outside the border, consumers have a great difficulty in enjoying the after-sales maintenance service. As for the traditional rights protection during the international trade, such as claims, returns, etc., due to its implementation costs being too high, some goods consumers are basically unable to safeguard their rights.

1．消费者权益难以得到好的保障

在跨境电子商务交易过程中，由于销售者或生产商身处国境之外，所以，消费者享受售后维修服务的难度很大，至于传统国际贸易过程中的索赔、退换货等维权行为，其实施成本很高，导致有些商品基本无法维权。

2. It is Difficult to Trace the Source of Cross-Border E-Commerce Products

Cross-border e-commerce overseas supply chain organization model tends to be like "overseas group purchase" "overseas buy". As a result, consumers only get the invoice for the purchase of goods, yet fail to get the certificate of origin as in the traditional international trade, making it difficult to trace the source of the products. Due to the virtual nature of cross-border e-commerce business and other characteristics of distribution services, it is difficult to implement the product recall in the event of product quality and safety accidents.

2. 跨境电子商务商品的来源很难追溯

跨境电子商务的海外供应链组织模式往往是"海外扫货""海淘",所以往往只能拿到货物商品的购货发票,而无法获得传统国际贸易过程中的原产地证明,导致产品来源难追溯。由于跨境电子商务经营环境的虚拟性和流通服务的跨国境等特性,一旦发生产品质量安全事故,对产品的召回难以落实。

3. Clearance Efficiency Needs to be Improved

Getting goods quickly is the general expectation of cross-border e-commerce consumers. According to the traditional way of inspection and quarantine, complicated procedures, long period and high costs tend to result in cargos being stranded at the port.

3. 通关效率有待提高

快速拿货到手是跨境电子商务消费者的普遍期许。按传统检验检疫方式,手续繁杂,周期长,费用高,往往会造成货物滞港压港的后果。

Section Three　Regulation Legal Issues of Cross-Border E-Commerce（跨境电子商务监管法律问题）

1. Consumer Rights Protection Issues

Under the cross-border e-commerce scenario, some domestic provisions on consumer protection are difficult to achieve and affect consumers' shopping experience. Therefore, overseas brands also provide the services like domestic businesses do, aiming to protect consumer rights by making reference to cross-border e-commerce standard.

1. 消费者权益保护问题

在跨境电子商务场景下,境内关于消费者保护的一些规定很难实现,影响消费者的购物体验,所以境外品牌商在做跨境电子商务时也在尽可能参照国内商家对消费者的服务标准来保护消费者权益。

2. Inspection and Quarantine Issues

The main basis for the inspection and quarantine of the bonded area is the departmental rules and regulations such as the Administrative Measures on Quarantine of Entry and Exit Postage. At present, the test of the bonded area only needs to apply the conformity testing standard, that is, according to the local production standards and the international mutual recognition standards, it is relatively flexible in actual operation.

2．检验检疫问题

保税区的检验检疫主要依据是《进出境邮寄物检疫管理办法》等部门规章。保税区的检验目前只需适用符合性检测标准，即按照当地的生产标准、国际互认标准，在实际操作中相对比较灵活。

3. Cross-Border Payment Issues

Cross-border payments mainly include two types: cross-border third-party payments and cross-border RMB payments. Cross-border RMB payment is characterized by settlement in RMB, eliminating currency conversion, reducing the payment cycle (T +3 days), but also to avoid the loss of exchange rate. Cross-border third-party payment means that consumers place an order with their local currency at a foreign website and pay the foreign merchant through a pilot payment agency into foreign currency.

3．跨境支付问题

跨境支付主要包括两种：跨境第三方支付和跨境人民币支付。跨境人民币支付的特点是以人民币结算，省去了币种兑换，缩短了支付周期（T+3日内），也避免了汇差损失。跨境第三方支付是指消费者用本国货币在境外网站下单，通过试点的支付机构转化成外币付给境外商家。

4. Platform's Responsibility

Domestic laws provide for a number of statutory obligations on the trading platform. In addition, cross-border trading platforms also need to consider issues such as whether foreign businessmen can enter the site, the choice of web servers and data centers and many other issues.

4．平台责任问题

境内法律对交易平台规定了多项法定义务，此外，跨境交易平台还要考虑境外商家能否入驻、网站服务器和数据中心的选择等诸多问题。

5. Tax Issue

With the issuance of the "Circular on the Tax Policy on the Import of Retail E-commerce in Cross-border E-commerce", cross-border e-commerce companies have gradually become equal in taxation terms with ordinary trade and the Customs and Excise Department will also carry out stringent enforcement in this field. Therefore, how to make the cross-border products fair and legalization in taxation while maintaining the advantages of cross-border e-commerce for ordinary import and export

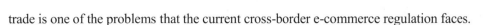

trade is one of the problems that the current cross-border e-commerce regulation faces.

5．税收问题

随着《关于跨境电子商务零售进口税收政策的通知》的下发，跨境电子商务在税收上逐渐与普通贸易同等看待，而海关也将在这个领域开展严厉的执法。所以，如何让跨境电子商务商品在税收上阳光化、合法化，同时保持跨境电子商务对普通进出口贸易的优势，是当前跨境电子商务监管面临的一个问题。

Section Four　Improving Cross-Border E-Commerce Supervision System（完善跨境电子商务监管制度）

1．Compulsory Quarantine System

For cross-border commodities that have a higher risk of transmitting epidemic or epidemic of human or animal diseases, they should receive compulsory animal and plant quarantine and quarantine inspection upon entry and exit.

1．强制性检疫制度

对传播动植物疫情或人类传染病风险较高的跨境商品，在进出境时，应实施强制性跨境动植物检疫或卫生检疫。

2. Source Tracking System

Cross-border e-commerce products should provide certificate of origin. For products that can not provide certificate of origin, the overseas purchasing team or buyers shall request the foreign authority to provide them with the certificate of origin, which serves as one of the documents of inspection and approval record.

2．源头追溯制度

跨境电子商务的产品应提供原产地证明。对于无法提供原产地证明的商品，海外购买团队或买家可以请求国外的权威机构对其予以产品来源认证，认证证书或标志作为国内通关验放的资料之一。

3. Integrity of Information Management System

Inspection and quarantine departments conduct good faith management to e-commerce enterprises according to the supervision implementation and the need to release the integrity of the relevant business information. By the establishment of cross-border e-commerce customs clearance service information platform, regulatory authorities can obtain,through the platform of cross-border, goods information, transaction information, logistics information, information exchange, mutual recognition of mutual recognition, law enforcement mutual aid.

3．诚信信息管理制度

检验检疫部门根据监管情况，对电子商务企业实施诚信管理，可以根据需要发布相关企业的诚信信息或违法失信信息。建立跨境电子商务通关服务信息化平台，监管部门可以通过该平台获得跨境电子商务的货物信息、交易信息、物流信息，实现信息互换、监管互认、执法互助。

4．Third-party Test Results Credit System

E-commerce trading platform or e-commerce enterprises shall submit to the inspection and quarantine authorities a qualified and valid third-party inspection report within the valid period, and the inspection and quarantine department shall verify the right of the third-party inspection report to conduct the random inspection.

4．第三方检测结果采信制度

电子商务交易平台或者电子商务企业应当向检验检疫部门提交有资质的并在有效期内的第三方检测报告，检验检疫部门对第三方检测报告有权通过抽查检验的方式实施验证。

Part B　Terminology Practice

1. **Regulation**: in business, industry self-regulation occurs through self-regulatory organizations and trade associations which allow industries to set rules with less government involvement.

2. **Consumer protection**: consumer protection is a group of laws and organizations designed to ensure the rights of consumers, as well as fair trade, competition, and accurate information in the marketplace.

3. **Market participant**: the term market participant is another term for economic agent, an actor and more specifically a decision maker in a model of some aspect of the economy. For example, buyers and sellers are two common types of agents in partial equilibrium models of a single market.

4. **Manufacturing**: the production of merchandise for use or sale using labour and machines, tools, chemical and biological processing, or formulation. The term may refer to a range of human activity, from handicraft to high tech, but is most commonly applied to industrial production, in which raw materials are transformed into finished goods on a large scale.

5. **Obligation**: an obligation is a course of action that someone is required to take, whether legal or moral.

6. **Rights**: legal, social, or ethical principles of freedom or entitlement; that is, rights are the fundamental normative rules about what is allowed of people or owed to people, according to some legal system, social convention, or ethical theory.

7. **Claim right**: a right which entails that another person has a duty to the right-holder. Somebody else must do or refrain from doing something to or for the claim holder, such as perform

a service or supply a product for him or her.

8. **Quarantine**: to separate and restrict the movement of people; it is a state of enforced isolation. This is often used in connection to disease and illness, such as those who may possibly have been exposed to a communicable disease.

9. **Inspection**: an organized examination or formal evaluation exercise. In engineering activities inspection involves the measurements, tests, and gauges applied to certain characteristics in regard to an object or activity. In international trade several destination countries require pre-shipment inspection.

10. **Parcel**: a package bearing the name and address of the recipient in order to be routed through the services of a postal service or by express package delivery service to the recipient.

11. **A certificate of origin**: often abbreviated to C/O , is a document used in international trade. In a printed form or as an electronic document, it is completed by the exporter and certified by a recognized issuing body, attesting that the goods in a particular export shipment have been produced, manufactured or processed in a particular country.

12. **Customs clearance**: in international trade, refers to the movement of goods through customs barriers.

13. **Bonded areas**: also known as Free economic zones (FEZ), free economic territories (FETs) or free zones (FZ) , which are a class of special economic zone (SEZ) designated by the trade and commerce administrations of various countries. The term is used to designate areas in which companies are taxed very lightly or not at all to encourage economic activity.

14. **Currency conversion**: it is, in finance, regarded as the value of one country's currency in relation to another currency. An exchange rate is the rate at which one currency will be exchanged for another.

15. **Tax**: a mandatory financial charge or some other type of levy imposed upon a taxpayer (an individual or other legal entity) by a governmental organization in order to fund various public expenditures.

Part C   Useful Expressions

1. with the emergence and rapid development of 随着……的出现与迅速发展

2. in terms of 以……形式

3. involve 包含，牵涉……

4. it is necessary to 有必要……

5. the import and export trade 进出口贸易

6. have the obligation to 有义务做……

7. be subject to 依据……

8. be obliged to 有义务做……

9. obtain a good guarantee 得到好的保障

10. trace the source of 追溯……

11. overseas group purchase 海外扫货

12. overseas buy 海淘

13. aim to 为了……

14. with the issuance of 随着……的发布

Part D   Exercise

I. Answer the following questions according to the information you have got.

1. What does cross-border e-commerce industry chain involve?

2. What are some regulation problems confronting the cross-border e-commerce?

3. What are some regulation legal issues confronting cross-border e-commerce?

4. How to improve cross-border e-commerce supervision system?

5. How to improve the source tracking system?

II. Match each one on the left with its correct meaning on the right.

1. Parcel   A. Free economic zones

2. C/O   B. mandatory financial charge by a governmental organization

3. Customs clearance   C. the movement of goods through customs barriers

4. Tax   D. certificate of origin

5. Bonded areas   E. a package bearing the name and address of the recipient

1. (   ) 2. (   ) 3. (   ) 4. (   ) 5. (   )

III. Translate the following terms and phrases into Chinese.

1. with the emergence and rapid development of

2. in terms of

3. involve

4. it is necessary to

5. the import and export trade

6. have the obligation to

7. be subject to

8. be obliged to

9. obtain a good guarantee

10. trace the source of

11. overseas group purchase

12. overseas buy

IV. Case study for cross-border e-commerce.

Case Description:

"Proprietary + Merchants" mode is equivalent to maximize enterprise inner advantage, including in advantage lacking or weak to take foreign investment to make up for its shortcomings.

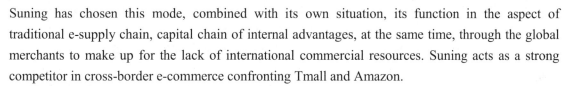

Suning has chosen this mode, combined with its own situation, its function in the aspect of traditional e-supply chain, capital chain of internal advantages, at the same time, through the global merchants to make up for the lack of international commercial resources. Suning acts as a strong competitor in cross-border e-commerce confronting Tmall and Amazon.

Questions:

Please comment on Suning's latest move on cross-border e-commerce.

案情介绍：

"自营+招商"的模式就相当于发挥最大的企业内在优势，在内在优势缺乏或比较弱的方面就采取外来招商方式以弥补自身不足。苏宁选择该模式，结合它的自身现状在传统电商方面发挥它供应链、资金链的内在优势，同时通过全球招商来弥补国际商用资源上的不足。苏宁进入跨境电子商务领域，也是继天猫、亚马逊之后该市场迎来的又一位强有力的竞争对手。

问题：

请评论苏宁云商在跨境电子商务方面的最新动态。

V. Please brainstorm with your fellow classmates or peers and try to find out some neat ideas about International payments scheme.

VI. Please determine whether the following statements are TRUE or FALSE. Then put T for TRUE or F for FALSE in the bracket at the end of each statement.

1. Cross-border e-commerce industry chain involves many market players, including: manufacturers or producers, cross-border e-commerce companies, cross-border e-commerce platform, cross-border e-commerce supporting services businesses (including payment enterprises, logistics firms, warehousing firms, etc. (　　)

2. Consumers, who purchase cross-border goods through cross-border e-commerce methods or platforms, do not have the obligation to declare actively and receive quarantine inspection for those goods that should be subject to quarantine inspection. (　　)

3. In the process of cross-border e-commerce transaction, since the sellers or manufacturers are located outside the border, consumers have a great difficulty in enjoying the after-sales maintenance service. (　　)

4. It is very easy to trace the source of cross-border e-commerce products. (　　)

5. Getting goods quickly is the general expectation of cross-border e-commerce consumers. (　　)

VII. Translate the following sentences into English.

1. 跨境电子商务的产业链中涉及许多市场主体，主要包括制造商或生产商、跨境电子商务企业、跨境电子商务平台、跨境电子商务配套服务型企业（包括支付、物流、仓储等企业）、跨境消费者等。跨境电子商务主体的多样性、地域的广泛性、交易的复杂性，导致各个市场主体的权利义务界限出现模糊甚至缺失现象，所以有必要厘清各市场主体的权利义务关系。

2. 消费者权益难以得到好的保证。在跨境电子商务交易过程中，由于销售者或生产商身处国境之外，所以，消费者享受售后维修服务的难度很大，至于传统国际贸易过程中的索赔、退换货等维权行为，其实施成本很高，导致有些商品基本无法维权。

3. 通关效率有待提高。快速拿货到手是跨境电子商务消费者的普遍期许。按传统检验检疫方式，手续繁杂，周期长，费用高，往往会造成货物滞港压港的后果。

4. 保税区的检验检疫主要依据是《进出境邮寄物检疫管理办法》等部门规章。保税区的检验目前只需适用符合性检测标准，即按照当地的生产标准、国际互认标准，在实际操作中相对比较灵活。

5. 境内法律对交易平台规定了多项法定义务，此外，跨境交易平台还要考虑境外商家能否入驻、网站服务器和数据中心的选择等诸多问题。

VIII. Multiple Choices.

1. Compared with traditional international trade, cross-border e-commerce presents the following features that traditional international trade does not possess (   ).

A. Multilating   B. Small batch   C. High frequency   D. Transparency

E. Digitization

2. Conducting cross-border e-commerce (   ).

A. is conducive to the transformation and upgrading of traditional foreign trade enterprises

B. shortens the intermediate links in foreign trade

C. provides new opportunities for small and micro enterprises

D. promote industrial upgrading

E. is conducive to China's manufacturing to deal with the new pattern of global trade

3. What are the main cross-border e-commerce participants? (   ).

A. Companies and individuals that conduct cross-border e-commerce operations through third-party platforms

B. Third-party platform for cross-border e-commerce

C. Logistics company

D. Payment company

4. What is the responsibility of determining the time of payment and place of delivery? (   ).

A. Website and background maintenance

B. Inquiry Orders

C. Order operation and documents

D. Production Arrangement and Document Management

5. Which of the following are the qualities that cross-border e-commerce personnel need to have? (   ).

A. Understand the concept of consumption and culture of overseas customers'online shopping

B. Understand relevant national intellectual property and legal knowledge

C. Be familiar with the different cross-border e-commerce platform different operating rules

D. Has "localization/localization" thinking

6. In the following description, what are the term risks? (   ).

A. Delivery Risk   B. Freight forwarding risk

C. Transportation risk   D. Property risk

7. In the following description, what is correct? (　　).

A. CFR = cost + shipping　　　　　　B. CIF = cost + shipping

C. CFR = cost + shipping + insurance　　D. CIF = cost + shipping + insurance

8. How can the long-tail words in Alibaba Station be obtained? (　　).

A. Hot search word　　　　　　　B. Industry perspective

C. Foreign trade express　　　　　D. Foreign trade post

9. How can Alibaba Station Foreign Minister's last words be obtained? (　　).

A. GOOGLE AD　　　　　　　　B. UOL

C. YANDEX　　　　　　　　　D. SINA

10. The main picture of Alibaba International Station is as follows: (　　).

A. master map is the first picture of the customer seeing our product on the list page

B. the main picture does not need to care

C. to highlight the main product when producing the main picture

D. the ratio of product size and proportion according to 61.8% golden points

Chapter Thirteen   China's Cross-Border E-Commerce Status

第十三章   中国跨境电子商务发展现状

Part A   Text

A Brief Introduction to China's Cross-Border E-Commerce Development History

Cross-border e-commerce refers to the exchange of information between trading entities that belong to different customs areas through e-commerce platforms or international commercial activities of commodity trading.

跨境电子商务，指的是分属不同关境的交易主体通过电子商务平台所达成的信息交换行为或是商品交易的国际商业活动。

Since China's Alibaba realized the use of the Internet connecting Chinese suppliers and overseas buyers in 1999, China's external export trade activities have become Internet-based. After that, China's foreign export trade experienced a transition from the information service to the online transaction and the whole-industry chain service cross-border e-commerce industry.

自从 1999 年中国的阿里巴巴实现用互联网连接中国供应商与海外买家后，中国的对外出口贸易活动就实现了互联网化。在此之后，中国的对外出口贸易经历了一个从信息服务，到在线交易、全产业链服务的跨境电子商务产业转型。

In recent years, China's cross-border e-commerce has accounted for an increasing number of China's total imports and exports, and the proportion of cross-border e-commerce in the overall e-commerce has also increased year by year. At present, the proportion of cross-border e-commerce accounting for e-commerce has far exceeded 30%.

近年来，中国的跨境电子商务占中国进出口总额的比重日益进入上升通道，跨境电子商务在整体电子商务的占比也逐年提升，目前跨境电子商务占电子商务的比重已超过 30%。

Section One   Main Driving Force of Cross-Border E-Commerce in China（中国跨境电子商务的主要推动力）

At present, China's cross-border e-commerce is still dominated by export e-commerce. According to the data released by China Industry Information Network (http://www.chyxx.com), its share is about 90%, while the import proportion is only 10%. In fact, this proportion has increased year by year. The reasons are as follows:

(1) With the appreciation of the Renminbi, the import growth rate will be higher than exports.

(2) Policy support will benefit the cross-border e-commerce, especially the standardized and large-scale development of imported cross-border e-commerce. A number of related policies on cross-border e-commerce have been introduced. While regulating the cross-border e-commerce industry market, cross-border e-commerce companies have also secured cross-border e-commerce services.

(3) Domestic large-scale e-commerce companies, such as Alibaba, Amazon, JD.com and Suning and No. 1 shop, have involved in Haitao, functioning as the most important driving force for promoting the explosive development of imported cross-border e-commerce.

当前，中国的跨境电子商务中仍然是以出口电子商务为主，按照中国产业信息网（http://www.chyxx.com）发布的数据，其占比约为 90%左右，而进口跨境电子商务占比只在 10%，实际上，这一占比有逐年上升的趋势。原因如下：

（1）随着人民币升值，进口增长率将高于出口。

（2）政策支持利于跨境电子商务，尤其是进口跨境电子商务的规范化、规模化发展。多项与跨境电子商务相关政策的出台，在规范跨境电子商务行业市场的同时，也让跨境电子商务企业开展跨境电子商务业务得到了保障。

（3）阿里巴巴、亚马逊、京东、苏宁、1 号店等国内大型电商涉足海淘，是推动进口跨境电子商务爆发式发展的最主要推动力。

Section Two　Traditional Logistics and E-Commerce Needs（传统物流与电子商务需求）

Traditional Haitao logistics mode is based on direct mail and transshipment. Among them, direct mail is a mode in which domestic consumers place orders and the goods are directly airlifted to China. They are cleared by four major commercial express delivery companies, postal companies, or foreign express delivery companies, and then delivered directly to consumers. The other type is transshipment, that is, domestic consumers in China must first register and register with a foreign transshipment company before placing orders. When placing an order, the goods will be sent to the transshipment company first, and then the transshipment company will send the goods by air to China for customs clearance. Finally, the domestic express delivery company is responsible for distribution.

传统海淘的物流模式是以直邮和转运为主。其中，直邮是国内消费者下单后，货物直接空运至中国境内，由四大商业快递、邮政公司或国外快递公司等进行清关，然后直接配送到消费者手中的一种模式。另一种是转运，即我国国内的消费者在消费前要先登记注册国外一家转运公司，下单时先将货物送到转运公司，然后由转运公司集中将货物空运至中国境内进行清关，最后由国内的快递配送公司负责配送。

The direct mailing mode is characterized by its simple operation and relative low risk of lost, damaged, and even stolen goods. The disadvantage is that direct mail is currently mostly carried by international express delivery companies. Although the delivery time is fast, the shipping cost is high. Moreover, there are still few overseas shopping websites that support cross-border direct mail service.

直邮模式的特点在于其相对于转运模式而言，操作简单，且货品丢失、破损，甚至被偷换的风险都相对较低。其缺点是，目前直邮大多由国际快递公司承运，虽寄送时间短，但运费很高；而且，支持跨境直邮服务的境外购物网站仍较少。

The advantage of the transshipment mode is its low price, which is 40% of the postal parcel price, and 20% of the direct mail mode. It is the main logistic method for goods with low unit price, high degree of standardization, and low requirement for logistics packaging. Transshipment is the mainstream Haitao logistics method.

转运模式的优点在于其价格便宜，是邮政小包价格的 40%，直邮模式的 20%，是货单价较低，且标准化程度高、对物流包装要求不高的商品的主要物流方式，也是目前主流的海淘物流方式。

The disadvantage is that the information flow and logistics are not connected and the logistics link becomes a "black box". The problem of "information asymmetry" occurs, leading to poor timeliness and security. On the one hand, the transhipment company system is not connected to the e-commerce system. As a result, consumers have no way to track parcels. If there are problems after the sale, they cannot be traced. On the other hand, the transhipment companies do not have docking with the customs system, and the tax clearance is extremely risky, which also leads to legitimate expectations. The mainstream consumers of customs clearance have concerns about sea scouring. There is no communication between the information flow and the logistics, which also leads to the inability to achieve large-scale operations. With more than one package, the transporter must consider the input-output ratio of the labor force and the increase in the cost of customs clearance.

其缺点在于信息流与物流没有打通，物流环节成为"黑箱"，出现"信息不对称"问题，导致时效性、安全性差。一方面，转运公司系统没有与电子商务系统对接，导致消费者没有办法追踪包裹，如果售后出现问题无法追踪；另一方面，转运公司与海关系统没有对接，完税通关风险极大，这导致期望合法通关的主流消费者对海淘产生顾虑。信息流与物流没有打通，还导致转运模式无法实现规模化经营。包裹一多，转运方就要考虑劳动力的投入产出比，以及通关成本的增加。

Obviously, the existing Haitao logistics mode can not meet the current Chinese e-commerce requirements for low logistics prices and high timeliness, and more importantly, with the large domestic e-commerce involved in Haitao, with the outbreak of Haitao scale growth, the existing logistics mode cannot digest such a large volume.

可见，已有的海淘物流模式无法满足现有中国电子商务对物流价低、时效性高的要求，而且更重要的是，随着国内大型电子商务涉足海淘，带来海淘规模的爆发式增长，已有的物流模式更是无法消化如此庞大的体量。

Haitao has become large-scale, and logistics has to solve two core issues: ① The e-commerce information flow and logistics shall be opened up, so that the logistics links can be traced; ② Docking with the customs system to improve the efficiency of customs clearance. To solve these two core issues, on the one hand, there is a need for top-level design of policies if balance between regulation and efficiency is achieved; on the other hand, large-scale, networked logistics companies are needed, especially logistics companies with better relations with customs shall participate.

海淘形成规模化，物流方面就要解决两个核心问题：① 电商信息流与物流打通，让物流环节"有踪可循"；② 与海关系统对接，提高完税通关效率。要解决这两个核心问题，一方面，如果实现了监管与效率的平衡，就需要制定政策的顶层设计；另一方面，需要大型的、规模化、网络化物流公司，尤其是与海关关系较好的物流公司参与其中。

Section Three　China's Cross-Border E-Commerce Market Competition（中国跨境电子商务市场竞争格局）

Under the background of globalized competition, China's professional B2C export cross-border e-commerce enterprises have faced full competition from local e-commerce providers in the target market, overseas cross-border e-commerce leading companies, and those domestic e-commerce leaders exported to overseas.

在全球化的竞争大背景之下，中国的专业 B2C 出口跨境电子商务企业面对来自目标市场本土电子商务、海外跨境电子商务龙头和国内电子商务龙头出海的全面竞争。

In fact, China's export B2C cross-border e-commerce and overseas local e-commerce (including overseas cross-border e-commerce) competition is not a full-scale direct competition, but indirect competition. At present, China's export B2C cross-border e-commerce is more competitive than overseas local e-commerce and overseas cross-border e-commerce. Its competitive advantage lies mainly in its strong domestic manufacturing capacity and its strong production capacity of cross-border electricity. Commodity categories can effectively open overseas differentiated markets.

实际上，中国的出口 B2C 跨境电子商务与海外本土电子商务（包括海外跨境电子商务）的竞争并不是全方位的直接式竞争，而是间接竞争。目前，中国的出口 B2C 跨境电子商务相对于海外本土电子商务、海外跨境电子商务的竞争优势主要体现在其依托中国国内的强大生产制造能力，并凭借其具有的强势生产能力的跨境电子商务品类，从而可以有效打开海外差异化市场。

"Light supply chain mode" of foreign cross-border e-commerce firms cannot provide sufficient competitive advantages in markets where prices and experience are highly sensitive. On the contrary, with a closer distance and deeper integration with the supply chain, China's cross-border e-commerce can provide products with higher cost performance and richer product categories, and can effectively integrate supply chain resources to achieve rapid response to production. The competitive advantage is, therefore, obvious.

国外跨境电子商务"轻供应链模式"在价格与体验高度敏感的市场中无法提供足够的竞争优势。相反的，凭借与供应链更近的距离和更深的整合力度，我国跨境电子商务可以提供性价比更高、品类更加丰富的产品，并能够有效整合供应链资源实现快速反应生产，竞争优势明显。

Section Four "Going Global" Strategy of China's Cross-Border E-Commerce（中国跨境电子商务"出海"策略）

At present, China's leading domestic e-commerce companies have chosen to go directly to overseas and are most likely to face the dilemma of the new market condition. The domestic e-commerce giants Alibaba and Jingdong have all tried to directly enter the overseas cross-border e-commerce market, yet they all faced the problem of large differences in domestic and international market environment. As domestic e-commerce sales strategies do not apply to foreign countries, when domestic giants are in the international market, their competitiveness tends to be limited. Therefore, Ali chose to enter the international market through the acquisition and holding of foreign local e-commerce. Jingdong is also planning to invest in foreign e-commerce companies and indirectly use local e-commerce.

目前，中国的国内电子商务龙头企业选择直接出海的路径，会面临新市场水土不服的困境。国内电子商务巨头阿里巴巴和京东都曾尝试直接进军海外跨境电子商务市场，但都面临国内外市场环境差异大的问题，由于国内电子商务销售策略并不适用于国外，所以国内巨头在国际市场上的竞争力有限。因此，阿里选择通过收购并控股外国本土电子商务企业来进军国际，而京东也在谋划投资国外当地电子商务领域，通过本土电子商务间接出海。

It can be seen that due to the professionalism of cross-border trade and the non-monopolistic nature of the target market within a certain period of time, localized operations have become a major issue for all domestic e-commerce companies to go overseas. The successful experience of domestic leading e-commerce companies can not be copied directly into overseas expansion and will soon create a comparable domestic monopoly advantage. In short, differentiation and decentralization will be the long-term pattern of future cross-border trade patterns.

可见，由于跨境贸易的专业性以及目标市场在一定周期内具有非垄断性，导致本土化运营成为所有国内电子商务出海面临的重大问题。国内龙头电子商务的成功经验并不能直接复制到海外扩张中，以使其很快形成可比国内的垄断优势。总之，差异化和分散会是未来跨境贸易格局的长期形态。

Part B　Terminology Practice

1. **Customs**: is an authority or agency in a country responsible for collecting tariffs and for controlling the flow of goods, including animals, transports, personal, and hazardous items, into and out of a country.

2. **Alibaba**: a Chinese multinational e-commerce, retail, Internet, AI and technology conglomerate founded in 1999 that provides consumer-to-consumer, business-to-consumer and business-to-business sales services via web portals, as well as electronic payment services, shopping search engines and cloud computing services.

3. **Customs**: an authority or agency in a country responsible for collecting tariffs and for controlling the flow of goods, including animals, transports, personal, and hazardous items, into and out of a country.

4. **Currency depreciation**: the loss of value of a country's currency with respect to one or more foreign reference currencies, typically in a floating exchange rate system in which no official currency value is maintained.

5. **Currency devaluation**: in modern monetary policy, a devaluation is an official lowering of the value of a country's currency within a fixed exchange rate system, by which the monetary authority formally sets a new fixed rate with respect to a foreign reference currency or currency basket.

6. **Fixed exchange rate**: sometimes called a pegged exchange rate, is a type of exchange rate regime where a currency's value is fixed against either the value of another single currency, to a basket of other currencies, or to another measure of value, such as gold.

7. **Transshipment**: is the shipment of goods or containers to an intermediate destination, then to yet another destination.

8. **Cross-docking**: a practice in logistics of unloading materials from an incoming semi-trailer truck or railroad car and loading these materials directly into outbound trucks, trailers, or rail cars, with little or no storage in between.

9. **Information asymmetry**: in contract theory and economics, information asymmetry deals with the study of decisions in transactions where one party has more or better information than the other.

Part C   Useful Expressions

1. the exchange of information 信息交换

2. overseas buyers 海外买家

3. external export trade 对外出口贸易

4. whole-industry chain service 全产业链服务

5. the proportion of ……的比例

6. have far exceeded 已远远超越……

7. dominated by 由……主导

8. with the appreciation of... 随着……的升值

9. direct mailing mode 直邮模式

10. meet the requirements 满足要求

11. core issues 核心问题

12. market competition 市场竞争

13. target market 目标市场

14. leading domestic e-commerce companies 国内电子商务龙头企业

Part D　Exercise

I. Answer the following questions according to the information you have got.

1. Since when did China's external export trade activities become cyber-based?

2. Which companies are the most important driving force for promoting the explosive development of imported cross-border e-commerce in China?

3. What is traditional Haitao logistics mode based?

4. What is the feature of direct mailing mode?

5. What is the drawback of direct mail?

6. What is the edge of transshipment mode?

7. What is the definition of Cross-docking?

8. What is the definition of information asymmetry?

II. Match each one on the left with its correct meaning on the right.

1. Customs	A. the way total output or income is allocated among individuals
2. Transshipment	B. detailed organization and implementation of a complex operation
3. Cross-docking	C. a practice in logistics of unloading materials from an incoming semi-trailer truck or railroad car
4. Logistics	D. the shipment of goods or containers to an intermediate destination, then to yet another destination
5. Distribution	E. an authority or agency in a country responsible for collecting tariffs

1. (　　)　2. (　　)　3. (　　)　4. (　　)　5. (　　)

III. Translate the following terms and phrases into Chinese.

1. the exchange of information

2. overseas buyers

3. external export trade

4. whole-industry chain service

5. the proportion of…

6. have far exceeded…

7. dominated by

8. with the appreciation of…

9. be based on

10. direct mailing mode

11. meet the requirements

12. core issues

13. market competition

14. target market

15. leading domestic e-commerce companies

IV. Case study for cross-border e-commerce.

Case Description:

"Proprietary" mode is that cross-border e-enterprises will be directly involved in the procurement, logistics, warehousing and other overseas goods buying and selling process. "Proprietary" mode boasts its very own logistics monitoring and payment system. At present, Henan bonded logistics zone has built tens of thousands of square meters for "Gather Beauty". The opening of bonded logistics mode will greatly compress the order delivery time, combined with the overseas direct service convenience and the whole process monitoring.

Question:

Please comment on the pattern.

案情介绍：

"自营"模式就是跨境电子商务企业将直接参与到采购、物流、仓储等海外商品的买卖流程，对物流监控、支付都有自己的一套体系。目前，河南保税物流区已为聚美优品开建上万平方米自理仓。保税物流模式的开启可以压缩消费者从下订单到接货的时间。同时海外直发服务具有便捷性，因此，对比常规"海淘商品"购买周期，聚美海外购周期可由 15 天压缩到 3 天，甚至更短，并能保证物流信息全程可跟踪。

问题：

请评论该模式。

The "Pier" is a cross-border electronic third-party trading platform for Chinese customers. The seller on the platform can be divided into two categories, one category is with individual of C2C pattern, and the other kind is with merchants of M2C pattern. It helps the foreign retail industry with Chinese consumers, in that the overseas retailers shall effect direct selling to Chinese consumers, Chinese consumers shall effect direct purchase, logistics is in the middle of the direct mail. The "Pier" boasts its Three "Direct" , namely "direct marketing, direct purchase, direct mail".

Question:

Please comment on the pattern.

案情介绍：

洋码头是一家面向中国消费者的跨境电子商务第三方交易平台。该平台上的卖家可以分为两类，一类是个人买手，模式是 C2C；另一类是商户，模式是 M2C。它帮助国外的零售产业跟中国消费者对接，就是海外零售商应该直销给中国消费者，中国消费者应该直购，中间的物流是直邮，即三个直：直销、直购、直邮。

问题：

请评论该模式。

V. Describe one or two cases about the latest development of China's cross-border e-commerce status.

VI. Please determine whether the following statements are TRUE or FALSE. Then put T for TRUE or F for FALSE in the bracket at the end of each statement.

1. Cross-border e-commerce refers to the exchange of information between trading entities that belongs to different customs areas through e-commerce platforms or international commercial activities of commodity trading. (   )

2. Since China's Alibaba realized the use of the Internet connecting Chinese suppliers and overseas buyers in 1995, China's external export trade activities have become Internet-based. (   )

3. In recent years, China's cross-border e-commerce has accounted for an increasing number of China's total imports and exports, and the proportion of cross-border e-commerce in the overall e-commerce has also increased year by year. (   )

4. At present, China's cross-border e-commerce is still dominated by export e-commerce. According to the data released by China Industry Information Network, its share is about 10%, while the import proportion is 90%. (   )

5. Traditional Haitao logistics mode is based on direct mail and transshipment. (   )

6. When placing an order, the goods won't be sent to the transshipment company, and then the transshipment company will send the goods by air to China for customs clearance. (   )

7. The direct mailing mode is characterized by its simple operation and relative low risk of lost, damaged, and even stolen goods. (   )

8. The advantage of direct mail is its being carried by international express delivery companies. (   )

9. Transshipment is the mainstream Haitao logistics method. (   )

10. Haitao has become small-scale.(   )

VII. Translate the following sentences into English.

1. 跨境电子商务指的是分属不同关境的交易主体通过电子商务平台所达成的信息交换行为或是商品交易的国际商业活动。

2. 随着人民币升值，进口增长率将高于出口；政策支持利于跨境电子商务，尤其是进口跨境电子商务的规范化、规模化发展，多项与跨境电子商务相关政策的出台，在规范跨境电子商务行业市场的同时，也让跨境电子商务企业开展跨境电子商务业务得到了保障；阿里巴巴、亚马逊、京东、苏宁、1号店等国内大型电子商务企业涉足海淘，是推动进口跨境电子商务爆发式发展的最主要推动力。

3. 直邮模式的特点在于其相对于转运模式而言操作简单，且货品丢失、破损，甚至被偷换的风险都相对较低。其缺点是，目前直邮大多由国际快递公司承运，虽寄送时间快，但运费很高；而且，支持跨境直邮服务的境外购物网站仍较少。

4. 可见，已有的海淘物流模式无法满足现有中国电子商务对物流价低、时效性高的要求，而且更重要的是，随着国内大型电子商务企业涉足海淘，带来海淘规模的爆发式增长，已有的物流模式更是无法消化如此庞大的体量。

5. 在全球化的竞争大背景之下，中国的专业 B2C 出口跨境电子商务企业面对来自目标市场本土电子商务、海外跨境电子商务龙头和国内电子商务龙头出海的全面竞争。

6. 可见，由于跨境贸易的专业性以及目标市场在一定周期内具有非垄断性，导致本土化运营成为所有国内电子商务企业出海面临的重大问题。国内龙头电子商务企业的成功经验并不能直接复制到海外扩张中，以使其很快形成可比国内的垄断优势。总之，差异化和分散会是未来跨境贸易格局的长期形态。

VIII. Multiple Choices.

1. What is the correct description of the product posted on the Alibaba International Station? (　　).

A. Accurate selection of product category

B. Product name must contain buyer search terms

C. Brief description of the equivalent product slogan

D. All the above are not correct

2. In order to create a high quality Alibaba platform product template, what can be included when describing a product? (　　).

A. Production line

B. Product Construction Diagram

C. Product Description

D. Product Certification

3. In order to create high-quality Alibaba platform product templates, what can be included when describing a company? (　　).

A. Company appearance

B. Factory Landscape

C. Factory floor plan

D. Cooperative customer or brand

4. Which of the following ways can be add keywords to Alibaba's background? (　　).

A. Search Keywords

B. System recommendation word

C. Manually add keywords

D. All the above are not correct

5. In the background of my Alibaba, you can view keywords by the following dimensions? (　　).

A. My Word

B. His Word

C. Top Search Word

D. Industry Perspective

6. What are the things that need to be done to make foreign trade on the Alibaba platform? (　　).

A. Increase the exposure for customers to find you

B. Increases your traffic to let customers know you

C. Increase the amount of inquiry for customers to fall in love with you

D. Increase orders to take customers home

7. What is correct as described below? (　　).

A. Generally speaking, B2C is the first goal of a deal

B. In general, B2B is the first goal of a deal

C. In general, B2B is based on the number of prospective customers

D. All the above are not right

8. When dealing with inquiries, which core points do we usually communicate with customers? (   )

A. Who are you?   B. What do you have?

C. What do customers want?   D. What do you give?

9. What is correct about responding to inquiries as follows? (   ).

A. Considering the time difference factor, try to reply to the customer's email when the customer goes to work

B. Considering the convenience factor, try to use picture format files when sending attachments

C. Consider language factors, you can try to use multi-language for inquiry reply

D. Considering professional factors, you can speak out possible problems, difficulties, and results in advance

10. About mailing samples, which of the following description is correct? (   ).

A. All customers need to post samples

B. Not all customers need to post samples

C. Some customers must send samples

D. All options are correct

参 考 文 献

[1] 易露霞，陈新华，尤彧聪. 国际贸易实务双语教程[M]. 北京：清华大学出版社，2016.

[2] 易露霞，刘洁，尤彧聪. 外贸英语函电[M]. 3版. 北京：清华大学出版社，2016.

[3] 尤彧聪，易露霞. 比较优势、交易成本与广东外贸制度创新驱动路径实证研究[J]. 社会科学. 2016（10）：100.

[4] 尤彧聪，易露霞. 外贸供给侧改革视角下企业科技创新驱动的转型方式实证研究：基于广东省外贸企业的调查[J]. 中国软科学，2017（12）.

[5] 尤彧聪，易露霞. 制度创新驱动广东省外贸竞争力的机理实证研究[J]. 当代经济，2017（7）：72-73.

[6] 尤彧聪，易露霞. 基于"供给侧改革"与创新驱动的广东出口贸易模型研究[J]. 中国市场，2017（16）：29-30.

[7] 尤彧聪，黄彩娥. "供给侧改革"视角下基于异构 MELITS 模型的异质性知识与跨境电子商务企业创新绩效的相关性实证研究[J]. 电子商务，2017（10）：40.

[8] 速卖通大学. 跨境电商：阿里巴巴速卖通宝典[M]. 北京：电子工业出版社，2015.

[9] 中国电子商务数据中心 http://www.100ec.cn/zt/data/

[10] 中国跨境电商网 http://www.100ec.cn/zt/wmds/